For the Morgans,

with best wishes.

Don

The Marquis de Morès

EMPEROR OF THE BAD LANDS

⚜ ⚜ ⚜ ⚜

The Marquis de Morès

EMPEROR
OF THE
BAD LANDS

by

DONALD DRESDEN

UNIVERSITY OF OKLAHOMA PRESS
NORMAN

BY DONALD DRESDEN

Le Chemin de Paris (Paris, 1946)

The Marquis de Morès: Emperor of the Bad Lands (Norman, 1970)

International Standard Book Number: 0–8061–0869–X

Library of Congress Catalog Card Number: 69–16720

Copyright 1970 by the University of Oklahoma Press, Publishing Division of the University. Composed and printed at Norman, Oklahoma, U.S.A., by the University of Oklahoma Press. First edition.

To
Marta, Chris, and Tony

CONTENTS

ILLUSTRATIONS

ACKNOWLEDGMENTS

I should like to thank Madame Athenaïs de Vallombrosa de Graffenreid, daughter of the Marquis de Morès, for her kindness in writing to me about her father and for photographs of him and books about him. I also thank Antoine de Vallombrosa, grandson of the Marquis, for his interviews and correspondence.

Thanks also to Charles Clegg, executor of the literary estate of Lucius Beebe, for permission to quote from *The Age of Steam*, by Beebe and Clegg.

My gratitude goes to the State Historical Society of North Dakota, whose director lent me the Society's complete file on the Marquis. My appreciation goes also to the distinguished house of Plon in Paris for permission to quote and use illustrations from books it has published about de Morès, all this arranged through Mlle Alicia Vejarano and M. and Mme Robert Aron, whom I also thank for arranging for the Duchesse de Sabran, niece of the Marquis, to supply me with illustrations, for which I thank her.

Thanks also to the widow of Herman Hagedorn for permission to quote from his excellent work *Roosevelt in the Bad Lands*.

Finally, I thank Marta Dresden, my wife, for reading the manuscript with understanding and critical eye.

DONALD DRESDEN

Washington, D.C.
March 15, 1969

The Marquis de Morès
EMPEROR OF THE BAD LANDS

I

THE EMPEROR OF THE BAD LANDS

On a blustery March day in 1883, the Northern Pacific Railway's *Pacific Express* rolled out of Chicago with an aristocratic young Frenchman aboard who was destined to become the most celebrated and the most shot-at man in the history of the Bad Lands of Dakota Territory. He was a *grand seigneur* with a burning ambition and a soaring imagination backed with plenty of cash, and the Old West gave him the opportunity to apply his resources to the fullest. His ranches, herds, and business enterprises became so vast, his competition with eastern robber barons so audacious, that newspaper reports dubbed him "The Emperor of the Bad Lands" and the journals of the day, including the best in New York, played his exploits on their front pages. Wherever he went, he was wrapped in a nimbus of controversy. He was admired or hated, praised or maligned, depending on the critic, but no one who knew him—or even knew about him—failed to have an opinion about the man. The impression he created on his contemporaries lived on for more than half a century after he left Dakota Territory. He cut a swath through the sagebrush incomparable for that part of the frontier, and his initial success seemed to forecast his parlaying a considerable fortune into millions. But he encountered formidable difficulties. Local gunmen and crooks tried to drive him out of the Bad Lands, and this led to gunplay and lynch threats that almost cost him his life and forced him to stand trial for murder. His moneyed eastern competitors reached out with tentacles of political influence, financial chicanery, and hired gunmen, all the way from Washington, D.C., to the Bad Lands, with resulting ruin to his business. Unbowed, he returned to France, where his career spluttered constantly and exploded frequently in a constant stream of violent episodes, including duels fatal to his opponents. It ended in Africa, in a fusillade of fire from the guns of assassins hired by his French political enemies.

This adventurer-entrepreneur, who was only twenty-five years old when he rode the *Express* that day in 1883, was born Antoine Amédée-Marie-Vincent Manca de Vallombrosa. When he reached his majority, he became the Marquis de Morès et de Montemaggiore, but since the latter part of the title was usually dropped, he was best known as the Marquis de Morès—and also by some unprintable names.

De Morès was a complex man. Above all, he was adventurous, endowed with the best qualities of an adventurer. Pierre Frondaie, a French author who devoted half of his book *Deux Possédés de l'Héroïsme* to de Morès, called him *"le Généreux, le Bâtisseur, le Provoquant, le Magnifique, le sans Peur (sinon sans Reproches) et avant tout, le Paladin."* No doubt he was generous, a fighter, and provoking. Frontiersmen quickly saw these qualities in de Morès. They also discovered he was completely without fear, and this without reproach. In several ways he demonstrated the qualities of a lower-case paladin: to many people of lesser means and position, especially in France, he was a champion and a legendary hero, and he repeatedly took the line that had been a byword of his mother, who said, "My birth confers no privileges on me; it gives me great responsibilities."

It would be difficult to conceive of a man who looked more the part he was living—not playing—than de Morès. A soldier and aristocrat, he bristled with the characteristics of a classical adventurer of the time. Six feet tall and with his 170 pounds well distributed, he was ramrod straight. Even in repose he looked as if he could leap into action in a second. He could. De Morès was strongly handsome, with an olive complexion, a determined chin, curly black hair, and long sideburns of that day. His dark eyes

4

were flashing bright. Although he was unfailingly polite, he was also aloof and somewhat imperious, a characteristic that was heightened by slightly hooded eyelids and a flaring black moustache that ended in needle-pointed waxed tips. De Morès exuded self-confidence. His appearance and bearing stood out in any crowd.

The trip was a fine bit of adventure for the Marquis, and part of the fun was the intriguing conveyance, so different from trains on the Continent. Called a 4-4-0 because of its four front wheels, four drivers, and no trailing wheels, the locomotive was a small, jaunty affair with a personality of its own. Lucius Beebe and Charles Clegg, America's leading railroad author-buffs, wrote in their *Age of Steam*: "Not even excepting the Yankee clipper ships . . . or the Concord coach . . . no devising of human genius for the conquest of time and distance was more beautiful or more useful than the American standard 4-4-0 steam railroad locomotive."

The 4-4-0 pulling the *Pacific Express* looked in mint condition with its brass work polished mirror bright and its iron painted in gay colors. Above its cowcatcher, on a tiny platform, stood an iron figure much like a hitching-post boy. Higher still was mounted a box, nearly the size of an orange crate, from which the great eye of the headlight stared ahead. The light box was decorated with elk antlers and painted on the sides to the taste of the engineer (he owned the light and took it home with him at the end of the run). A bell, lustrous as ormolu, dangled from an ornate cradle, clanging a pleasant note when the engineer pulled the cord. From one of the two teapot-like formations above the boiler a steam whistle sprouted. The high driving wheels, almost half as tall as the locomotive, clacked with a metronomic beat as they bore down on the rails, the connecting rods flashing in the sun. On upgrades, the locomotive's exhaust puffed from a smoke-stack that rose first as a cylinder, grew, then diminished to form a diamond shape in profile—a diamond stack, it was called, and it was pert as a cockade.

Back of the engine was the tender, filled with wood, followed by a combination baggage and smoking car and several coaches, the latter so jammed with westbound settlers that many stood in the aisles. Then came the diner. Finally there was "the varnish," as the sleeping and private cars were called because of their high gloss. In one of these de Morès rode with his man William van Driesche, who has been described as a secretary-valet by some writers but actually was more of a business manager (the French would have called him an *homme de confiance*, with the confidences directed largely to financial affairs). A well-educated Frenchman, he was the third generation of his family to serve the de Morèses, with loyalty running both ways. The de Morès children and grandchildren were fond of van Driesche, too: they called him Mr. Willie.

The *Pacific Express* continued its run to St. Paul, Minnesota—it took twenty hours from Chicago, more than triple today's running time for the 425 miles. After a layover of twelve hours, during which the diner was stocked with buffalo meat and other game and the supply of potables was reinforced, a new crew took the *Express* over the next leg of the trip. Skirting many lakes, the train chugged on through heavy woods, its cars swaying and vibrating when the speed exceeded thirty miles an hour.

When the *Express* rattled across the bridge over the Red River of the North, the Marquis was in Dakota Territory. From the wooded countryside of Minnesota, the landscape changed abruptly and de Morès saw the prairies unfold before him as the train bored into the West; the tiny *Express* seemed swallowed up in plains extending on every side to the horizon, so vast they seemed infinite. Sod huts of early settlers literally sprouted out of the prairies, standing out, with more substantial frame buildings, in lonely defiance. A few trees bordered the infrequent streams. But for miles and miles nothing broke the monotony of this part of Dakota, so flat it was hard to believe that landscape could repeat itself with such obstinance. For a newcomer—and this was de Morès' first trip to the Great Plains—the outstanding impression was space compounded by space. And what a contrast to France, with her pocket-sized fields, prim rows of poplars guarding ancient roads, and stone farm buildings generations old.

Here and there potholes and sloughs dotted the land, and from them great flocks of wild ducks and geese rose to join thousands of others on their way to the myriad lakes of Canada. Skeins of Canada geese undulated, higher, then lower, and changed direction in the wind. Closer to the ground, coveys of grouse and prairie chickens rocketed into the air, then coasted to feeding grounds near by. Dozens of rabbits bounded over the prairies. Badgers peeked out of burrows. And everywhere gophers flicked their tails and ran—this was to become the Flickertail State: North Dakota.

Soon great waves of immigrants would surge over Dakota (many had already arrived), but in 1883, railroads and land companies were turning every phrase at their command to induce settlers to come to the Territory. One of the most eloquent rhapsodizers of the time was Patrick Donan, who produced a 75-page apotheosis entitled *North Dakota, The Land of the Golden Grain, The Lake-Gemmed, Breeze-Swept Empire of the New Northwest.* "No region in the United States or the world," he wrote, "is attracting more widespread and favorable attention today than Dakota, and none is or could be more worthy of such regard. In vastness of extent, variety and exhaustlessness of resources, infinitude of natural advantages, intelligence, energy and enterprise of population, marvelous rapidity of growth and improvement, universal and unbounded prosperity for the present, and golden promise for the future, Dakota unites in herself all the capabilities of a glorious statehood, all that is requisite to render her, ere long, the imperial commonwealth of the New Northwest, and the cherished home-land of contented and happy millions."

Warming to his subject, Donan went on to say that Dakota "is a land fair enough to tempt the angels in their flight to pause and wonder whether a new and better Eden has not been formed

7

and roofed with sapphire skies. . . . Its climate unites all that is bracing and inspiring. . . . People who have come here to die of bronchitis and consumption have lived to become glowing embodiments of soundness and strength, with throats like firemen's trumpets, and lungs like blacksmiths' bellows. The howling blizzards, of which outside worldlings delight to prate, blow all miasma and contagion from Dakota's favored plains and valleys, and breathe new life into dilapidated nostrils. . . . The productive capacity of Dakota is as limitless as her extent is great. . . . Any land will pay for itself at present prices in one or two crops."

Whether de Morès fell under Donan's spell is moot. His primary interest in the Territory was cattle, yet its agricultural potential interested him, too. Already some of the land de Morès saw was under cultivation, but a great deal more remained unbroken prairie where thick wild grass was now just beginning to turn green. Eventually, de Morès would direct some of his boundless energy and seemingly inexhaustible supply of capital into farming. He, too, would try to persuade settlers to buy the land he owned and to pay for it with their crops. The thoughts of those future operations must have been on his mind as the prairie continued to unfold before him.

Leaving aside the glow that can come from the prospect of making money, the trip pleased the two Frenchmen, for it was replete with new sights and sounds.

As night began to fall, guttering lamps and candles gleamed from windows in the little false-fronted towns where people came to the depot for the big event of the day: the train passing through or, better still, stopping to take on or let off a passenger. The typical station was a one-story building whose outstanding external feature was a protruding window which gave a view of the track in both directions to the man who acted as stationmaster, telegrapher, ticket seller, express agent, and baggageman. Inside, the building was pleasantly warmed by a potbellied stove, glowing red. High-backed benches were ranged around the stove, and the plain floor was liberally sprinkled with spittoons—

the accuracy of the users was notoriously bad. Kerosene lamps on brackets threw light on railroad advertising posters covering the walls. "Wanted" notices had their place on a special board. The station smelled strongly of smoke and tobacco juice. Train watchers gathered around the stove to wait for the locomotive's warning whistle, then poured out onto the platform as the *Pacific Express* thundered through, its engineer waving cheerily.

At several of these stations, de Morès' train stopped. The dining car and the sleepers were always objects of great interest, for many people in the little towns had never enjoyed anything more opulent in travel than the red-cushioned coaches. Then the 4-4-0 was off again, the beam of its kerosene headlight glistening on the rails ahead. At night, the whistle took on a haunting note, its who-wuuuuuuuuu sailing across the prairie but not echoing, for there was nothing in the distance to reflect the sound waves. There were other sounds in the night: when de Morès and van Driesche stepped out of their car at depots and water tanks, they could hear the off-key wail of the coyotes' ki-yi-ki-yiiiiiiiiiiiii.

The *Express* clattered over the bridge spanning the Missouri Slope country. The scene quickly changed from that of the prairies. Towns became scarce, farms were farther apart, and the billiard-table plains began to roll in gentle hills and valleys.

Soon left behind were the last outposts of law and order: Mandan, on the western bank of the Big Muddy, and Bismarck, presently to become the capital of the Territory, on the eastern bank. Ahead lay de Morès' empire-to-be, the area along the Little Missouri River and its tributaries called the Bad Lands, a part of the Old West where only the six-gun and vigilantes ruled and where lynch law was common.

The train's conductor contributed to the popular conception of the "Wild West" when he came through the cars and announced, with obvious satisfaction, that the *Express* would soon be passing through country celebrated for its wild game. Waiting for this information to sink in, he then invited the passengers to break out their firearms, open the windows, and blast away.

9

This awakened slumbering travelers and keyed everyone to a high pitch. For most of the passengers, especially easterners, this was high adventure: a direct participation in action in the Wild West. Nothing like it could possibly happen in the effete East. What a conversation piece when the easterners got home!

Windows were jerked up. Passengers scrambled for guns and ammunition. If buffalo were the targets for marksmen firing from the cars, the easterners were enthralled, but the great shaggies, as they were called, also interested westerners sufficiently to induce editors to run stories about them in frontier newspapers. At about the time de Morès was headed for the Bad Lands, the *Bismarck Tribune* reprinted on its front page a story from the *Glendive Times* about the antics of two buffalo, the *Pacific Express* engineer and the passengers aboard.

"Conductor Hulet tells us," the story went, "that Monday evening when his train was a short distance from Terry, two large buffaloes made their appearance, and nearing the locomotive, kicked their heels in the air, evidently with disdain at the iron horse's speed, and seemingly, bantering for a race. Pulling the throttle wide open, the engineer turned his steed loose, and for nearly a mile the racers were neck and neck, but steam overcame animal endurance and wind, and the buffaloes stopped, looking crestfallen and thoroughly ashamed. The excitement among the passengers, who were nearly all Eastern people, was intense. . . . Mr. Hulet stopped the train. . . . The passengers in their anxiety to get a shot at 'the wild cow of the plains,' tumbled, jumped and rolled out of the cars in one confused mass (firing rifles, shot guns and) every variety of pistol from a toy gun to a selfcocking six. After several fusillades the buffaloes were killed and a head of one secured." The train resumed its journey.

The Northern Pacific's mobile shooting gallery did not earn the approval of all passengers. Take the case of a Scotsman, Gregor Lang, and his sixteen-year-old son Lincoln, who rode the *Pacific Express* for the first time in the spring of 1883. In his *Ranching with Roosevelt*, Lincoln Lang says that when the train stopped at Dickinson, it was boarded by a number of professional buffalo hunters in buckskin clothes. They carried heavy Sharps rifles, which were standard weapons for their calling. He describes what happened:

> Suddenly from behind a low hill close to the track, there ran a small herd of buffalo, startled by the train. . . . Swiftly, with lowered heads they made off up an open draw, at their characteristic bobbing gait.
>
> Instantly all was excitement in our car. Almost before I could realize what was happening, those hunters—save the mark—had the windows up and were bombarding them. Before the fleeing animals could make their getaway, it became evident that a couple of them, at least, had been hit. Clearly we saw one stumble forward on its knees, to recover thereafter and keep on, while a second dropped back, evidently in sore distress. That was the last we saw of the buffalo, an intervening butte cut them from view, putting an end to the criminally insensate shooting.
>
> A little further along . . . a large band of antelope numbering perhaps two hundred head, was seen to the south of the track, but a short distance off.

Startled, the animals began to run, but they chose a line of flight parallel to the railroad tracks:

> Apparently the engineer decided to give them a race. Such a chance to show off—to impress us "tenderfeet"—was too good for the slayers. Promptly they again went into action. . . . By the time the train had pulled far enough ahead to render further shooting futile, at least five had been killed outright and perhaps twice that number crippled, to become, later, the sure prey of their natural enemies, if they did not die in the meantime.
>
> I recall the conductor was in our car, apparently enjoying the fun and making no effort to stop it. When father and one or two others . . . protested, appealing to him to stop the train and pick up the dead animals, at least, he flatly refused. "What in hell do they amount to anyhow?" he inquired.

Curiously enough, it was the wildlife, then being slaughtered from the train windows, that had first attracted de Morès' attention to the Bad Lands. Count Fitz-James, his cousin, had hunted there and told him about the abundance of furred and feathered game. An ardent nimrod, the Marquis was fascinated—so was the Marquise, who was a crack shot and loved the outdoors. But the essential reason for de Morès' journey to the Bad Lands was the cattle industry, now developing because of such apparently diverse elements as Indians, buffalo, settlers, and railroads.

The Indians had resisted the westward advance of the white man because their hunting grounds were being usurped. The government, pressed by business and railway interests, wanted the West settled, but Indians scared many prospective settlers away. There were two ways to get rid of the red men: fight them directly or deny them their principal means of living, the buffalo. The Indians had always taken only a sufficient number of the animals to provide the food they needed; they used the skins for clothing and shelter, the bones for implements. The Indian wars of the 1870's broke the military power of the tribes, and in that decade the development of a process for preserving and tanning buffalo hides brought armies of commercial hunters to the plains. Buffalo robes in that era of horse and sleigh, when house heating was rudimentary, were quite popular at a cost of about $8.50 each. The herds were enormous: the entire population of the great beasts was estimated to be some forty to fifty million (on one occasion a train was halted for nine hours to let a herd cross the tracks). Then the slaughter began. A good marksman could kill more than a hundred a day with a .50-caliber Sharps rifle. The skinners characteristically took only the hide, although sometimes they carved out the best pieces of the animal, such as the tongue and the hump, the latter a particularly succulent morsel. Usually, however, the carcasses were left to rot.

Conservationists objected to the wholesale killing of the animals. They appealed to state, territorial, and federal governments, but to no avail. Indeed, those bodies encouraged the annihilation, for it speeded the day when all the Indians would be forced by hunger to surrender and live on reservations.

The elimination of the buffalo herds would also open the

country to cattle. The two kinds of animals could not have been grazed together, for the buffalo so dominated the ranges that the cattle would have been dispossessed. More important, interbreeding would have produced a beast sometimes known as cattalo—hardly a desirable animal from which to cut a filet mignon.

Southwestern cattlemen plumped for clearing the plains to the north, for their ranges had been crowded following the Civil War and even if they had not been overgrazed, the grass tended to wilt early in the summer because of the species and climate. In the early 1870's, Texas ranchers started to drive their herds into Kansas and Nebraska prairie feeding grounds and to the railheads established there for shipping stock to the East. Then they eyed the plains of Dakota, and the railroads supported the cattlemen's wish to see that region opened for grazing. Not only would the railroads benefit from the cattle traffic going east, but they would also sell their property along the right-of-way to settlers.

By 1879, when the Northern Pacific Railway reached the Little Missouri River in Dakota Territory, most of the buffalo in that region had been killed, the Indians relegated to reservations, the Sioux to the south, the Gros Ventres to the north. The Dakota ranges were lightly stocked, and the native grass, called bunch or buffalo, was much more nutritious than that of the Southwest. Moreover, because of the hot, dry Dakota summers and the natural qualities of the grass, it cured on the stem, becoming, in effect, uncut hay that lasted all winter, even under snow. Cattle could graze nearly the year round, with little or no supplemental feeding. So it was that stock from the Southwest poured into Dakota in ever increasing numbers until, in the summer of 1883, an estimated 250,000 cows and steers had been driven into the basin of the Little Missouri and its tributaries.

De Morès knew about all this bovine activity. The ranching part of the cattle industry appealed to him, but his interest was not confined to the range. In 1883, almost all the cattle from the western ranges were shipped east of the Mississippi to be slaughtered, and much of the finished beef then was returned to the West. De Morès proposed to revise this wasteful process by slaughtering at an abattoir he would build near the range, then shipping the finished product east. Basically, his reasoning was sound, for with such an arrangement he should have been able to deliver meat to the consumer at a price lower than his competitors could offer. This was no open-and-shut case, but in common with every likely appearing business proposition, it seemed, on the surface at least, to be promising. De Morès wanted to make a killing, and he possessed the capital to start his venture on proper footing. He had a fortune of his own—about $1,000,000, a handsome sum in 1883—and his father was well off, although it must be said that in the light of subsequent parental action in France, it would have been miraculous if he could have tapped that source. Then there was de Morès' father-in-law, who was highly solvent. Finally, the Marquise enjoyed an annual income of $90,000 from a portfolio of blue-chip securities.

Was de Morès just money grubbing, or did he have some more lofty reason for wanting to parlay his fortune? After he left the United States, the *Sioux Falls* (now South Dakota) *Press* quoted him as saying that with the money he would make in the cattle business and his other enterprises, he would return to France. There he would finance and manage a coup d'état, in which he would be helped by his friends in the army, and he would mount the throne in a new French monarchy. Fantastic as that might sound, de Morès did have, through his mother's side of the family, a relationship with the Orléans hierarchy. Moreover, he was a plotter: he eventually became embroiled in French politics as an active supporter of General Boulanger, who nearly rode his horse up the steps of the Élysée Palace. So it is possible that de Morès had regal aspirations, but even if he did, it would have had little bearing on his exploits, except that perhaps his schemes might have been slightly less grandiose without such a spur. But even that is doubtful.

Whatever de Morès' long-range aims might have been, he was

determined to achieve his immediate objective of plunging into the cattle business. This was not a hunting trip, as some accounts would have it, but, rather, a combination of venture and adventure that he hoped would earn a lot of money for him.

On the Frenchman's long trip, another bridge was significant —the span over the Little Missouri River—for when the *Pacific Express* crossed this one, the journey was ended. On the west bank of the Little Muddy, the 4-4-0 shuddered to a halt, steam sighing from its escape valves. The conductor jumped down from the open vestibule and put a stepping stool on the station platform. Up ahead, the baggageman pitched a mountain of trunks and valises onto a four-wheeled cart. De Morès and van Driesche descended. The conductor swung his lantern in a wide arc to signal the engineer, and with a polite clanging of the bell, the engine's exhaust coughed hoarsely as the *Express* gained momentum.

Van Driesche checked most of the luggage at the station, then he and de Morès carried a tent down to the banks of the Little Missouri—the Marquis had been warned about the fleabags that passed for hotels in this part of the world. It was now so dark that the two Frenchmen could see little of the wild beauty of the valley, but both were impressed by their surroundings and the feeling of being completely alone. They pitched their tent, watched the last rays of light fade, and then, exhausted after their long trip, fell asleep. They didn't hear the coyotes' yip or the deeper howl of the wolves.

II

DE MORÈS' BACKGROUND

That de Morès should have cast his lot—and a pile of money—in the Old West was natural, considering his background. He came from a long and illustrious line of adventurers, soldiers, and soldiers of fortune. De Morès was thoroughly French, but his Spanish ancestry constantly burst forth, notably in his explosive reaction to any slighting remark, no matter how mild, which kept him literally at sword's point defending the honor of his name.

De Morès' Spanish forebears fought in the conquest of Sardinia in the fourteenth century. In payment for their services, the King of Spain presented them with two Sardinian villages, which made up the Marquisate of de Morès, and he also gave them the title. For generations the family enjoyed life on Sardinia, even though the island changed hands several times among Spain, France, and Italy. De Morès men served in the military and were important members of the royal court.

In the nineteenth century, a conspiracy to unseat the King of Sardinia was uncovered by some of the King's agents before the coup could be pulled off. At that time, Vincent Manca, grandfather of de Morès, was a colonel of cavalry and a first gentleman of the King's court. It was not Manca, however, who was instrumental in discovering the plot, and as punishment for this act of omission, the King exiled him and confiscated his property. But Manca had influence, and soon he was back in the good graces of the King; his property was restored to him.

Whether this palace contretemps influenced Manca's next

move is obscured by time, but whatever the reason, he migrated to France soon after the event. It was natural that he should associate with French aristocracy, and in 1831 he married Claire de Galard de Grassac de Béarn, an heiress from a family related to Henry of Navarre, who was the French King Henry IV. Mademoiselle de Béarn's lineage went back to Caius Mucius, the Roman who bravely set out across the Tiber to slay King Porsena but in error killed the king's secretary instead, an act of which he was so ashamed that he burned off one of his own hands.

From the Vincent Manca–de Béarn union was born Richard Manca, who took the title Duc de Vallombrosa. He married Geneviève de Perusse des Cars, daughter of the Duc des Cars, who was a lieutenant general in the French army and one of the top commanders in the conquest of Algiers. Their son, the future Marquis de Morès, was born in Paris on June 14, 1858, at 9 rue de Grenelle, in the heart of the fashionable Faubourg St. Germain. The house, built in 1713 for the Duchesse d'Estrées, had been passed down through generations in de Morès' mother's family. It was a lovely old place with a deep court and a patina of graceful age. Throughout de Morès' life, his surroundings, regardless of how crude the country might be, always had some of the cachet of the Faubourg St. Germain.

De Morès' mother was not in the best of health, so his father bought the Villa des Tours in Cannes, on the Riviera, where the climate was milder than in Paris. Since he was a highly sensitive and imaginative boy, it is easy to understand that young de Morès should be impressed by the locale, with its marks of various peoples from the first days of Mediterranean civilization.

De Morès' early education was classically French: nurses and governesses, along with his parents, taught him French, English, Italian, and German by the time he was ten years old. Then he was entrusted to the best tutors, who put him through an excellent schooling. He was a brilliant student, combining a quick, analytical mind with an unrelenting determination to excel—characteristics he carried throughout his life.

In this formative stage of his life, de Morès enjoyed the guidance of a mother who, although not robust physically, was vibrant with strong ideas about how a man of her son's position should conduct himself. She believed in the Pascalian thought that "the pleasure of the great is to make happiness for others," and she constantly impressed on her son the importance of recognizing and discharging his responsibilities to the state and to those less fortunate than he. It was during this time that de Morès was studying catechism; surely parental religious influence must have been strong, for the seeds of Catholicism were sown deeply, and flourished, in the young man.

Religion also had a part in de Morès' higher education. When he had completed the tutorial stage, he entered Stanislas College in Cannes, where he studied under the Abbé Raquin and was graduated in 1873. Considering his ancestry, it was natural that de Morès should want to carry on the family military tradition. He was also a patriot, and the humiliating defeat France suffered in 1871 in the Franco-Prussian War could well have had a bearing on his following a career of arms. De Morès wanted to enter the navy and had prepared for the entrance examinations at the College of La Seyne-sur-Mer. He surely would have passed the tests, but he was stricken with brain fever and was therefore unable to complete them in time for matriculation. This was the first crucial point in his life, for it is possible (albeit improbable) that the active life of a naval officer, with sea duty and shore leave in distant lands, could have satisfied his craving for adventure. Whatever might have been de Morès' thoughts about the navy, he dismissed them and entered the Jesuit College of Poitiers in southwestern France.

Again he turned in a brilliant academic performance. The military still had a powerful attraction for him—or was it the idea of service to the state? Whatever the reason, upon graduation from Poitiers, he entered St. Cyr, the West Point of France, where he performed with his usual éclat. A young man of high spirit, de Morès was a devil at St. Cyr. Timid classmates idolized him, for he not only possessed the necessary intelligence and daring to play pranks, but always performed them with such finesse that he kept out of the clutches of the martinets who ran the academy.

At St. Cyr, religion still gripped de Morès strongly. In discussions with classmates, some of his contemporaries expressed doubts, but he never wavered in his firm belief. He was a close friend of Charles de Foucault, who renounced the army in favor of the Trappists and became a monk; de Morès saw de Foucault often in his new calling.

Several of de Morès' fellow cadets distinguished themselves in the army, among them Durtas, Mazel, and Pétain, and the odds are that he would have been with them in high command during World War I had he stayed in the army. And, had he lived until that time, it would be hard to picture de Morès as anything but a violent opponent to the World War II Vichy regime of his old classmate Pétain.

In 1879, de Morès was graduated from St. Cyr. He was then twenty-one years old. He chose the cavalry as his branch of the service, the usual selection of the most intelligent and adventurous military academy graduates before the invention of the airplane. The young lieutenant was immediately ordered to Saumur, then the finest cavalry school in the world and possessing the added advantage of being located in the Loire Valley, with its exquisite cuisine and the delightful wines of Vouvray nearby. De Morès was brilliant at Saumur, both in the classroom and in the field. He easily met the academic requirements, and he rode as if he were a part of the horse. As a one-man army, he was practically invincible, for he combined the coolness and courage that were essential to the aggressive handling of broadsword, *épée*, and pistol, and his superb coordination never failed. This early training was to stand de Morès in good stead in the years to come.

From Saumur, de Morès was posted to a regiment of cuirassiers at Maubeuge near the Belgian border—a duller town would be difficult to imagine. (A picture of the lieutenant at that time, in a stiff, choke-necked army uniform, shows him looking arrogantly down his aristocratic nose and past the waxed tips of his haughty moustache.) His next post was with the Tenth Hussars, and he enjoyed a brief bit of action in helping to put down an uprising in Algiers. De Morès was promoted to first lieutenant. Following the Algiers tour, he returned to garrison duty near provincial towns such as Nancy and Luneville, which did nothing to relieve the boredom of a peacetime military career. His life was enlivened by two duels, both of which he won at the cost of his opponents' lives. Little is known today about those two early encounters, much in contrast to his duels on the field of honor in the 1890's, which commanded headlines in Paris and New York.

With no prospect of action in sight, de Morès couldn't bear the army any longer, so in early 1882, he resigned, although he continued to maintain a reserve commission. He probably had no idea of what he was going to do when he quit the army, but, considering his means, he surely didn't have to worry. However, there soon occurred an event that profoundly influenced his life for the next few years: with his handsome appearance, courtly manners, and social standing, de Morès was in constant demand at the leading salons of Paris, and in one of them he met an American, Medora von Hoffman, the daughter of a wealthy New York banker. Miss von Hoffman's maternal grandmother had been one of the most celebrated belles of New Orleans; the granddaughter had inherited her beauty. Medora was tiny, about five feet tall, with pale skin, delicate features, and lustrous titian hair. For her and de Morès, it was a *coup de foudre*, and on February 15, 1882, they were married at Cannes in the Church of the Stained Glass Windows, with the Bishop of Fréjus performing the ceremony.

If the new Marquise de Morès thought she was going to continue to live in Cannes, where her parents had a villa—or any other place in France for that matter—she was mistaken. A few years after the marriage, the Marquis was talking to a newspaper reporter in New York about the de Morès place of residence. "It's the funniest thing in the world," he said. "My wife married a European to live in Europe, and yet we have spent almost all of our married life in the Wild West of America."

There was an intermediate step, however, between the tame Mediterranean coast and the wild West. The young couple spent most of the summer of 1882 on the Continent and in mid-August sailed for the United States; de Morès had agreed to work in his father-in-law's bank in New York. Incongruous as that might seem for an adventurous young man, it was logical: the von Hoffman bank, one of the leading institutions financing outstanding enterprises of the day, would be a fiscal promontory from which he could survey the American business scene and pick a good place to invest his money.

When the Marquis and Marquise arrived in the United States, Manhattan was being braised in the canicular heat of August, which was particularly enervating for those accustomed to cool European summers. To escape the climate in town, they went to live at the von Hoffmans' home at Stapleton on Staten Island. Life there was very pleasant. The von Hoffmans had two servants and the de Morèses added five of their own, so the Marquise had little to do but amuse herself and supervise the household. The latter she did with Germanic thoroughness; her household books were frequently in German, although her extended exposure to life in France also showed in her accounts with *rosbif*, *boeuf*, *côtelettes*, and *saucisson* figuring.

Although the family was well off, Madame de Morès didn't waste a cent. It is easy to picture her in her study, figuring out what they were going to eat. One grocery bill shows how carefully she scrutinized everything: she found an undercharge of 1½¢ on a five-pound pail of lard. Time after time she worked out total prices, as, for example, 4¾ pounds of chicken at 28¢ a pound, which came to $1.33. Having been charged 45¢ for a cauliflower, the Marquise wrote firmly in black ink beside the item the word "dear"—and she underlined it. She also under-scored, in red pencil, two items that apparently jarred her: sherry at $8.70 and wines and cigars at $48 (she noted that her husband had paid for these himself).

In another book the Marquise used for keeping track of meat and grocery purchases, she listed under the heading "Cheap Viandes" rump, shin, round steak, corned beef, and stew beef, and then, apparently thinking with her pencil, she wrote: filet? For ready reference, she penned a list of prices of various cuts of meat in cents per pound: veal cutlets 18, pork chops 11, porter-house steak 20, sirloin 15, mutton chops 15, soup meat 10, lamb chops 35, veal chops 18, sweetbreads 35. Grouse and partridge were $2 a pair, woodcock $1.75, plover and squab $4 a dozen. A 3½-pound lobster cost 53¢, and oysters were less than a penny each.

Everything went down in the little account books—the 10¢ to "a blind man when in New York," the 25¢ and 50¢ on two occasions when "a poor old lady" asked for help, the $10 to charity for a hospital, the $12 a month for carriages to church, and the 25¢ put in the collection plate.

Let it be said that neither the Marquis nor the Marquise was parsimonious. Tiffany's bill in December of their first year in New York totaled $750. Hanft Brothers, the florists at 224 Fifth Avenue, sent an accounting for a pink rose corsage at $5 and daily deliveries of a large bunch of violets and a boutonniere at $3.25, which brought the monthly charge for flowers to about $100. Just in case the Marquis were to suddenly return to Paris, he kept up his membership in the exclusive Société d'Éscrime at 4 rue d'Anjou St. Honoré, which cost the equivalent of $250 a year and assured him of fencing opponents.

It was a pleasant life for the young couple, she coming back to the family home, he exploring an exciting city, New York, and seeing Americans for the first time on their home soil. They were a glamorous pair, a most handsome addition to any party, and so they were in constant demand for balls, Germans, dinners, and other social affairs. They went to Manhattan frequently, and when the opera season opened, they used the von Hoffman box at the Academy of Music, which was at Fourteenth Street and Irving Place. August Belmont, William R. Travers, and others of such social standing had boxes near the von Hoffmans'—$30,000 couldn't buy a box in the 1880's. In her spare time, the Marquise was perfecting her French, which she spoke quite well; she also took painting lessons and was rather accomplished.

But all was not inside activity. The de Morèses combed the beaches around New York in the late summer and early fall. Then with autumn came the shooting season, and they journeyed up the Hudson and elsewhere for wildfowl. On these expeditions they were well supplied with hampers of food and wine put up for them by Park and Tilford.

Meanwhile, de Morès was playing the boy banker, for he had immersed himself in the operations of the von Hoffman bank at 50 Wall Street and was striving to master the intricacies of finance. He did very well. De Morès had a keen mind and an enormous capacity for work, qualities that endeared him to his new American colleagues. He soaked up finance so thoroughly that when he returned to France, he wrote a book entitled *The Secret of Exchange*, and he was able to talk with authority and ease on economics. The von Hoffman bank did an international business, one part of which was arbitrage, the buying and selling of currencies or securities in, say, London and New York to make a profit on the difference in price between the two markets. De Morès worked on these trades, which required quick thinking and acting. But trading, especially in a slow market, can be boring unless one has trading in his blood. De Morès didn't. Moreover, arbitrage usually yields only a small profit on each transaction, so it was difficult for the Frenchman to reconcile this phase of banking with his objectives. De Morès always thought and frequently acted on a grandiose scale, and his work in the bank soon began to pall.

Although de Morès was wedded to von Hoffman's daughter,

he wasn't married to the bank. And in 1882, the American business scene presented many attractive business (or speculative) opportunities that could generate substantial sums. Industry was mushrooming, the railroads were pushing to the Pacific, and the population was expanding.

De Morès was an unusual investor-speculator, for he enthusiastically embraced the idea that his moneymaking should be fused with adventure. In those days, adventure in America was synonymous with the Old West. That left a wide territory from which to choose, but the Marquis, partly because of the stories told by his cousin, Count Fitz-James, had riveted his attention on the Bad Lands of Dakota Territory. Most of his cousin's yarns centered on hunting, but de Morès knew about ranchers moving into the Bad Lands and about the great cattle drives from the Southwest penetrating the area. Soon he was delving into the economics of raising cattle, slaughtering them, and selling the finished product.

De Morès convinced himself that the cattle business was just about the greatest potential bonanza in the United States, which was exactly what he wanted to believe. He wrote an analysis of the industry, and when he came to the reasons for which he thought it was lucrative, he posed the question: "And why?" He answered by saying: "Because cattle serve first the need for nourishment repeated twice a day and every day; second, another necessity required several times a year, that of clothing coming from sheep, and leather from cattle. When these two necessities are assured, man need think of nothing more but shelter."

De Morès was thinking of something else, making money, and on the basis of his initial success, he hoped to persuade French friends to join him as investors in expanding his American enterprises. His optimism was unquenchable, and in fairness to his business sense, it must be said that his estimate of the cattle business was solidly based. The nation's meat stocks were not keeping pace with the increasing population. Moreover, waves of immigrants were still to come, and they would unbalance the supply and demand for meat still more.

As the winter wore on, de Morès became increasingly impatient with the onerous aspects of the banking business. For a kinetic man, the canyons of lower Manhattan grew more and more confining. Life away from the bank was pleasant enough, but neither de Morès nor his wife was captivated by society doings. Both were intrigued with the prospect of living in the Old West, and while Medora was not about to be transformed into a pioneer wife in a sunbonnet, she was ready to face the good and bad fortune that might befall one on the frontier. Stories from the West were common in newspapers and magazines; these yarns whetted the interest of the two. Only the year before, the Earp brothers had shot it out with the Clanton-McLaury outlaws at the OK Corral in Tombstone, Arizona Territory, killing three of them. The outlaws later assassinated Morgan Earp, crippled Virgil for life, and almost got Wyatt. Wyatt took out after the murderers and killed two of them; the others scattered, never to come back within gun range. Dakota was not quite so lurid, but only because there were fewer cattle and therefore fewer cowboys, which meant less trouble. But the Bad Lands were just about as tough, man for man, as the country to the south, although not until de Morès arrived did the area become prime copy for eastern publications.

The Marquis and his wife could talk of nothing but Dakota. In January, 1883, the die was cast. One day after the bank closed, de Morès walked up Broadway to Thompson & Sons, where he bought two pairs of high boots, a tackle box, a trunk, two revolver holsters, a carbine sling and holster. He went home and started to pack.

The Marquis had met Commander Henry Gorringe, a former U.S. Navy officer whose private business deals had forced his resignation from the service. Gorringe was a great promoter. He traded on his naval career, which he felt was distinguished by his having brought the Needle of Cleopatra from Egypt to New

York, a feat hardly worth the importance Gorringe attributed to it. In the fall of 1881, he had traveled through the northwestern part of the country with Henry Pender, son of Sir John Pender of London. While the two were in the Bad Lands, the United States government offered to sell a piece of real estate and some buildings along the Little Missouri that had been used by the army. Gorringe and Pender bought the property and with this asset formed the Little Missouri Land and Cattle Company. They hired Gregor Lang to turn out a small herd of cattle on the land to show their ownership. Gorringe had some sort of idea about developing a tourist and hunting headquarters with the buildings and the real estate, but when de Morès began to talk about the cattle business, Gorringe assured him that the Little Missouri Land and Cattle Company holdings were just the thing for the operation the Frenchman wanted to start.

Much as Gorringe and Pender liked their investment, Gorringe agreed to sell de Morès an option on the holdings. If the option were exercised, it would bring the land and buildings to de Morès for $37,000 (Gorringe and Pender had paid only a few hundred dollars for the property, but there was no reason for its appreciating several thousand per cent). De Morès bought the option. He would have been lucky if he had never set eyes on Gorringe.

Early in March, armed with a letter from General William Tecumseh Sherman asking all army officers in Dakota and Montana to afford de Morès protection and assistance—plus a safe-conduct communication to Indian agents from the Commissioner of Indian Affairs—the Marquis and his man van Driesche set out for the Bad Lands of Dakota Territory. The Marquise said she would follow after the baby she was expecting had been born.

III

THE TOWN OF LITTLE MISSOURI—
THE BAD LANDS

When de Morès and van Driesche awakened in their tent on the west bank of the Little Missouri River, the sun was just beginning to rise. Both came out of the shelter to take in the view that had tantalized them the night before when it had been so dark they could see only a bit of the fascinating new country. They looked upon a peaceful Bad Lands scene: the valley of the Little Missouri where the river looped lazily along a course fringed with cottonwoods that were just beginning to bud. Back from the water's edge the land sloped gently to a wall of high, steep bluffs that had been the banks of the river centuries earlier when it was a wide, brawling torrent. The first rays of the sun were striking the deeply serrated bluffs; in their form and multitude of colors, they suggested that a miniature Grand Canyon might have developed if the waters of the river had been stronger and more plentiful. De Morès and van Driesche could hear the river's waters chuckling over the rocks.

The air was dry and bracing at this 2,000-foot altitude, and the breeze was spiked with the pungent odor of wild sage. Van Driesche had a fire of twigs glowing in a few minutes, and soon the aroma of bacon, coffee, and wood smoke wafted around the tent. De Morès sliced some of the bread van Driesche had bought in St. Paul and toasted it over the coals. While the toast was not the *croissant* and *brioche* to which he was accustomed for breakfast, food mattered little, for already de Morès was feeding on excitement that generated in him a state of euphoria.

Good soldier that he was, de Morès wanted first of all to make his own reconnaissance of the land where he hoped to ranch and build his slaughterhouse. For this he and van Driesche needed horses, so they set off for the town where they had got off the train the night before. The place was officially called Little Missouri, but it was known equally well as "Little Misery." The town's *raison d'être* was the building of the Northern Pacific, which had reached this point in 1879. The United States Army was detailed to protect the construction crews from the Indians, who were constantly on the warpath against the encroaching white man, with a company of fifty men and several officers being assigned to the sector where de Morès found himself. The outfit was called the Bad Lands Cantonment, a term that also applied to the log barracks, officers' quarters, and other army buildings. The cantonment sparked the beginning of the town.

The first entrepreneur in Little Missouri was Frank Moore, who had given up his job as purser on a Missouri River steamboat for the more lucrative calling of sutler. According to Webster, a sutler was first a "man who takes on low offices," but that status became elevated in time to "one who follows an army and sells to the troops provisions, liquors, and the like." Moore's sale of "provisions, liquors, and the like" was limited, but his business prospered, for immediately after the Bad Lands Cantonment troops had unrolled their bedding, they claimed that the alkali dust had parched their throats unmercifully and that they needed quick relief. While there is no record of the quality of the refreshments Moore served, it was common practice in his time to compound a witches' brew by diluting alcohol of dubious quality with river water, adding a plug of tobacco for coloring and a slug of red pepper for firepower.

Moore's place also served as a recreation hall for the soldiers, trappers, buffalo hunters, cowboys, and others who drifted into Little Missouri. If things were dull, something was quickly cooked up. Sometimes the entertainment was a bit macabre, as in the case of Paddock and Livingston. Those two Little Missourians were not friends, yet they were not confirmed enemies, either. Given that premise, the soldiers thought they could have some fun. They told Paddock that Livingston was out to gun him down and vice versa. When Paddock approached Moore's, a soldier would run out, slamming the door behind him. His companions inside would raise a noise, as if they were restraining someone. The soldier outside would tell Paddock that Livingston was inside (which was not true) and that Paddock should leave if he wanted to live because there was no telling how long the soldiers could hold Livingston. The soldiers would then play the same trick on Livingston. Tension between the two men grew as the supposed threats were carried back and forth. It was great fun for the enlisted men, and the officers did nothing to stop it.

Neither Paddock nor Livingston wanted to hurt the other, but each was finally goaded to the point where he felt he had to act or be called a coward. One day as Paddock was sitting in front of his shack, Livingston came riding down the road, filling the magazine of his rifle. The ensuing action was short and decisive. Presumably, Paddock fired the first shot, for Livingston was killed.

In most towns of the Old West, including the toughest, a killing usually resulted in some kind of legal action, even though the affray might patently appear to be self-defense. Writing of the Livingston shooting, an old-timer said: "There seemed to be no talk of a trial or anything of that kind—it was an incident closed."

While life—and sometimes death—centered around the cantonment buildings and the sutler's store in Little Missouri, there were scattered around several shanties belonging to squatters, rustlers, and others who, if not outlaws, were barely inside the law. By far the most substantial structure was the Pyramid Park Hotel, a jumping-off place for sportsmen, a place where they could outfit themselves for the rigors of the field. (The Northern Pacific called the Bad Lands "Pyramid Park" in the hope that name would attract tourists, even though there was nothing pyramidal or parklike about the place. Finally, in the 1930's, even the railroad beat a semantic retreat from "Pyramid Park" to "Bad Lands.")

Moore's sutlership soon had competition: six other saloon-keepers arrived in Little Missouri, and while their booze was no better than Moore's, some of them provided diversions other than drinking and shooting, such as faro games, dancing partners, and sporting departments with prostitutes summoned on the tom-tom.

Bill Williams was the leading dispenser of what was known as Forty Mile Red Eye. He was a dumpy-looking man with piglike eyes, red hair, a flushed complexion which he constantly kept fueled, and an animal leer. One of the thoroughly disreputable inhabitants of the town, he was willing to make a fast dollar in any way, including cattle rustling. In spite of his despicable character, Williams could be amusing when slightly inebriated, but it was hard to find him in that relatively benign state, since he was usually loaded. He hated to be alone, and on the infrequent occasions when his place was deserted, he would line up several rows of chairs, as if for an audience, then deliver a sermon to the empty seats. Jess Hogue was Williams' partner; a shadier individual would be difficult to imagine. He would do anything for money. Then there was a third-ranking rapscallion in Little Missouri, a friend of Williams and Hogue, named Jake Maunders. One of the most feared men in the Bad Lands, he was a cold-blooded killer and extremely crafty. Curiously enough, he was to influence de Morès' stay in the Bad Lands—and all for the worse.

Little Missouri was no place to bring a maiden aunt for a visit. Certainly some respectable citizens lived there, but they were a minority. Prostitutes outnumbered the other ladies, a population statistic that helped to explain some of the town's rowdiness. Gamblers, drifters, rustlers, con men, common thieves, and gunmen lived off the soldiers and unlucky innocents who came through en route to what they hoped were greener pastures. Cowboys from Texas were good prey; they frequently stopped in Little Misery while driving cattle into the Bad Lands. Shooting was almost as common as breathing, with drunks galloping up and down the main street, firing their guns in wild abandon. It was considered great sport to wait for the conductor to descend from the *Pacific Express*, then shoot at his feet to make him dance. It is highly possible that the amount of brass in the streets from discharged revolver and rifle cartridges would have been enough to cast a memorial of sorts in honor of the best shot in town. For hundreds of miles around Little Missouri there was no law and no lawman; the only way anyone could enforce order was with a .45.

By the time de Morès arrived, the army had been moved from the cantonment to another post. This reduced the number of roisterers, but did nothing to inhibit those who remained. The permanent population of Little Missouri was probably about two dozen, with the census going up at night. No one would ever have been so brash as to take a count. The last thing many of the Bad Lands inhabitants wanted was to be counted and identified.

It was only eight o'clock when de Morès and van Driesche walked into Little Missouri. The dusty street was deserted, except for a couple of stray dogs and two forlorn cow ponies tied to a rail in front of a saloon, their riders having forgotten them in the previous night's revelry. It was easy to spot the livery stable, with its hitching post in front and a corral in back. De Morès pounded on the door. It was opened by a sleepy man, tall and bronzed, with a droopy moustache, black goatee, and shifty eyes. He was E. G. (Gerry) Paddock, they learned—the man who shot Livingston. He rented horses to the Frenchmen, and off they rode into the heart of the Bad Lands, following the map de Morès had obtained from the military in Washington, D.C.

De Morès knew that French-Canadian explorers had named the region and that they had meant nothing deprecatory by calling it the Bad Lands. The name evolved quite simply, really. The Bad Lands are a jumble of topography, about two hundred miles long and fifty miles wide, that sprawls along the course of the

Little Missouri and its tributaries but lies mostly in what is today western North and South Dakota. The Little Missouri's course is sinuous, doubling back repeatedly like hairpin turns on a mountain road. Its tributaries follow the same kind of snake-like flow. When these waterways were cut eons ago, they formed valleys and ravines, and because of the twisting water courses, successive valleys and ravines run at angles to each other. Following a subsidiary valley might well lead the explorer to a dead end and far off his intended course. This is what happened to the early French-Canadian *voyageurs*, and when at last they pushed across the difficult terrain to the level prairies beyond, they wrote across their crude maps, *"Mauvaises terres à traverser,"* for it had indeed been bad land to traverse. Soon the "traversing" part of the translated French name was dropped and the area was called simply the Bad Lands. The Sioux Indians called the region *macha sicha*, which means "bad lands," because they said a hostile tribe once was wiped out there in a cataclysm of fire and lightning as divine punishment for having denied the area to peaceful tribes that had hunted there before. The Bad Lands were the end result of the Great Spirit's conflagration, the red men said.

Indians swarmed over the Bad Lands after the first French-Canadian explorers went through early in the nineteenth century. This was the stronghold of the Arikaras, Gros Ventres, Sioux, and Mandans. They trapped and hunted all over the area, and by 1845 the fur trade was so brisk that the American Fur Company built a trading post, Fort Berthold, about fifteen miles below the confluence of the Little Missouri and the Big Muddy.

Americans had heard little of this area until 1864, when Brigadier General Alfred Sully took on the Sioux for a double purpose. His first task was to retaliate for Sioux attacks on settlers in Minnesota, then he was to escort a wagon train of prospectors and their families from Bismarck to what they hoped would be fabulous wealth in the gold mines of Montana and Idaho. When Sully reached the mouth of the Little Missouri, he learned that the Sioux were on his right in the Killdeer Mountains at the edge of the Bad Lands. He went after them, won the engagement, then plunged through the Bad Lands, which he described as "grand, dismal, and majestic," adding that they looked like "hell with the fires out."

That was not the last of the Sioux. In the fall and winter of 1875–76, Sitting Bull's forces holed up in the Bad Lands about fifty miles northwest of present-day Medora. In the spring, Lieutenant Colonel George A. Custer and the Seventh Cavalry went after Sitting Bull; while organizing his campaign, he camped at what is now the Custer Trail Ranch near Medora. Custer's scouts scoured the Bad Lands looking for the Indians, but found none. The vagaries of the weather stopped military operations, for on June 1 and 2 a raging blizzard swept over the Bad Lands, forcing the regiment into camp. When the weather cleared, Custer led his men out of the Bad Lands and finally to their annihilation in the Battle of the Little Big Horn. Later that year, Brigadier General George Crook pursued some of the Indians who had fought Custer, chasing them through the Bad Lands, then south, and finally defeated them in the Battle of Slim Buttes in what today is South Dakota.

By 1879, the Sioux were either dead or on reservations, except for a few bands that held out, and when de Morès and van Driesche rode through the Bad Lands in 1883, only a smattering of stray red men were on the loose. These could be dangerous, but most of them were hungry people to whom an appeal could be made with food or whiskey.

The two Frenchmen were fascinated by the strange topography surrounding them as they cantered along. Nowhere on the globe are the weird formations of the Bad Lands duplicated. To some people, the Bad Lands seem part of another world—and in a way they are, for they were created centuries ago and have changed very little since.

When prehistoric seas receded from the area, they left vast swamps and lakes. Since the climate was tropical, plant life flourished: great forests covered the soggy land, and a tangle of jungle growth filled the space between the trees. As this profusion of plant life died, the debris fell into the water and formed peat. With the passage of time, the peat was compressed into lignite. Millions of years passed, with layer after layer of soil, clay, limestone, and rock being deposited atop the lignite. Then the region dried, and from the center of the earth volcanic fires erupted, igniting many of the lignite beds. Eventually, the fires died, leaving behind ashes, limestone, rocks, and the baked clay, called scoria.

When the newborn Little Missouri and its tributaries came frothing out of their sources, they cut through the lignite ashes, washing away the soft soils and clays that had not been baked. As the waters receded, they left behind stark, deeply serrated bluffs; rain and wind carved countless ravines leading into the main channel of the Little Missouri. The surging waters also left behind baked-clay buttes, a fantasy of cones, obelisks, spheres, mushrooms, domes, and an infinite extent and variety of other shapes that look as if they were models for a surrealistic painting.

The buttes are freakishly colored in horizontal layers of multi-hued clay, with a predominance of scoria, much of it brick red but some also pale pink. Veins of black lignite run through them, contrasting with clays of ocher, gray, and brown. Like the valley floor from which they rise, the buttes are usually barren, standing stark against the sky. But some wear on their sides a patina of green stuff that grows where hospitable soil has lodged, and some are whiskered on top with prairie grass; cedar and juniper trees cling stubbornly to others, their bright green contrasting with the subdued colors of the mass from which they wring their nourishment. The buttes frequently are grotesque, even garish, yet they flare in a kind of wild beauty as they change colors when the sun plays on their many facets. Under a cloudy sky, they stand brooding and menacing; in moonlight, they cast ghostly shadows over the tousled landscape and the eerie scene is lighted in hellish reality by the carmine glow from a burning lignite vein.

The Little Missouri and its tributaries did more than carve out the Bad Lands: they left a layer of rich soil along their banks for a considerable distance inland. Here de Morès saw buffalo grass rising knee high. Trees—elm, box elder, ash, cottonwood, and evergreen—grew in profusion. Draws and ravines leading to the Little Missouri were especially lush with grass and other vegetation; for this, beavers were responsible. The little animals had dammed the streams, thus conserving water for plant life and preventing erosion that otherwise would have washed the topsoil away in a wild runoff.

De Morès saw that the ravines not only offered food for livestock, but, because of their deep sides, also provided shelter from wind and snow. This was important, for Bad Lands winters can be brutal, with howling blizzards and temperatures as low as sixty degrees below zero.

A white-tailed deer bounded across de Morès' path; two mountain sheep stared down from atop a butte. In the distance, an elk tossed his majestic antlers and disappeared over the horizon. In addition to the wildlife, some Longhorn steers were feeding in one of the draws. All of these animals living off the land were fat, and this pleased de Morès; as he and van Driesche rode along, he could picture herds of his own beef cattle fattening there.

At noon the Frenchmen stopped by a small stream, where van Driesche cooled a bottle of white wine and spread the contents of his saddlebags on a flat rock. There were tins and jars of *pâté de foie gras*, sardines, potted meat, cheese, and bread. Nothing was left to carry back. The two stretched out in the sun, smoking cigarettes and watching a hawk glide on the air currents, then plummet to the ground and rise with a prairie dog in its claws.

When they reached their tent that night, they had traveled about fifty miles. For the next two days they did the same thing, but over other ground, with de Morès noting carefully the areas he thought would be best suited for his operations.

At the end of the reconnaissance, de Morès was delighted with

35

what he had seen. It seemed to him that the place where the Northern Pacific crossed the Little Missouri River was ideal for the kind of cattle-raising, buying, and slaughtering enterprise he wanted to establish. In writing about the selection of this locale, de Morès said it had the advantages of "eastern limit of the range; shortest haul to market; railroad facilities; water and ice to any extent; abundance of fuel in the shape of lignite; immense amounts of range, shelter and grass along the Little Missouri River, allowing the beef crop to be concentrated and without loss of substance, but with constant increase of same; possibility . . . to own a permanent right of way to . . . [the] shipping point . . . ."

In addition to these business considerations, the Frenchman liked the Bad Lands; the vastness of the territory greatly appealed to him. He wrote the Marquise about his reaction to the wide open spaces, saying: "I like this country for there is room to move about without stepping on the feet of others." It is ironic that he should have expressed himself in that way, for although he certainly had no intention of stepping on anyone, some of the people in the Bad Lands soon thought he was going to trample them out of existence, and this led to serious trouble.

Since the town of Little Missouri, such as it was, already existed, de Morès felt he should take whatever advantage there might be in opening his operations there. When Gorringe sold the option to de Morès, he remarked that a building he owned might serve as a ranch house, so the Frenchman now went to see it. He was met by Frank Vine, who worked for Gorringe. The building turned out to be the old cantonment, and from the moment the army left it, the elements had taken their toll. Patently, it wouldn't do for anything and de Morès told Vine so, which raised Vine's ire.

De Morès went to the land office in Bismarck to search the title on the Little Missouri Land and Cattle Company land for which he held an option. What he found made his moustache twitch: the only property Gorringe and Pender owned was the set of old cantonment buildings; title to the rest of what Gorringe claimed was nonexistent. Frank B. Allen, a young attorney in Bismarck, helped de Morès with the title search. He suggested that the Marquis could buy all the land he wanted for his ranch and corrals from the Northern Pacific and others and that he could also acquire property on the east bank of the Little Missouri for his packing plant.

Back in Little Missouri, the Marquis told Vine of his findings in Bismarck and added, somewhat unnecessarily it would seem, that he was not exercising the option on the land Gorringe purported to own. Vine was further incensed. He insisted that the option was binding on de Morès to buy the land. De Morès was icily aloof. Vine frothed. Vine said he was going to organize others in the Bad Lands to drive de Morès out for his failure to exercise the option. De Morès, who was fearless to a fault, replied that he had no intention of being bullied by anyone, much less a man of Vine's ilk.

The threat to drive him from the Bad Lands angered the Frenchman, but it did nothing to deter him from carrying out his plan. To attempt to operate in Little Missouri was out of the question, but as de Morès himself had remarked, the Bad Lands abounded in space. There was, indeed, a fine townsite across the river from Little Missouri. Why not build his own town?

De Morès and van Driesche struck their tent and walked across the railroad bridge to the east bank of the river, where they promptly pitched it again. Then, with van Driesche standing at attention beside him, de Morès cracked a bottle of wine over an iron tent peg and christened the place where his town would rise Medora—for his wife. The date, in 1883, was prophetic: April 1.

IV

THE BUILDING OF MEDORA

Never before had the people of the Bad Lands seen such a whirlwind of activity as that blown up in the building of Medora. Carloads of construction materials began to arrive from the east, and with them platoons of carpenters, bricklayers, and masons. The journeymen's helpers were loaded with the masters' tools. Industrious and skilled, the workers proudly claimed they had learned their trade in the Old Country. Accents and pride in their work showed their long apprenticeships and the demanding standards to which they were accustomed. Wads of chewing tobacco bulged from their cheeks, or, if they were Scandinavians, their lower lips swelled with snuff, which they called "snoose" to rhyme with moose. They were a goodnatured lot, singing and whistling while they worked.

Since there was no place for the men to stay, de Morès brought in tents, and soon the building site resembled an army camp. The canvas attracted attention for miles around. One of the first to see what was going on was A. C. Huidekoper, whose ranch was a few miles from Medora. He came to the Bad Lands from Pennsylvania on a hunting trip in 1879 and was so taken by the country and its prospects for ranching that he returned in 1882 and bought a large tract (it rivaled the Marquis' holdings). "I remember my first sight of Medora," he wrote. "George Woodman, a Boston man . . . and myself, had ridden in from the logging camp. We were hot and had an alkali thirst. As we dropped down into the flat where Medora now stands we saw a lot of tents. . . . We rode up to a larger tent that seemed to be headquarters. A little Frenchman came out and announced that he was William van Driesche, secretary to the Marquis de Morès. He asked if I was Mr. Huidekoper [Huidekoper would have been difficult to mistake with his drooping blond moustache, deerslayer cap, and puttee-like leggins] and said that the Marquis had left word that if I arrived he was to entertain us the best he could. I told him that we were very thirsty. He went into the tent and brought out two big goblets of cold champagne. My, but it did taste good!"

Some of de Morès' detractors have sought to leave the impression that he welcomed the support of the roughnecks and crooks of the Bad Lands; that he enlisted the friendship of Huidekoper is only one indication of the facts. He knew that his gesture to Huidekoper in absentia would help him. At the same time, he realized that on the basis of mutual interest, the man from Pennsylvania was on his side. Both were substantial landowners and had everything to gain by making the Bad Lands a place where law at least was recognized, if not in order.

(Later, de Morès saw Huidekoper frequently. Both were ardent huntsmen and loved nothing better than to take off over the prairies and draws after game. Huidekoper was critical of de Morès, but only with regard to his business judgment and some of the things he did, such as building a hunting coach to duplicate the one Napoleon used on the fatal Russian campaign. No doubt the two men had more in common than they shared with the scum of the Bad Lands. But then that wouldn't have been difficult.)

Building personal political fences was only one job facing de Morès—building his town of Medora demanded much attention. Huidekoper and other Bad Lands "superintendents" soon saw the first structure in the new community rise: de Morès' office, where van Driesche set up the accounts and ran the enterprise. Then the general store, also a part of the de Morès plan, was built. It was stocked with all manner of merchandise, including groceries, dry goods, harness, saddles, tobacco and cigars, flour and feed, felt shoes, and overshoes. Hunters' supplies were also a specialty.

De Morès constructed other buildings, including a hotel, and soon other entrepreneurs arrived in Medora to try their luck. The first, of course, were the saloonkeepers, for the thirsts to be slaked in the community were growing constantly in number and seemingly were unquenchable. Several of the saloons that blossomed in Medora had originated in Little Missouri—moving across the river was simple. The competition between the two towns was intense, but it was clear that Medora, with the money the Marquis was pouring into it, was the better bet. Their relationship soon degenerated to a deplorable state. Lincoln Lang wrote: "The air fairly seethed with rivalry and factional feeling. Like a pair of bulldogs on a leash, aching to be at each other's throats, the two communities glowered at each other from opposite sides of the river."

De Morès wasn't trying to drive Little Missouri out of business but such was the result of his building Medora, and the animosity from the west bank of the river was directed at him. One of the heaviest losers in the competition would be Henry Gorringe, for his dream of mounting a great tourist operation in Little Missouri faded with each hammer blow in Medora; the Gorringe faction was a rallying point for others who had come to detest de Morès.

The Marquis' most ambitious building project, by far, was the slaughterhouse, sprawling structure close by the river and the railroad. Huge boilers and machines for it arrived and a brick chimney taller than anything in the surrounding countryside began to rise. The abattoir was scheduled to be completed and ready for operation in the fall of 1883, and the deadline was met. A spur track was built from the slaughterhouse to the main line of the Northern Pacific. Corrals for cattle were constructed near by.

Houses were started for the employees who eventually would staff the packing plant, and de Morès put up a recreation hall for them that included billiard rooms and bowling alleys. While the house de Morès was building for himself and his Marquise had ample room for the von Hoffmans when they visited, he constructed a brick house for them in town.

In all this bustle of activity, de Morès was everywhere, supervising, giving directions, and pushing everyone on to work. But even though he was busy, he was always readily accessible in his office, and, knowing the way to the heart of most of the workers and others, he always had "something for the snake bite," as he quickly learned to call the refreshment he served his callers (he drank sparingly himself).

The Marquis tired of living in the tent, and since he would be traveling a great deal by railroad, he rented a private car, *The Montana*, from the Northern Pacific and spotted it on the siding. To the consternation of his father-in-law, who thought de Morès was roughing it on the frontier, the Marquis and van Driesche moved into the car, where they lived in splendor pending the completion of enough of the Marquis' house so that he could occupy it.

The house has been called a château, a term which bears little relationship to the structure, for it was more of a ranch house than a French country place. In keeping with de Morès' seigneurial position, it perched atop a high bluff on riverbank opposite Medora, so that it commanded a view of all its owner controlled in the immediate vicinity—and that was just about everything. The first excavation at the site was for that facility without which a Frenchman would find life impossible: a wine cellar. Eventually, the place would have twenty-eight rooms, not counting the coachman's house, which was outside the main building. Nothing remotely near this size had been seen on that part of the frontier. Work was being rushed so that the Marquise and the new baby could come out for the summer.

Despite the attention he had to devote to construction, de Morès was beginning, as early as May, to organize his enterprises in accordance with territorial and state laws. On May 12, 1883, he incorporated the Northern Pacific Refrigerator Car Company (NPRCC) with Herman Haupt, Jr., and C. Edgar Haupt, both of St. Paul, Minnesota. The firm was capitalized at $200,000; of the 500 shares of stock, de Morès held 330 and the Haupts 85 shares each. The company was incorporated in New Jersey, to do business there, and in eight other states and five territories. It was empowered to raise, slaughter, and sell cattle, sheep, and hogs and ship the meat in refrigerator cars it would build; it could also use the rolling stock for shipping perishables other than meat, such as game, fruit, vegetables, and dairy products.

Having bought about four thousand acres where the town of Medora was rising, plus a parklike area on the other side of the river where his house was going up, de Morès turned his attention to acquiring, personally and through the NPRCC, land for a ranch where he could raise his own livestock and keep cattle he bought until they were ready for slaughter. Remembering his personal reconnaissance on horseback and the advice of Frank Allen, the Bismarck attorney, he bought strips of land on both sides of the Little Missouri. Each was about twenty to twenty-five miles long and stretched five miles inland from the riverbank, that being the maximum distance cattle could be expected to walk for water.

The holding was vast. Not only was the acreage immense in itself, but because of water rights, it effectively controlled several thousand acres that abutted de Morès' property. The Frenchman was not the kind of person who would buy up property with water rights in order to deny the use of the river to his neighbors, and even if he had entertained such an idea, he certainly wouldn't have publicized it. Yet the fact remains that with his strategic land holdings, de Morès did look down the throats of his neighbors, and being the people they were about such matters, they fumed and exploded.

Not only were de Morès' neighbors angry about water rights, but they also objected to the way the Marquis obtained some of his land. He bought nearly nine thousand acres from the Northern Pacific for about $23,000, but part of it was acquired through the purchase of scrip, which some Bad Landers didn't understand or didn't want to understand. Scrip was a document issued by the federal government authorizing the holder to acquire a specified acreage of unoccupied public land, the location of which he chose. It was issued for a number of reasons, among them, to compensate people who had been legally dispossessed of their lands, such as the Choctaw Indians, who were given scrip for more than a million acres in lieu of the land to which they were entitled under the Treaty of 1830. Up to 1907, when the government ceased to issue it, there had been authorized enough scrip to cover more than two and a half million acres, and some of it is still outstanding.

In effect, scrip is a deed to a specific amount of land, and so it has been bought and sold much as if it were land. De Morès purchased Valentine Scrip, named for the man to whom it was originally issued, which the Frenchman used to acquire public lands along the Little Missouri. The legality of transactions in scrip was never challenged, yet when de Morès began to take over property to which he was entitled by the purchase of Valentine Scrip, there were rumblings about the Marquis' expropriating the Bad Lands as if he had paid nothing. This was nonsense, but the criticism shows how deeply the Marquis was resented by those who didn't have his means, for they too, could have bought land through the purchase of Valentine Scrip if they had had the funds.

Among the loudest in their criticism of de Morès' scrip purchases was Lincoln Lang, who wrote: "We began to hear much from across the river about certain more or less mythical 'Script Rights,' whatever they might be . . . de Morès was buying up land in quantity under them, proposing thus to take title to anything and everything that appealed to his fancy. Nobody, it appeared, had any rights now except himself, so that we would all have to knuckle down accordingly." Lang *père* also vented his

43

spleen against de Morès, which could well have been on orders from Gorringe, who never got over his pique when the Marquis refused to be duped into buying the Little Missouri Land and Cattle Company.

Then de Morès bought twelve thousand acres of wheat land near Bismarck. This purchase bore no relationship to his operations in the Bad Lands—it was more than a hundred miles away—and moreover he paid cash for the acreage. Yet de Morès' critics pointed to this acquisition as further evidence of his desire to run everything in the western part of the Territory.

The charge of land grabbing and attempting to monopolize the Bad Lands was fantastic. In the first place, it is doubtful that de Morès really wanted more land than he actually owned; his property was sufficient for the operation he envisioned. True, many ranchers with large herds owned no range land at all, but only the real estate on which their home buildings stood, if that. Huidekoper had about the same acreage as de Morès; there was a difference, however, in the owner's nationality. In the minds of the suspicious residents of the Bad Lands, de Morès was a menace because he was a foreigner.

In addition to buying land, the Marquis was making some sizable cattle deals. Far from opposing the Marquis, ranchers in the Bad Lands and in Montana were delighted to have a local buyer for their livestock. Soon de Morès' purchases were being discussed far and wide, even to the point of becoming the subject of editorials. This one appeared in the *Mandan Pioneer*:

The Marquis de Mores has bought of the Concord Cattle Company 3,000 steers. . . . He has also purchased of Joseph Leighton 800 head of cattle and 200 horses. Besides he has 1,200 head of cattle being contracted for. . . . Receipts and vouchers are on hand to show that the Marquis has invested $300,000 in this western country. When the Northern Pacific Refrigerator Car Company gets to work it will call for 2,500 to 5,000 cattle a month. It is impossible to over-estimate the value of this industry in the West Missouri country. The stockmen of the Bad Lands, and for hundreds of miles around, will have a market for their cattle right at hand instead of having to send them to some remote point in the east. There will be economy in this in many ways. In the first place, cattle that travel east in cars lose flesh on the way, while being slaughtered near the ranches they will yield to the owners the full value of their weight. Then too, money will be kept in the country tributary to Mandan, which would otherwise be paid to eastern slaughterers and dressers. So delighted are the western stockmen with the prospect, that Miles City, Montana has given forty acres of land to the company, of which the Marquis de Mores is president, on which to erect buildings. In the spring a branch office will be put up at Miles City.

De Morès was not at all bashful about telling people of his plans to buy cattle in quantity. One of the Marquis' confidants who passed his stories on was Howard Eaton, who, with his brother Alden, ran a dude ranch called the Custer Trail. The Eatons were about de Morès's age, fine young men who had been in the Bad Lands since about 1880. De Morès told Howard he was going to buy all the livestock that came over the Northern Pacific, slaughter it in his abattoir at Medora, and ship the finished product to Chicago and points east. Eaton then asked de Morès if he had any idea how many cattle the railroad shipped. According to Herman Hagedorn, in his *Roosevelt in the Bad Lands*, de Morès replied:

"It doesn't matter. My father-in-law has ten million dollars and can borrow ten million more. I've got old Armour and the rest of them matched dollar for dollar. Do you think I am impractical? I am not impractical. My plan is altogether feasible. I do not merely think this. I know. My intuition tells me so. I pride myself on having a natural intuition. It takes me only a few seconds to understand a situation that other men have to puzzle over for hours. I seem to see every side of a question at once. I assure you, I am gifted in this way. I have wonderful insight."

Hagedorn, it should be remembered, idolized Teddy Roosevelt, who wasn't too fond of de Morès, so the language of the quote might be somewhat exaggerated. And Howard Eaton must have been in his sixties when he recalled the remarks de Morès had made about forty years earlier. Nevertheless, de

45

Morès' confidence crops up in other instances, and no doubt this characteristic did nothing to endear him to the people of the Bad Lands. Howard Eaton, however, was not influenced by de Morès' bragging; at least he stood by the Frenchman when he was in trouble.

If de Morès was affected by either criticism of himself or his plans, he didn't show it. He continued building his empire.

In addition to the carpenters and other builders, de Morès needed men to run his packing plant and cowboys on his ranch. Eventually, his indoor staff numbered 150, with an equal total in the saddle.

For the ranch, de Morès hired Johnny Goodall as foreman, a choice that no one would have argued, for the man knew his business thoroughly, both in handling men and beasts. It was Goodall's job to hire cowboys, a tricky business because rustlers liked nothing better than to infiltrate an honest outfit and then ply their trade.

As a driver and sort of general foreman around the abattoir, de Morès took on Gerry Paddock, the Little Missouri liveryman from whom he and van Driesche had rented horses for the first ride through the Bad Lands. De Morès also engaged, as two of his most trusted lieutenants, Dick Moore and Frank Miller. They were cowboys and general handymen; both stood by de Morès throughout his days in the Bad Lands, especially in the gun-fighting.

Thus far, de Morès seemed to have chosen as well as he could in the scantily supplied labor market. But then he picked as one of his assistants a man who had just about the most unsavory reputation of anyone in Little Missouri—and he deserved it. He was Jake Maunders.

Maunders was a powerfully built man with a scowling face set off by a slack jaw and eyes one would instinctively distrust. One of the early settlers in the Bad Lands, he had first worked as a commercial hunter, but when foreign and eastern sportsmen discovered the Bad Lands, he soon found he could earn far more by guiding them to the game. His rates were fierce. He prospered. He was a squatter par excellence, and he immediately occupied any cabin that was left for even a short time, claiming it and the surrounding land. When anyone attempted to settle near by, he said he owned the land and extracted a fee for it. Human life meant nothing to him. He had shot MacNab, one of the first pioneers, as MacNab walked innocently away from Little Missouri, and everyone knew of another murder he had committed. In addition to those two homicides, a man to whom Maunders owed a sizable sum of money was found dead. Maunders claimed the man had been kicked to death by a horse, an explanation that never would have stood up in court—but there were no courts in the Bad Lands. Little wonder, then, that with such murderous tendencies Maunders should be anything but a thief, which he was, and his skill as a forger with a branding iron was well known.

Whatever reason de Morès may have had for hiring Maunders remains a mystery. De Morès was dealing with people completely different from those he customarily associated with, yet he wasn't naïve. The most logical explanation is that the shrewd Bad Lander (and bad actor) convinced de Morès that because of his long residence in that part of the country, he was uniquely equipped to advise on any subject that might arise. De Morès could therefore have overlooked Maunders' unsavory character in the supposed interests of business. But hiring Maunders damaged the Frenchman's standing with the honest people of the Bad Lands, for they despised Maunders and his ilk.

De Morès was drawing criticism from another source: the outlaws and roughnecks of the Bad Lands. They saw in Medora, now in its second month of building, exactly what they didn't want. The growth of the community would inevitably mean that the county would be organized, which would bring law to the doorstep of their domain. The county had not been organized before because the lawless element was able to use its superior influence against those who wanted law and order. But with the slaughterhouse, the accompanying arrival of the workers' wives and others, things would be different. So it was that the people who lived by their wits began to find fault with everything the Marquis was doing. At first, the remarks were simply foul-mouthed criticism which anyone with a clean shirt would have drawn: cutting a dude down to size in rough talk. Then, as the buildings in Medora continued to rise and more people arrived, de Morès' became an execration in the mouths of the toughs. They knew their days were numbered unless they did something.

The commercial hunters sided with the lawless. There was still sufficient game in 1883 to provide a living for men who shot deer, elk, antelope, buffalo, and wildfowl and sold the meat to army posts, construction crews, and railroad dining cars. Civilization would spoil this business, for the wildlife of the region had its balance with nature. Once that balance was destroyed, the game would diminish, as indeed it did when the great herds of cattle invaded the Bad Lands.

De Morès was well aware of the scorn being heaped upon him by the crooks of the Bad Lands, and he wanted to enlist some of the honest people on his side. He already had Howard Eaton. Then he went after Gregor Lang, a dour Scotsman whose sanctimonious appearance was intensified by muttonchop whiskers and tiny eyes that peered through equally small glasses. He was the sort of man who probably disliked more people instinctively than he liked, and he was bristly as a porcupine. Lang was backed by Sir John Pender, yet he was allegedly opposed to aristocracy, which was said to be the basis for his reaction to de Morès. Herman Hagedorn says Lang simply did not like "the grandiose Frenchman." Despite Lang's well-known disposition toward the Marquis, de Morès proposed that they join forces against the outlaws, for he thought, quite logically, that personal feelings should have nothing to do with establishing law and order in the Bad Lands. Lang's reaction to de Morès' proposal was quick as litmus: he said he wanted nothing to do with the Frenchman or his plan. De Morès was flabbergasted. "I am sorry," he said to Lang politely. "I desire to be friends with every man." Lang's refusal must have been a bitter potion for a man accustomed to having people ask *him* for favors.

The incident with Lang was one of the first indications that de Morès was up against forces he had never dreamed of. The young Frenchman, old for his years, realized that he could do nothing to change Lang's attitude, nor could he do anything to alter the opinion of people in general. Yet the Marquis himself was responsible for some of the local antipathy. If Maunders and others hired by de Morès had been performing their duties, they would have warned the Frenchman that the barbed wire he had just ordered was a stick of dynamite with a short fuse.

V

DE MORÈS FENCES HIS LAND

When de Morès bought his ranch along the Little Missouri, he immediately did something that would have been perfectly natural in Europe but was anathema on the frontier: he fenced his land. To be sure, he owned the property and there was no territorial law against fencing, but at that time no one fenced. Cattle roamed the open range, owners claiming them and their offspring at roundup time. If the Marquis had dug a moat around his place and erected a stone wall inside it, he could not have erred more egregiously than he did with the wire. He had broken the tradition of the open range, an unforgivable sin.

The air in Little Missouri and Medora crackled with protests over the fencing. Here was proof, de Morès' enemies cried, that the Frenchman was trying to monopolize the Bad Lands and run things the way he wished. To some extent, the fences lent a bit of credibility to the charge, for the Marquis owned one of the largest ranches and he was the only rancher to fence his land.

Surely de Morès didn't realize how galling his barbed wire would be to the people of the Bad Lands. It has been said that he hated to be told anything that conflicted with his own ideas. No doubt he did rely on his own thinking, frequently to the exclusion of outside advice. It is also possible that his men told him what to expect if he fenced and that he ignored them; he could be mulish when he made up his mind. Had he provided gates in his fences, he might have averted some of the trouble, but not all, for the fact that he had fenced was enough to alienate many of the Bad Landers.

The fences brought wrath upon de Morès because of some practical complaints from people who were inconvenienced by the wire. They probably didn't have a legal leg to stand on, but then there was no law in the Bad Lands, and moreover, people there were accustomed to settling such matters without the benefit of the bench. The complaints grew out of the fact that the Bad Lands were covered by a web of trails, free for anyone to use. Now these were cut off by the Frenchman's fences, which necessitated detours up or down the Little Missouri. That anyone had to detour at all was highly offensive to the frontiersmen, who thought they had a natural right to move anywhere they pleased without hindrance—it had always been that way, and they saw no reason for a change. To some ranchers, the wire was an acute stricture: cattle on ranges abutting de Morès' land had to be driven some distance for water, since they could no longer use the trails leading to the river. In some instances, ranchers themselves were denied the routes they normally used to go to the ranges, to their neighbors, or to their favorite settlement on the Little Missouri.

Some of the loudest protests came from a smattering of small cowmen who had settled on plots of ground now enclosed in the property de Morès had bought and fenced. These operators were called "nesters," being squatters who "nested" on public or private property. They were known as "dogiemen," too, because they raised dogies (calves which at roundup time neither claimed nor were claimed by a cow); they also ran cattle brought into the Bad Lands from Minnesota and other places to the east.

The nesters admitted they were squatters, but in their minds this did nothing to lessen the validity of their claims: they felt they were entitled to the land by virtue of having lived on it. The odds are that de Morès would not have minded their staying where they were, provided they behaved. In fact, their presence lent a seigneurial air to his domain which he might have thought fitting—he later offered them sheep, to be raised on a generous share arrangement. But the atmosphere around the Bad Lands had become so miasmic with generated ill will that troublemakers carried stories to the nesters of de Morès' plans to evict them. None of the dogiemen talked to de Morès, who would have assured them that he had no such designs. Rather than speak to him, they chose to fume and protest to the people who told the stories. Their reply was that if the Marquis or anyone representing him came to their places with the idea of sending them away, he would be met by gunfire. They undoubtedly meant it.

The hunters were only slightly less vituperative. Their blood pressure had risen over de Morès' mere presence in the Bad Lands, for what he was doing represented the encroachment of civilization, which meant the demise of wildlife in the area. While this might not happen overnight, the end of commercial game hunting loomed as a certainty. Add to that dolorous eventuality the fact that some of the hunters' trails had been blocked by the Marquis' fences. This meant long detours to reach their favorite hunting grounds.

One of the most vitriolic critics of the Marquis and his fences was a hunter named Frank O'Donald, better known as O'Donnell. He was tall and bony, light complexioned, and the prototype of the frontier hunter in a fringed buckskin suit and the usual armament in a belt around his hips. An English journalist wrote that O'Donnell "was the sort of man that, if choice were thrust upon me, I should prefer to have as a friend rather than an enemy. But if that made no difference, I should like to strike him off my visiting list altogether." O'Donnell wouldn't have cared if he were on or off anybody's visiting list, for he was an independent cuss who was accustomed to roam over the prairies as freely as the game he pursued. When in his cups, which was frequent, O'Donnell could be one of the meanest men in the Bad Lands. The wire he now discovered across one of his trails had the same maddening effect on him as booze.

O'Donnell shared a claim down the river with two other hunters, Reilly Luffsey and Jack Reuter, better known as Dutch Wannegan. Luffsey was an Irishman with the typical features of his countrymen and long black hair that flowed from under his big cowboy hat. Wannegan was noted for being smooth shaven (at least when he once had his picture taken) and for his thick accent (he was German born). He claimed to have fought in the Franco-Prussian War, and that was his reason for wanting to join O'Donnell in his vendetta against the Frenchman; he wanted another crack at the enemy.

The three hunters were furious about the fences. In Little Missouri, they cursed the Marquis and his wire, finding a ready audience among people who bristled at the slightest intimation of anyone's infringing on what they felt were God-given rights. Lincoln Lang was one of their most willing listeners, and he became, almost automatically, a sympathizer with the hunters because they were against a man his father disliked. Writing about the three hunters' complaint, he said: "Their inalienable rights were being infringed upon. They were not going to stand for it. That was all there was to it." Lang didn't explain what the "inalienable rights" were, for although de Morès' fences might have cut off a hunting trail, he did own the land, which he had a perfect right to protect from trespassers.

As if the wire were not enough to rile O'Donnell, Luffsey, and Wannegan, a busybody told them the blatant lie that de Morès planned to buy their claim down the river with Valentine Scrip and oust them immediately. The trio reasoned such an act would be the same as claim jumping. They exploded. "Ever jump us," shouted O'Donnell to Gregor Lang, and he'll "jump right into his grave!" In a masterpiece of understatement, A. C. Huidekoper remarked: "There was bad blood all around."

Enter Jake Maunders. He had long been on the outs with O'Donnell, and the feeling was mutual. Nothing could please Maunders more than to build up the ill will O'Donnell held for de Morès and thus provoke a fight in which O'Donnell would be killed; the possibility that the Marquis might be the loser in a gunfight was of no consequence to Maunders. One day Maunders ran into O'Donnell in a saloon. Both had been drinking to

53

the nasty stage, but just short of becoming reckless. Maunders, in his usual crude way, began to needle O'Donnell about de Morès, saying he had heard that the hunter had accepted an invitation from the Marquis to go hunting. The printable part of O'Donnell's reply was that he planned to shoot de Morès on sight. When Maunders told de Morès about the threat, the Marquis shrugged it off as saloon braggadocio.

Gregor Lang now joined the hunters in their verbal war against the Marquis. As a polemicist, Lang's son Lincoln was far from expert, but he reflected the family point of view accurately when he said: "The cause of the hunters was our cause, just as ours was theirs. Soon we found ourselves practically sleeping on our guns in almost hourly expectancy of the breaking forth of blue flame. Nor did we have long to wait."

Shortly after the first of the Marquis' fences was strung, it was cut. By whom? No one knew. De Morès' men put it back up. The next rancher or hunter to come along snipped it again. The process continued until it was a literal tug of wire between the Bad Landers and the de Morès forces. Most of the cutting was done at night, but in the deep ravines, where cover was good, the fences fell during the day. The Marquis' hands rode the fences, but it was easy for a man to lie in the tall grass, wait for the rider to pass, and then snip.

Gunplay began, first only sporadic shots fired from a distance at de Morès and his men as they rode the fences. Then it became more intense, the gunmen always under cover when firing, and although the Frenchman and his forces returned the lead, they drew no blood. The tactics of de Morès' enemies were clearly designed to scare the Marquis so that he would at least let his fences down and at best leave the Bad Lands. The people taking on the Frenchman obviously didn't know him. Bullets continued to whistle around de Morès, but he didn't scare. Knowing the way de Morès died, it is easy to understand that he would have spat upon anyone in the Bad Lands who might have suggested that he run in the face of fire.

It was now mid-June, only two and a half months since the day the Marquis broke the bottle of wine over the tent peg to christen his town Medora. Although he owned a ranch and cattle, his slaughterhouse was not yet finished. It seems logical, therefore, that the trouble he encountered was not inspired by meat packers in the East, which was subsequently the case. Gorringe and his cohorts were still smarting under the rebuff de Morès had given to their phony land scheme, and they undoubtedly influenced others against him.

Aside from the hostility generated by Gorringe and that which arose from the fencing, many Bad Lands people hated de Morès from the day he arrived. Nothing he might have done, including the removal of his fences, could have changed that feeling. Moreover, the attitude of the Bad Landers was not temporary. As late as 1946—sixty years after de Morès was in Dakota for the last time and fifty years after his death—old-timers in western North Dakota still held him in contempt. There seemed to be little residue of good feeling, despite Howard Eaton's and A. C. Huidekoper's regard for de Morès, but of course they were long since gone. Animosity toward de Morès was almost congenital.

Why the animosity? There are a number of reasons, most of them revolving around the fact that de Morès was so completely different from anyone else in the Bad Lands. While the 1880's were supposed to typify the age of rugged individualism and nonconformity, the fact is that even then people tended to dress, appear, and act alike. This resulted in a general leveling of everyone to a standard several cuts below the aristocratic. De Morès couldn't change his bearing, dress, speech, or attitude toward people, much as he might try. Then there was his nationality. It might seem strange that xenophobia should thrive in the Old West, but it did. Many frontiersmen were foreign born and many others were only first generation in America, so there was little logic in their judgment of de Morès. Had the Marquis been, say, Scotch or English, the attitude toward him might not have been so critical, for then he would not have been quite so different from people the Bad Landers were accustomed to. But that he was French set him apart even more. The crowning irony of this scorn based on nationality was that many of the de Morès haters would have been hard put to identify their fathers and others would just as soon have forgotten the maternal side of their parentage.

Another sore spot was de Morès' title. In the first place, many of the Marquis' critics weren't quite sure what a title was, but they knew it set the holder apart. Some vilifiers said de Morès' title was phony and that he had merely invented it to make him appear important in the Bad Lands. Others charged that even if the title were authentic, the frontier was no place to be using it, since everyone there was supposedly equal (some were apparently more equal than others). Finally, the Frenchman obviously had loads of money, and stories of the von Hoffman wealth also got around quickly; it was natural that he should be envied by people who could count their assets in dollar totals of two or three digits. Envy can quickly turn to hate.

And so the combination of being different, French, titled, and moneyed made de Morès a pariah in the eyes of many frontiersmen, in spite of his possessing many qualities that were normally admired by most people in the West. He was every inch a man, and all who met him were struck by that fact. No one could question his courage or integrity. He was consummately skilled with firearms, knives, and horses. In his own way, he tried hard to be friendly with everyone. All these were attributes, Americans have been led to believe, that frontiersmen respected, for supposedly a man was judged on the basis of what he was and what he could do rather than his outward appearance or his ancestors. That theory, for de Morès at least, was as phony as the mythical "melting pot" for immigrants in the big American cities. The threats against the Marquis, the shooting at him from ambush, and the fence cutting continued.

VI

OPEN WAR ON DE MORÈS

On Saturday night, June 18, 1883, the first organized and open move to drive de Morès out of the Bad Lands was made. A cowboy named MacCauley rode into Little Missouri from Lang's ranch, where he worked, and loaded himself with the usual overcharge of Forty Mile Red Eye. MacCauley mounted a stool in a saloon and proceeded to harangue his fellow drinkers on the iniquities of foreigners—the British as well as the French —charging that these interlopers from overseas were coming to the Bad Lands and seizing privileges for their exclusive benefit, to the detriment of everyone who had lived in this part of the Old West from the earliest days. He continued in this vein for some time, much to the joy of his listeners, for most of them were the toughs and thieves who would lose by the Bad Lands' becoming civilized. MacCauley ended his ranting by saying that anyone (meaning de Morès) who tried to come in and take over the Bad Lands should be taught a lesson, which was another way of saying that he should be lynched. (Although MacCauley worked for Lang, who hated de Morès, it is difficult to believe that Lang would have been a party to a lynching.)

Exactly what happened later that evening was obscured in an alcoholic haze, but it is clear that a group of would-be enforcers of order, euphemistically called vigilantes, decided that de Morès should be run out of town. First, a few gunmen were sent to the Marquis' house, high on the bluff, where he was now living in a section which had been finished. They surrounded the house and fired through the windows with rifles and pistols. As soon as the shooting started, de Morès and van Driesche extinguished the lamps and the Marquis returned the fire. While the shooting was in progress, one of the vigilantes slipped up to the front of the house and slid a card under the door.

The following morning, de Morès was just about to leave the house when he saw the card. On it was a roughly drawn skull and crossbones and the cabalistic numbers "7–11–77." Neither de Morès nor van Driesche knew what the card meant. Although they were disturbed over the previous night's shooting, they gave no more thought to the card or its possible connection with the gunfire. Later in the day, however, Frank Miller, one of de Morès' most trusted men, came to the house and the Marquis showed him the card. Miller explained that the card meant de Morès would have to get out of town within twenty-four hours or be killed.

De Morès was not prepared to run in the face of possible trouble, and besides, how did he know all this was not just a bluff? He went about his business. In the middle of the week, he left for Montana, nothing untoward having happened since the shooting. He returned in a couple of days to find that all hell had broken loose.

De Morès learned that the three hunters, O'Donnell, Wannegan, and Luffsey, had ridden into town one day, sluiced down a Niagara of booze, and shot up the town. Said Howard Eaton: "These men held a perfect reign of terror in the town . . . firing promiscuously into hotels, business houses and saloons." A grindstone near the hotel was a favorite target, for the whine of bullets ricocheting off it was particularly piercing. The trio had another sitting duck—or, rather, rows of them—in the sticks that held up windows in the hotel. Shooting these out was great fun: not only was there a banging and a splintering, followed by the yelling of the person in the room, but the crashing down of the window lent an added and final note. That the son of Mr. Haupt, general manager of the Northern Pacific, was in one of the hotel rooms made the shooting even more of a topic of conversation.

It was quite natural that the three gunmen should wreak their vengeance on the Marquis; they rode across the river and blasted the half-finished house. On the final day of the spree, the hunters rode over to the Marquis' abattoir, which was nearing completion. O'Donnell, with his .45 drawn, ordered Frank Miller to stop all work on the packing plant and told him he was going to shoot de Morès on sight. The three then rode off into the Bad Lands, but they were not to be gone very long.

When de Morès returned from Miles City on Saturday evening, O'Donnell was waiting for him at the station, gun in hand. By some strange coincidence, de Morès got off the train on the side opposite O'Donnell. Not finding his prey, O'Donnell rode off, and de Morès, without knowing how narrowly he had escaped, went home. There, van Driesche and Miller told him about O'Donnell's latest threat against his life. Up to this point, it had been difficult for de Morès to take the threats seriously, for he had been a good friend of O'Donnell when he first arrived. He had hunted with him, offered him a job, and had proposed that he stake O'Donnell to some livestock. He had also told O'Donnell he would always be glad to grant any favor the hunter might ask. And now this man was threatening to shoot him on sight!

Since O'Donnell was a fairly simple man, there arises a question: Was the cutting of the hunting trails by the Marquis' fences the real reason he was out for the Frenchman, or had he been egged on, even hired, by people in the Bad Lands and in the East (Gorringe) to do the dirty work? In a tract on the Marquis published in 1929, the late Representative Usher L. Burdick of North Dakota says the shooting by O'Donnell and company was more than just their idea. "There is no doubt," he wrote "that many of the so-called law abiding citizens of the district gave at least tacit support . . . and while there was no plan to injure the Marquis personally . . . the demonstration was an open act of hostility." There might not have been any plan, but certainly O'Donnell's threat was not to be taken lightly, especially in a country where such talk usually was far from loose. De Morès knew this as he debated his course of action.

Frank Miller suggested that he get out of town for a while. De Morès interpreted that to mean running away; he had never bowed in the face of danger and he didn't propose to start now. Maunders was consulted. He advised de Morès to be careful and to be sure to get in the first shot. Of course, the Marquis might well have sent word to O'Donnell that he was ready to shoot it out. The Frenchman was not only a crack shot with a pistol, but he was also fast on the draw and, as Huidekoper put it, "game as a pebble." With all the choices of action before him, de Morès preferred to stand on the law. But there was no law in Billings County, where Medora and Little Missouri were located. The nearest peace officer was in Mandan, 130 miles east, which was the seat of government of Morton County. Not wanting to waste time, de Morès took the train for Mandan the following day, Sunday.

De Morès was dismayed to find that both the sheriff and his deputy were out of town on official business: he had hoped to have the sheriff swear out a warrant for O'Donnell's arrest. In the absence of the lawmen, de Morès went to a territorial justice of the peace, Mark Bateman, and explained the situation, including, of course, the fact that O'Donnell had threatened to shoot him on sight. He asked what he should do. Bateman, accustomed to letting the law of the frontier write itself where there was none, replied unhesitatingly, "Why, shoot."

De Morès thanked the justice, although he must have asked himself for what, except that he now had judicial sanction of sorts for protecting himself. This was somewhat of a refinement on the frontier, where most people felt that they had a perfect right to shoot in self-defense.

The Marquis was still uncomfortable about his position, so he went to see his attorneys, Allen and Burns, in Bismarck, just across the river. They were unequivocal: the best thing to do was to skip the country and let the hotheads cool down. They felt de Morès shouldn't even return to Medora, but take off immediately from Bismarck. De Morès rejected this idea. Not only would it be running away, it would also mean leaving van Driesche in Medora at the mercy of the hunters, and that was something the Marquis could never do. He thanked his advisers and left for Medora on the *Pacific Express.*

When he arrived in Little Missouri—the station in Medora had not yet been built—de Morès got off the train with his .45 in hand, fully expecting trouble. There was none. This was a strange and ominous sign. De Morès went to his house, where van Driesche, Dick Moore, and Frank Miller were waiting. They told him the three hunters had returned to town and that, in a saloon, O'Donnell had repeated the threat he had made before: he was going to kill de Morès the first chance he had.

The five men sat down to an evening meal, with de Morès chatting amiably and seemingly unconcerned, even though three men were somewhere within gunshot and apparently determined to kill him. After the sun dipped behind the twisted buttes of the Bad Lands, darkness fell rapidly, and with it the cover for O'Donnell and company, plus other reinforcements. Slowly they crept up the steep hill to the Marquis' house; when all were within rifle range, but not so close that they couldn't get away quickly, they opened fire. Bullets cracked through the house and around the Marquis and his men. They quickly armed themselves and returned the fire through the slits in the shutters. Some reports have it that O'Donnell taunted de Morès, yelling at him to come outside and settle the feud, which the Marquis did, shooting the gun out of O'Donnell's hand. This is unlikely, for de Morès was too smart to expose himself in the dark under those unequal conditions; he was brave but not foolish. The barrage continued spasmodically all night, and when the sun was beginning to show over the bluffs to the east, the gunmen slunk away.

In Bismarck the next day, the *Tribune* headlined the story on its main news page:

ARMED DESPERADOES
ARE MAKING MATTERS UNPLEASANTLY
LIVELY AT LITTLE MISSOURI

From information received at an early hour this morning, it is very evident that a deplorable state of affairs exists at Little Missouri [Medora and Little Missouri were used interchangeably]. On Sunday night the desperadoes inaugurated a reign of terror in the town. They surrounded the hotel, riddled the windows with bullets and acted like demons turned loose from pandemonium's most disreputable district. Everything points to a desperate state of affairs up there and some startling news may be expected this morning.

It was startling, all right, and de Morès was right in the middle of making the news.

The *Tribune* story was picked up by other papers and the wire services, and soon there was editorial comment about the de Morès–O'Donnell feud, some of it extremely acid. The *American Nonconformist* of Tabor, Iowa, carried a story headed "Outlaws on the Rampage":

Desperadoes! Outlaws! Ah indeed! Well, we sincerely hope that desperadoes, outlaws or whatever the old party ravishers of their countrymen may choose to call them, will set their foot down [in order] that counts, marquises, dukes and any other foreign aristocrats shall not establish . . . ranches in Dakota or in any other part of this country. The soil of America belongs to American citizens only, and if the citizens of England or of any other country have bought it they shall not directly or indirectly establish themselves or anyone else on it. We hope the class of desperadoes will increase who will steadily resist the settlement of this country by foreign aristocrats.

There was plenty of shooting by O'Donnell and his crowd on the day following the night bombardment of the Marquis' house. At midmorning, the three hunters came back and began firing again. They were soon joined by other riflemen. De Morès knew he had a chance to shoot it out then and there, but he still wanted to stand on the law if he could. There being no law, however, he proposed that it be sent for. He got in touch with Howard Eaton, who said he sympathized with de Morès and would stand by him. De Morès composed a telegram to Frank Allen, his attorney in Bismarck, saying: "Desperadoes together and armed. Shoot at everything. Cannot muster enough men to meet them. Send Harmon [the sheriff] with armed posse or soldiers in shortest possible time. [Signed] Morès, Howard Eaton, E. G. Paddock."

To get the message to the telegraph office in Little Missouri was a problem, since O'Donnell and his men were waiting to fire on anyone who came out of the big house on the hill. De Morès put his military training to work and soon figured out a route through a draw that would make it possible for Frank Miller to get to the station. Miller crawled on his stomach through the depression, partly masked by sagebrush. It looked safe. Then gunfire broke out, the lead whistling overhead and some of the bullets thudding into the bank near Miller's head. He inched forward, then snaked through the last of the ravine and, at last able to stand upright, sprinted to the station door. He filed the message.

While Miller was gone, de Morès was suddenly aware of someone creeping through the bushes at the foot of the hill. Watching intently, he saw the man advance. It was O'Donnell. De Morès waited for him, rifle at the ready. The Marquis was startled to hear van Driesche run from the rear of the house. He said another man was coming up from the back, also crawling. That was Luffsey. Before Luffsey could get any farther, de Morès ran out of the house to face O'Donnell, fully expecting him to fire. The Marquis was flabbergasted to see O'Donnell turn and run. Not being a man to shoot anyone in the back, even someone retreating from a fight, de Morès held his fire.

While all this gunfire erupted around the Marquis' house, the sheriff in Mandan was immediately dispatching his deputy, Henry Harmon, with a warrant for O'Donnell's arrest, along with a posse, said to range in number from three to twenty, a statistic that mattered little in the light of what the posse did, or, rather, didn't do.

De Morès' attorney in Bismarck knew about the departure of

the lawmen. Thinking the news might cheer de Morès, he wired his client, saying that everything would be fine when the deputy sheriff and the posse arrived in Little Missouri. Unwittingly, Allen thereby contributed to the fight that followed. When the lawyer's message stuttered out in Morse code in the station at Little Missouri, the telegrapher's face lit up. He transcribed the dots and dashes on a pad, scratched the finished result on an official yellow form in ink, and set off. But the addressee was not his first stop. He looked for O'Donnell, an old friend, and, finding him, showed him the message. O'Donnell, feeling confident on the basis of the past week's events, scrawled a note across the back of the telegram, saying that any help the Marquis was expecting from the sheriff could be put in his eye and that he, O'Donnell, and his men would meet the lawmen when they arrived in Little Missouri.

There were three reactions to the telegram and O'Donnell's note on it. First, Howard Eaton was worried about Harmon, so he wired him, the message to be delivered when the train stopped at Sully Springs, six miles east of Medora. Eaton's telegram said that if Harmon were killed trying to arrest O'Donnell, de Morès and his men would consider themselves deputized and would pursue the murderers. Second, Harmon was a coward compared to his brother, and Eaton's wire scared the wits out of him—he could picture himself in a gunfight with the desperadoes, and his fear spread like a disease among the possemen. Third, the intention of O'Donnell and his crowd was clear to Miller and Moore, de Morès' men. They told the Marquis that the message O'Donnell had written on the telegram showed he would never allow anyone to take him prisoner; if he escaped arrest, he would hide out in the Bad Lands, where he would be a constant menace to de Morès and his men. In short, the war O'Donnell had started would continue, with the Frenchman the prime target.

All this added up to a chilling fact: unless the deputy sheriff arrested O'Donnell and company, de Morès and his men would have to stop them. But where to do this? De Morès wanted to give Harmon a chance to make the arrest, but if he failed, then the Marquis and his men had to be in a position to act. There was one trail from town that the O'Donnell crowd was most likely to take if it escaped arrest. De Morès and three of his men planted themselves along that route. They were not merely setting an ambush, as some writers have charged. Rather, they were planning to demand that O'Donnell and his men surrender, but if O'Donnell didn't, then force would be used.

De Morès' preoccupation with legality surfaced again. Despite Eaton's telegram to Harmon, de Morès sent Miller to the station with a message for the sheriff, telling him of the plan to stop O'Donnell and also saying that he, de Morès, and his men would consider themselves a part of the sheriff's posse. Fuzzy as the law was on such matters in those days, the odds are that the Marquis and his men could not legally have become members of the posse without having been formally sworn in. But that was a minor matter.

De Morès and his men waited. Van Driesche had been left at the house, so there was Moore, Miller, and Paddock to help the Marquis. De Morès deployed them in strategic spots along the trail and took up a position where he could not only command but also fight if the need arose. It was a warm summer day, with all the overtones of peace, at least as far as nature was concerned. The Marquis and his men had not long to wait: the *Pacific Express* clattered across the bridge. De Morès whistled his men to attention—they were already on the alert.

When the *Express* braked to a halt in Little Missouri, Harmon and his posse stepped off as if they were a platoon lining up for inspection by a visiting dignitary. They were being inspected, all right, but not in a ceremonial way: O'Donnell, Wannegan, and Luffsey were astride their horses a few feet away, their rifles cocked and aimed at the deputy and his men. O'Donnell told Harmon that if anyone jerked a gun, he would be shot down. At that range, it was clear that anyone reaching for a revolver would be killed in a split second.

The sheriff answered by saying that he had a warrant for the arrest of the three and that his orders were to take them back to Mandan for trial. O'Donnell replied that he would never be taken alive by any lawman and challenged the sheriff to arrest him and his companions. Harmon didn't move. What could he do?

Nothing. But O'Donnell could and did. He ordered the sheriff to go to the nearest saloon and bring back three drinks, which Harmon did. The three gunmen downed their booze and tossed the glasses away. Keeping everyone covered, they backed their ponies for a distance, then wheeled and fired several salvos into the air. They spurred their mounts, yelling and shooting as they rode—and laughing too, for they knew Harmon couldn't get horses quickly enough to overtake them. They were soon out of sight and out of range of the deputy's guns.

When de Morès heard the firing and yelling, he knew the sheriff must be in trouble. Then, in an instant, he saw O'Donnell, Wannegan, and Luffsey galloping over the trail, rifles cocked and at the ready. Seeing no one in pursuit, de Morès naturally reasoned that the three hunters had disposed of the lawman and his posse. The Marquis took cover. When the three horsemen rode into view, de Morès held up his hand to signal them to halt, a final gesture for a peaceable end to the feud. It was answered by gunfire. Seeing his adversaries' weapons being aimed, the Marquis hit the dirt and rolled into position to return the fire. According to some accounts, de Morès fired first, but who squeezed a trigger before the other matters little, for there now could be no doubt of O'Donnell's intent to kill.

Both the O'Donnell and de Morès factions were using lever-action Winchester rifles, the standard weapon of the frontier at that time, and everyone knew how to handle his piece. The hunters' ponies went down quickly. The riders then used the fallen animals for cover, firing from behind them. The air was filled with lead, some bullets thumping into the bodies of the fallen horses, others ricocheting off rocks. De Morès stood up to aim deliberately and fire, then ducked for cover, drawing plenty of fire. His clothes were pierced, the butt of his rifle was hit, and a near miss cut his face with flying rock, causing him to bleed freely. Miller and Moore were pouring shots toward the three hunters; they, too, drew fire.

O'Donnell, Luffsey, and Wannegan were giving nothing. They continued to fire from behind their fallen mounts, stopping only to reload. The fight raged for about a quarter of an hour. Considering the short range and the marksmanship of the men involved, it is a miracle that casualties were so light.

Luffsey raised himself a bit to aim. Two slugs hit him: one in the throat, the other in the chest. He fell back, calling for Wannegan. De Morès later said of Luffsey: "His horse was shot from under him, and it was really a sight to see him fight. He was very nervy. He lay behind his horse with his black hair flowing in the wind. He did his best, but he was soon killed. No one knows who fired the shot that killed him."

Someone on de Morès' side shot O'Donnell's rifle out of his hands and also put a bullet into his right thigh. Wannegan, seeing O'Donnell wounded and Luffsey lying still, got up to run, followed closely by O'Donnell, who was having a bad time because of his wound. The two didn't get very far. In the face of this rout, de Morès and his men must be credited with great restraint: in the Old West, more men were shot where their suspenders came together than in any other spot on their anatomies. But no one fired. Instead, the two were taken prisoner and marched into Little Missouri, where they were turned over to Harmon, the deputy sheriff.

The story of the gunfight on the banks of the Little Missouri was flashed all over the nation. On June 28, 1883, the *New York Times* ran a story about the encounter on its front page, saying the outlaws had been captured and that "threats of lynching are freely made." The threats were against de Morès.

The *New York Sun* also ran a column-long, front-page story under this head:

MARQUIS DE MORÈS' FIGHT

How a Titled Cattle Raiser Disposed
Of His Enemies

His Life Threatened by Desperadoes, He
Asks a Justice What He Shall Do

The Justice Told Him to Shoot and He Did Shoot

The Marquise and her father read the news with astonishment, for de Morès, who was a bad correspondent, hadn't hinted that trouble was afoot. Moreover, he wouldn't have worried his wife under the circumstances, especially in view of the pending birth of their child. Von Hoffman wired de Morès to ask how he was and what might be done for him. The Marquis replied by saying merely that he was fine.

He was, for the moment, but the feeling against him in Little Missouri and Medora was bitter and violent. "De Morès probably never knew just how narrowly he escaped lynching," Lincoln Lang wrote, "for there were hot heads among Riley's friends who were hard to control." Lang probably contributed to the mob's attitude toward the Frenchman, for he claimed that de Morès had about ten men with him at the shooting and that the Frenchman was across the river, where he fired on the three hunters from ambush. Lang is alone in his version of the fight.

The citizens around the two Bad Lands towns were in a turmoil over the shooting. The *Bismarck Tribune* reporter said three times in the same story from Little Missouri that "excitement here is great," then went on to report that the consensus was that the deputy sheriff should have arrested the three hunters when he arrived. No doubt Harmon had been stupid in stepping off the train as he did, staring into the muzzles of rifles held by O'Donnell and company; why he didn't look out of the train first, then fire, or let some of the posse off on the opposite side, no one knows. Undoubtedly his brother, a much tougher man, would have behaved differently. Yet once Harmon was off the train and dominated by the hunters' guns, it is understandable that he should not want to provoke a showdown that certainly would have resulted in casualties among the posse.

Such speculation served no purpose. De Morès was in a tough spot. To be sure, Howard Eaton and other substantial citizens were squarely behind him when they learned the facts. But the Langs and Luffsey's friends were after the Frenchman's scalp, and they wanted nothing to get in their way.

VII

JUSTICE-OF-THE-PEACE JUSTICE

Only a few years had passed since Paddock drew a bead on
Livingston, with fatal results, and Maunders had done the same,
with MacNab as his target. In neither instance had a coroner's
inquest been called, much less a preliminary hearing preparatory
to a jury trial. The shooters went free. But there was a difference
between them and de Morès: he was an outsider. And he was
also the object of intense ill will. Moreover, the shooting to which
he had been a party provided a convenient excuse for the further
machinations of those who opposed him. De Morès' attorney
noted: "The Lang party did not propose that the Marquis should
escape responsibility for the killing of Luffsey, and they did hope
to use that act as a means to get him out of the country without
further bloodshed." (Just why they should have been worried
about further bloodshed—unless it would be their own—is a little
mysterious in view of the gun grabbing that went on.)

Legal action against de Morès came quickly. A coronor's jury
was whistled up; it decided that Luffsey had died from shots
fired by de Morès or one of his men or both. On this finding, it
was easy to have a justice of the peace issue warrants for the
arrest of the Marquis, Frank Miller, and Dick Moore. They were
quickly taken to Mandan, where O'Donnell and Wannegan were
also being held pending a hearing.

Frank Allen, de Morès' attorney, knew the kind of rough-and-
ready justice dispensed in Mandan and how prejudiced it could
be. Despite the evidently solid case de Morès had for self-defense,
long honored on the frontier as a valid reason for shooting, he was

still in a precarious position, for lynching was a constant menace. That year alone in the United States, 134 men died at the hands of lynch mobs—and open threats to lynch de Morès had been made. The Frenchman would be in a particularly dangerous spot if he were held in the Mandan jail, a log cabin that could be easily fired and was hard to defend. Allen wanted to keep his client out of jail at all costs during the preliminary hearing; at the same time, he hoped to get a quick, favorable verdict that would preclude de Morès' being held on a murder charge, which was not bondable, for a trial by jury.

Speed in this legal proceeding would depend somewhat on the official before whom it was to be held, but whoever he was, he would be a justice of the peace. In many instances, the justices on the frontier were as arrogant and ignorant as their counterparts of today who prey on motorists ensnared in speed traps. That they could be bought was common knowledge, but there is nothing to indicate that Allen tried to buy his client out of trouble. He reviewed the qualifications of the two justices who could hear de Morès' case, and finding that only one met the requirements of the county, he knew the Marquis would have to appear before him. The man was Mark Bateman, the justice who, only a week before, had advised de Morès to shoot in self-defense.

Witnesses were called at the hearing, and Bateman heard the story of the shooting unfold. It was a short session. Bateman ruled that de Morès and his men had been threatened by O'Donnell and company and had fired in self-defense. The murder charge against them was dismissed. Normally, this would have meant the case was closed—but it was not.

O'Donnell and Wannegan were still being held for manslaughter because they had provoked the fight in which Luffsey was killed, even though they were on Luffsey's side.

De Morès naturally thought the affair was over for him and his men, but he had failed to take into account the animus of the Lang crowd. He didn't even get out of Mandan. Two days after the Bateman hearing, he wired his attorney in Bismarck: "I am arrested and in jail. Come." For the second time, he was being held on the charge of killing Luffsey, as were Frank Miller and Dick Moore. The following day, the *Bismarck Tribune* headlined the story on its front page:

THE PLOT THICKENS
ARREST OF THE MARQUIS DE MORÈS ON A
CHARGE OF MURDER
The Warrant Issued by a Rural Justice
Of the Peace
An Examination Set for 10 O'Clock
This Morning
The Latest Development

Mandan, July 2—Special—Quite a sensation was caused at the Inter-Ocean Hotel at 9 o'clock tonight by the arrest of the Marquis de Morès by a constable . . . . The warrant for his arrest was issued by Daniel Collins, a justice of the peace who lives on his farm some distance from town. The warrant ordered "any constable into whose hands it might fall" to arrest the Marquis, Frank Miller and Dick Moore on a charge of murder of Reilly Luffsey. Information of the murder, the warrant stated, was given by O'Donnell, who is now in jail awaiting a hearing tomorrow morning. . . . Justice Collins has set his hearing of the Marquis for 10 o'clock tomorrow morning, the same hour that Justice Bateman has appointed to hear the charge against O'Donnell. It is supposed by some that this is a move on the part of O'Donnell's friends to get the Marquis in jail for a night and prevent his appearing as a witness against O'Donnell in the morning. . . .

This new legal move was the brainchild of Gregor Lang, according to de Morès' attorney, who said: "The second Justice of the Peace [Collins] had been discovered by the Lang party and he had proved to be an acquaintance of Luffsey, and, like the latter, an Irishman and a Catholic. He had been persuaded to issue a warrant for the Marquis' arrest; the Lang party had hired a lawyer at Mandan, and secured the services of a well-known criminal lawyer named Campbell in Minneapolis, and de Morès was technically in the Sheriff's hands for examination."

This time de Morès was in the log jail, and the threats of lynching had not abated. Allen had to do something to get him out of that precarious position. After talking to a number of leading citizens about the very real danger to the Marquis if he were left in jail, Allen pleaded with the sheriff to let him and a selected list of citizens be responsible for the Marquis' appearance in court and not to confine de Morès in the jail. Allen pointed out that to incarcerate a man of the Frenchman's stature in a log hovel would be a black eye for the Territory, especially since the Marquis had demonstrated his faith in Dakota by investing a large sum of money there. The sheriff agreed, and the hearing began.

On July 4, 1883, the *Bismarck Tribune* headlined its lead story:

THE LITTLE MISSOURI
Sensation Still Foaming, Boiling
And Seething
Attorneys for O'Donnell Threaten to Make
The Contest Warm
Operations at the Marquis' Farm Almost
At a Standstill

The story went on to describe the tactics being used by Campbell, prosecuting attorney for the Territory, who had been imported from Minnesota at the insistence of the Langites. Campbell was something of a dandy, with a long beard and flaring moustache, and for the frontier he was well turned-out in a fine suit and Prince Albert coat. "There is no plea necessary," he said to the court. "We are not here to try these men, but to have a preliminary examination, and to ascertain if a crime has been committed and if there is a proper ground for holding them." (He meant holding them for a trial by jury.)

De Morès' counsel had engaged George P. Flannery to handle the case. The courtroom lawyer was in his early thirties, handsome, light complexioned, with blue eyes and brown hair. He wore a neat moustache, much in contrast to many of the soup

strainers so common in those days. Flannery was a skilled attorney, with a manner before the bench that had proved successful for many clients.

Flannery began the defense presentation with some plain facts
which should have brought an immediate dismissal of the charge.
"The court should understand," he said, "that if these defendants
have been arraigned and examined on this charge and have been
acquitted, there must be some limit to the number of times that
they can be brought forward and arraigned on the same charge.
The statute rules that if the justice finds insufficient evidence
against a defendant he must be discharged. Now as a matter of
fact these men have been arraigned and examined upon this
identical charge. Unless that is a protection to them—unless the
demands of the law so far as a preliminary hearing are concerned,
have been satisfied, where will it all end? If this court is to sit here
and take up a case that has been discharged by a co-ordinate
court, what is to prevent some other court after this one taking
it up again and so on throughout the utmost extent of the justices' courts within Morton, Stark and Billings counties?"

Campbell replied that "it is not the intention of the law that a
party should be shot down in cold blood, and then an examination be procured before some justice, who for aught I know, was
partial to the defendants. . . . If that were possible, all it would be
necessary to do would be for a man to kill another, get a partial
justice to hear the case and get acquitted. . . . If I live I will satisfy
a jury of Morton (county) that it was not only a murder, but a
diabolical murder, by a man who laid in wait." This was mild
compared to Campbell's ranting later in the trial.

It was a bitter hearing, with Justice Collins openly hostile to
the defense: he constantly ruled on legal points, about which he
knew nothing, in favor of the prosecution. About twenty witnesses were called by each side, and the courtroom spectators
hung on their testimony. By word of mouth and the papers,
stories of the proceedings were spread around Mandan as if they
were choice gossip. Mandan became practically an armed camp,

with the factions for and against de Morès ready to leap at each other's throats. One observer said it would have taken little provocation to turn the town into a battlefield. At the end of each day's session, de Morès was escorted back to the Inter-Ocean Hotel, where he was the constant object of attention and topic of conversation.

The hearing dragged on for twenty-six days, with Collins saying he would sit for a year, if necessary, "to get at the bottom facts," as he put it.

Despite the open hostility of many Mandanites and the Lang crowd, at least one newspaper editor was objective enough to see the hearing in its true light—and also had the courage to say what he thought. The *Mandan Pioneer*, in an editorial on July 3, 1883, remarked:

The Pioneer may as well say now as at any time, that its sympathy in the Little Missouri trouble is with the Marquis. We have here a spectacle of a gentleman of capital endeavoring in a legal fashion to bring a vast and fertile piece of country under cultivation. He has a large amount of capital at command. He has seen fit to come to a region that especially needs capital, and he is welcome. The Bad Lands for years have been the rendezvous of a lot of desperadoes, and they are causing a deal of bother. All decent people agree that the desperadoes must go. As surely as civilization must prevail over barbarism, so surely must this desperate element be put down. The Marquis may rest assured that all decent people are with him.

Just across the river, the *Bismarck Tribune* had a slightly different point of view. It said editorially on July 11:

The de Morès case is a sad one, and the Marquis doubtless regrets his hasty action which resulted in taking a human life. Had he seen more of life in the west he would have known better how to estimate the rough talking fellows he had to deal with. The hunters and herders of the plains have the utmost contempt for titles, and but little respect for wealth and refinement. Toward those well-dressed, and [those] who hold themselves aloof from them, they are very apt to show a feeling of jealousy or contempt. It affords them pleasure to irritate the "high toned," and they attain the high-

est degree of glory if they can intimidate one who has made a reputation for bravery. Among them it means nothing to shoot or
threaten to shoot, unless they succeed in frightening, [and] serious
consequences are very likely to follow, particularly if the one they
are playing proves to be a man of nerve. In this case, jealousy had
ripened into hatred, and the O'Donnell party, being on a wild
débauche, sought to amuse themselves by loud threats against the
Marquis and his men, and by shooting into the buildings. O'Donnell
admits that he shot at the chimney of the hotel, and it has been
clearly proven that the balls passed through the rooms occupied
by guests. As these threats related to the Marquis, he had abundant
reason to suppose they meant business, and he did the most natural
thing in the world—armed himself and was prepared to protect his
life and property. He knew the sheriff had attempted their arrest,
and that they had galloped off in contempt, and as they were
carrying their arms before them it was easy enough to assume that
they were prepared for an attack in view of the threats made against
his life and that of his men. He had abundant cause to believe his
life was in danger. He was justified in arming himself and should
he be held for trial the verdict of the jury and the judgment of the
court will surely be justifiable homicide. The law is so plain on the
subject that he who runs may read.

Still, knowing O'Donnell, as the writer has for years, he believes
he would have confined his shooting to his mouth, for he is really,
as the Marquis concedes, a whole-souled fellow who is genial
enough when not in liquor. The unfortunate man who was killed
was at least as good as the average frontiersman, while the other
is said to be very quiet. Indeed, none of the trio are the desperadoes
that the cowboys of the plains are usually pictured to be.

De Morès' council knew that neither editorial nor public
opinion was going to influence Collins, and it had already been
demonstrated that he was impervious to reason in the courtroom.
The prosecution had based its case on the fact that de Morès and
his men had been parties to a shooting in which they claimed to
have been members of a posse, which they were not. Flannery
was arguing that de Morès was merely protecting himself and
his property against open threats. But it was clear that was not
enough. The defense had to find some way to save de Morès
from a charge which would entail a long imprisonment in the

log-cabin jail before a jury trial could be held. The threat of lynching, rather than becoming less ominous, undoubtedly would increase if the Frenchman were held.

Lawyers Allen, Burns, and Flannery decided that there was only one way to extricate their client. If Collins would not listen to reason, he would bow to influence, so de Morès' attorneys set out to find the best lever to apply to "Uncle Daniel," as several newspaper accounts referred to him.

On the evening of the hearing's twenty-sixth day, de Morès was seated at a dining-room table next to a window of the Inter-Ocean Hotel where he could be clearly seen by all passersby. His guests were the governor and the attorney general of the Territory. The dinner was a long and pleasant one, with several prominent citizens dropping in to pay their respects to de Morès and the territorial officials. Later in the evening, the attorney general was seen to meet Justice Collins and go with him for a long walk. The attorney general's exact words to Collins were not recorded, but in the light of subsequent events, it is not difficult to surmise that he must have given Uncle Daniel some instruction in the law as he saw it.

Collins reconvened the hearing that night. According to de Morès' counsel, it was a most unusual session:

The scene in the courtroom that evening was a remarkable one. The Langites were exasperated to find that they had not been able to get into prison the man who had killed one of their number, while two of their own friends were in jail for the part they had taken in the proceedings. The witnesses on both sides had had an almost free run of the barrooms, the prisoner toyed with a bowie knife, and almost every man in the room, except the justice and the lawyers, had a weapon in sight.

The address of the prosecuting attorney, Mr. Campbell, was a scathing one. Describing the killing of Luffsey, he proceeded in this strain: "Great God! Has it come to this, that every foreign pretender and dudish upstart can run rough-shod over the poor of this community without fear of punishment? What if we are poor? Was the Saviour rich? If He despised mammon, shall we bow down and worship the Golden Calf, especially when we know he was a poor, inferior, foreign-bred, fed and fattened on American gold . . . by selling his supposed title to an American girl that he may have a fat and easy time of it off her money?" There was much more of the same sort, which aroused in de Morès an indignation that led his counsel to fear an outbreak at once.

Having finished this part of his speech to the audience, the lawyer addressed himself to the court and said, "Your Honor, I shall now proceed to advise you as to what constitutes murder," and he opened a volume of *Wharton's Digest of Criminal Law*. But the first line was not finished when the justice called out to him, "Put down that buk."

"Your Honor," proceeded the prosecutor, "this is *Wharton's—*"

"Put down that buk Misther Campbell. Ye can say anything ye want, and ye can tell me anything ye want, but I don't want you to read to me a word out of any buk. This crime with which this honorable young man, this member of the French nobility, this Marquis de Morès, is charged with having committed, in the Territory of Dakota at Little Missouri, was committed in an unorganized county, a county where they have no protection, and I am informed by the highest authority that crime, homicide or anything that was committed in an unorganized county can't be governed by what is said in a buk. What the law buk says relates to what takes place where they have officers and protection, but where they shoot at the drop of a hat, ye don't have anything to do wid buks. Go on, Misther Campbell as long as ye want, but don't dare unless ye want to be in contempt of this court to read anything out of a buk."

Mr. Campbell looked in a deprecating way at the counsel for the defense and was heard to say under his breath, "The—old fool. They've bought him." He took his seat. The Justice, looking over the audience then said, "I find this a very grave and important case, and one which has been fairly tried on both sides. It has taken these gentlemen twenty-six days to present the testimony, and it is quite impossible for this poor, plain Justice as I am to arrive at an immediate decision. And besides, whatever way I decide this case, I can't please all, and ye've all been kicking, and the court thinks ye all feel bilious and as it is quite late, the court reserves its decision."

On his way to the depot that night, the counsel for the Marquis felt a gentle tug on his coat sleeve, and looking around, there was the Justice. "Wasn't the boys hot?" was his first remark. "Yes, Justice, they were hot." "Yes," he continued, "and we might have had trouble. I want you to bring the Marquis around to my house tomorrow morning by a quarter to six and I will discharge him."

Whether de Morès knew about the discharge that was to be made the following morning has been lost in time, but when he returned to his hotel that night, he asked one of his friends where he could find Campbell, the prosecuting attorney. When asked why he wanted to see Campbell, de Morès replied: "I intend to kill him on sight. Do you suppose I will allow any man to live after talking about me as he did, and after what he said about my coming over here and marrying a rich wife?" At that moment, the door to an adjoining room opened and Campbell appeared. De Morès drew his revolver and aimed at Campbell, but as he squeezed the trigger, a friend struck his gun arm and the shot went high. De Morès, now livid with rage, was lucky, for had he hit Campbell, to say nothing of killing him, all bets for the following morning might well have been off. But de Morès never forgot Campbell's insults. (A year after the hearing, Campbell saw de Morès in a hotel at St. Paul, Minnesota, and came up to shake hands. De Morès glared at him and said: "Campbell, you dare to speak to me? I give you just one minute to get out of that door, and I don't want you to speak one word while you do so." Campbell left.)

The morning after the final arguments, de Morès and his counsel appeared before Justice Collins. The charges against him and his men were dismissed. The Marquis was free, but the Lang crowd, Luffsey's friends, and the hangers-on who thought all along that O'Donnell had been right, still harbored their hatred. The discharge was not the last de Morès was to hear of the affair.

The *Bismarck Tribune* summed up the case editorially in a pro–de Morès way, noting that

O'Donnell's life was no doubt saved by his pretending to be badly wounded. He surrendered and was turned over to the sheriff with whom and for whom the Marquis and his party were acting. After examination it was decided that the homicide was justifiable and the people generally applaud the judgment of the court. De Morès had reason to believe his life was in danger; he was warned that he must defend himself, and so he did, and there is no court or jury under heaven having any regard for the rights of a fellow man that would hold him blamable no matter what the consequences to those assailing him might be. The case of O'Donnell will be decided tomorrow. He will, no doubt, be held over for assault with intent to kill, possibly for riot, and for resisting an officer, and can esteem himself very lucky indeed if he does not, when it comes to trial, get from five to ten years imprisonment on each count.

No doubt the *Tribune* was right about O'Donnell's just fate, but justice had little to do with what happened. O'Donnell was back in Medora almost as soon as de Morès.

Rid for the moment of ballistic and legal skirmishing, de Morès turned to his enterprises, for he wanted to be sure that his slaughterhouse would be in first-class operating condition by roundup time in the fall.

VIII

MEDORA IN 1883 AFTER THE FIRST TRIAL

Now that de Morès was free from ballistic skirmishing (a respite that wouldn't last long) and legal battles (which would be resumed), he refocused his attention on the enterprise in Medora that had ground to a halt when threats and lead began to fly. He must work fast. It was late July. The fall roundup was only a few weeks away, and range cattle would soon be ready to market.

Carpenters, bricklayers, and machinists again swarmed over the partly finished slaughterhouse and, spurred constantly by de Morès, quickly pushed the building and its components to completion. Corrals were set up near the plant, and a spur was built to connect with the main line of the Northern Pacific.

The Marquis soon added materially to his already substantial herds and arranged to buy animals outside the immediate vicinity. Well he should have, for he envisaged dressed-meat sales that would demand many more cattle to process than roamed the near-by ranges. Word quickly spread that de Morès was in the market for steers—and at prices more advantageous than ranchers could get by shipping to St. Paul or Chicago.

There was no legerdemain in de Morès' quote for beef on the hoof at Medora. He merely took the price at Chicago stockyards, deducted something for the shrinkage that live animals suffered en route from the ranges, and calculated a profit for himself. Despite his figuring a return of some 10 to 12 per cent on invested capital, which the Marquis considered just under the circumstances, the ranchers who sold to him thought his deal was fair. Aside from price, they enjoyed the advantage of a market literally on the range: many of the sellers drove their steers only a short distance to the Marquis' corrals near the Little Missouri and were paid on the spot.

But de Morès' suppliers were not restricted to the immediate vicinity. Some came from points farther west. For example, Mason and Lovell operated a sizable spread in Wyoming Territory's Big Horn Basin, and having been forced to cope with the problems that beset ranchers dealing with Chicago packers, they were delighted to learn of the Frenchman's market.

One day in the fall of 1883, Lovell wired de Morès that he was coming through Medora on the *Pacific Express* and asked if they could meet at trainside to work out a deal on some steers. To the cautious purchaser, accustomed to examining livestock carefully before buying, this may have seemed rash. Not for de Morès. The prospect of a trigger-quick transaction appealed greatly. He wired Lovell, saying he would be at the station.

The train braked to a halt. Lovell was at the railroad-car door and leaped off as the train stopped. The conversation was brief, limited to the time required to take on water for the locomotive and for the engineer and fireman to squirt oil from long-spouted cans into the vital parts of the 4-4-0. In that short time, de Morès agreed to buy 3,000 head of cattle at $45 each; the total bill, $135,000, represented a considerable sum in those days. But perhaps more important was the way in which de Morès conducted business: he was taking the seller's word for the quality of the animals, looking nothing in the mouth—except, perhaps, the seller.

The *Express*, with Lovell aboard, chuffed off, the buyer and seller waving their farewells, each convinced that he had struck a good bargain. Each had.

(It was in this operation that de Morès hired Johnny Goodall; he brought the first thousand animals from Mason's and Lovell's ranch to the railhead. Why Mason and Lovell wanted to let Goodall go has never been explained, but it could have been that de Morès simply outbid them for Goodall's services.)

De Morès negotiated a number of other deals for cattle, and while they were neither so precipitate as the one with Lovell nor as large, they added substantially to his herds and to his prestige as an entrepreneur whose slaughterhouse could boost the fortunes of cattlemen and others in the area. The Frenchman was building good will among the ranchers, and it spread to a few others in the Bad Lands.

Then de Morès did something that seems almost inexplicable, especially since he himself was a cattleman: he bought some fifteen thousand sheep. Neighboring ranchers exploded. They objected that the sheep nibbled the grass right down to the roots, often killing it; cattle would leave enough stem for the vegetation to recover and regrow. The ruckus de Morès raised with his herds of sheep almost precipitated another of the wars between cattlemen and sheep owners that were so common in the Old West.

In an effort to take some of the sting out of the sheep operation, de Morès farmed the animals out on shares to about twenty small ranchers. His terms were generous. He agreed to give his partners the yield for the first seven years, during which time he would take nothing for himself. Almost from the start, the people with whom he made the deals pulled the Marquis' own wool over his eyes: the alleged depredations of coyotes and wolves rocketed in direct ratio to a growing popularity of mutton stew.

This question arises: had Maunders and the others who worked for the Frenchman advised him of the consequences of running sheep, or did he merely decide it was a wise move and go ahead without any consultation? In the light of what happened to the sheep later that year, it seems probable that the Marquis paid no attention to anyone in the matter, if indeed he even bothered to ask.

Summer had turned to fall. The nervous leaves of the aspens shimmered in the pale light as the leaves of the cottonwoods shuffled, brown and crisp. Across the great spaces of the Bad

Lands, now rumpled and tan, clouds of dust rose from the herds of cattle being rounded up.

Early in October, Johnny Goodall and his men brought the first of de Morès' steers, bawling loudly, in from the range and herded them into the corral near the abattoir. (A French author says: "They caught them with the lasso and drove them to Medora.") The slaughterhouse was ready. So were the butchers and other employees, imported from Chicago and elsewhere. Outside, the brand-new rolling stock of the Northern Pacific Refrigerator Car Company waited on the spur, packed with ice and ready. Soon quarters and halves of beef were being loaded into the cool cars. Off they rumbled to Chicago.

It was quite a remarkable feat for the Marquis to build his slaughtering operation literally from the ground up and ship dressed beef six months later. Not only had he launched the business with great dispatch, but other plans reflected the vigor with which he was ready to carry out an ambitious expansion. He had blueprints for icehouses at several points en route to Chicago, and negotiations were afoot to build or buy other refrigerating plants in the East. He was also eyeing the route to the Pacific Coast—the Northern Pacific had pushed its line through and its trains were rolling daily to the westernmost shores of the nation. And what about other abattoirs west of Medora? Could he sell his product locally in, say, central Montana, and compete favorably with meat merchants who shipped there from Chicago slaughterhouses?

De Morès' beef sold well on the wholesale market in Chicago. When his product first hit the meat stalls there, it spoiled several luncheons of prime steak being eaten by old-time meatmen. Some of the muttonchop-whiskered men scoffed, but sharp-eyed traders, the fighting troops of the beef trust, recognized de Morès as a real threat. But if they disagreed about the Frenchman's competitive power, harmony prevailed on the main issue: no one, much less an upstart Frenchman, was going to break into the beef trust.

84

The Marquis de Morès off on a hunt. He was armed with an over-and-under long gun, pistols, and a knife (stuffed into the chap on his right leg). It was said that he armed himself like a battleship.

A portrait of the Marquis de Morès, perhaps exaggerating his imperiousness.

Courtesy Librairie Plon

A parade celebrating the patron saint of the Sardinian village of Tiése. The Marquis is at the center of the photograph. His ancestors received their title for helping Spain in the conquest of Sardinia.

Courtesy Northern Pacific Railway

A Northern Pacific wood-burning 4-4-0 engine (four leading wheels, four drivers, and no trailers) with a diamond stack, at Fargo, Dakota Territory, in 1883. An engine like this pulled the Pacific Express that de Morès rode that spring to the Bad Lands.

Courtesy Southern Pacific Company

A diamond-stacked 4-4-0 engine rumbling through the countryside over the Southern Pacific lines in 1884. De Morès's private car would have been hitched to such a train.

Ceremonies celebrating the completion of the Northern Pacific Railway at Gold Creek, Montana, September 8, 1883, only a few months after de Morès founded Medora, Dakota Territory, and his beef empire. It is impossible to make a positive identification of the train, but it probably was a prototype of the Pacific Express that de Morès rode to the Territory. It was powered with a 4-4-0 locomotive.

Courtesy North Dakota Travel Department

The Bad Lands, where de Morès engaged in his enterprises, hunted, and rode. The name Bad Lands derives from early French explorers, who named the area *les mauvaise terres a traverser*, for the lands were, indeed, difficult to traverse.

Courtesy State Historical Society of North Dakota

Medora, Dakota Territory, sometime between 1883 and 1905.

The château of the Marquis de Morès, now a museum. Restored but not altered, it has been maintained as it was when the de Morès family lived there.

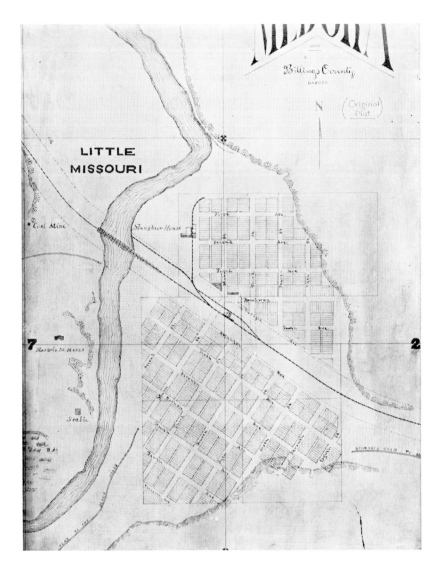

The original plat of Medora, showing ambitious plans for growth. The Marquis de Morès named the site for his American-born wife, Medora von Hoffman.

De Morès was prime copy for newspapers all over the United States, as these clippings from New York show.

Medora von Hoffman, the Marquise de Morès, as painted by an unidentified artist. Her Titian hair set off a pensive face.

The de Morès children. From the top, Paul, Athenaïs, and Louis, Duke de Vallombrosa.

This photograph of a gathering before the hunt was shot at the side of the château some time between 1883 and 1885. Although the people were not identified, it is clear that the Marquise, in a white scarf and broad-brimmed hat, is at the left foreground, riding sidesaddle. The Marquis probably is the man on foot in the center. The two teams of horses in the background apparently are drawing the famous hunting coach of the Marquis.

The Marquis de Morès' packing plant, at Medora, the first and only one on that part of the frontier in the 1880's. The sprawling structure burned, and today all that remains is the yellow brick smokestack, shown at the left.

Arthur T. Packard, founder, publisher, editor, reporter, and space salesman of *The Bad Lands Cow Boy*, published in Medora, Dakota Territory.

Theodore Roosevelt, known by Medorans as "Old Four Eyes," loved to ride the range and was a good horseman, but probably not so skilled as the Saumurian-trained de Morès.

Advertising a stagecoach line took imagination in the days of de
Morès. This flyer indicates how alluring the idea of riding a stage
was, especially from Medora to Deadwood, where gold riches
beckoned.

No doubt the objective of the Chicago meat dealers, backed by the major packers, was to cut down de Morès. At the same time, it must be recognized that the Frenchman inadvertently goaded them with some freewheeling talk.

The Marquis was enthusiastic about the Bad Lands and his operation. He constantly plugged the idea of developing the cattle and meat-packing industry in Dakota Territory, suggesting that opportunities were almost boundless. Moreover, some of the old-time meat packers were obviously annoyed by his remarks about the way in which he was going to revolutionize—indeed, take over—the business. Their reactions, fused in Chicago and points east, became increasingly ominous. Coupled with this challenge to his enterprise, his life was again threatened.

Late in the summer of 1883, the Marquise arrived in the town that had been named for her. It was a revelation. The town, the Bad Lands—just about everything—were like nothing she had seen before. Nor had the eastern-seaboard publications, enthusiastic as they may have been, really described the Old West accurately. Besides, seeing the wild country firsthand was of course quite different from reading about it or, as in the case of the Marquise, hearing about it from the few in New York and elsewhere who had been in that part of the world. She was enchanted.

Soon the house on the bluff began to show her touch. Furniture and furnishings arrived by the carload. Servants bustled about. And all over the place, the charm of the Marquise glowed. To the Medorans who saw the Marquise, she was an intriguing person, reserved but not aloof. She did not pat people on the back and her manner of dressing was far from frontier, but most of the people found a friend in this lady of New York, Paris, and other cities on the Continent.

To the Marquis and his wife, the Luffsey shooting seemed distant history, but neither anticipated the deep-seated enmity of the Lang crowd and Luffsey's friends. It was not long before the crack of rifle fire interrupted the Frenchman when he rode the range. Many times he was out long after dark, and thus made an easy target. Hired guns? Probably.

At this point, one must ask about marksmanship, or the lack of it, in the West of 1883. By way of comparison, it would seem that Annie Oakley was an exceptionally fine shot. Nevertheless, that the Marquis led a charmed life is demonstrated by his grandson's story of the hat his ancestor wore: it was riddled with bullet holes. (Later, in France, de Morès and his political followers wore wide-brimmed cowboy hats and shirts to complement them.)

Many stories have been told of threats against de Morès life. According to one account, enemies of the Marquis had marked him for hanging, which piece of information got back to de Morès through van Driesche. De Morès told his *homme de confiance* to guard the Marquise, and over her protest, he rode into Medora to look for his would-be executioners. He didn't find them in the places they normally frequented, but was told that they had ridden out of town. De Morès took up the trail.

According to the story, he found the lair and, dismounting some distance from it, marched in with a .45 in each hand. He is reputed to have told the leader of the mob that he understood the plan was to hang him and if that were the case, here he was. It is easy to believe that de Morès could have done this, and unless he were confronted with several adversaries, there is no reason to think he could not have come off quite well in a gunfight. Whatever the circumstances, legend has it that the lynchers followed de Morès' suggestion to forget the idea and come to the hotel in Medora and work on some ancient bottles of whiskey which the Frenchman had stocked. It is possible that such an incident occurred, for the Marquis was endowed with a charismatic quality which could work wonders in people of the most diverse callings, including, perhaps, lynchers.

When de Morès returned home that night, his wife was nearly frantic. The story is that she told him she wanted to return to Paris and give up the Bad Lands properties. No doubt she was frightened—who wouldn't have been?—but de Morès talked her out of leaving. She went to New York for a visit with her parents, then returned to the Territory later that year.

That O'Donnell and Wannegan had anything to do with the new outbreaks of violence against de Morès in those months seems improbable, even though they had been released from jail soon after de Morès' second hearing before Justice Collins. Both had returned to Medora almost immediately, and while nothing was said about the speed with which the charges against them had been dismissed, it was obvious that money or influence, or both, had been used. The prediction of the *Bismarck Tribune* editorial writer—that O'Donnell would be lucky to get out with less than several years in jail—failed to take into account the justice of frontier justices of the peace.

O'Donnell was broke when he came back to Medora; his only asset was a downriver claim with a stand of hay on it. And who should buy it just as it stood? None other than the Marquis de Morès, the man O'Donnell would gladly have killed. What was behind this transaction? One version theorizes de Morès paid O'Donnell much more than the crop was worth as a sort of penance for having been on the opposing side when Luffsey was killed. Another angle is that de Morès, well aware that he might yet be tried before a jury for Luffsey's death, wanted O'Donnell to be as friendly to him as possible in that event. Wannegan freelanced around as a cowboy and general handyman, and there is some evidence that de Morès helped him, too, even to the extent of hiring him as a cook. A Frenchman hire a German as a *chef de cuisine*? Well, strange things happened in the Old West.

Compared with the earlier part of the year, the winter season came with considerable peace. De Morès knew he would have to close the packing-plant operation for the season, which he did, and with that, he and the Marquise left for the East. Their first stop was St. Paul, Minnesota, ostensibly to break the journey but also for business reasons.

De Morès wanted to establish general offices for the Northern

Pacific Refrigerator Car Company in a city where financial and other institutions were readily accessible. St. Paul was such a center. (The Frenchman would continue to operate out of Medora but remain sufficiently mobile to go where he pleased, especially along the route of the Northern Pacific.) A second reason for locating the offices in St. Paul was that the Haupt brothers, officers of the company, lived there. Finally, St. Paul was a division point and home office of the Northern Pacific Railway, with which de Morès would have considerable dealings. Access to the top men would be important.

It took only a short time to finish the St. Paul business, and then the de Morèses boarded the train for New York. This time, they decided to stay in Manhattan, so they took up residence at the Brunswick Hotel on Fifth Avenue between Twenty-fifth and Twenty-sixth streets, at that time a fashionable part of town.

Meanwhile, de Morès' sheep were in trouble. Nearly half of the fifteen thousand he had put out on shares were gone. Fantastic stories about what caused the death of the animals were circulated. One had it that enemies of de Morès had poisoned them. This was patently impossible. Poison some seven thousand sheep scattered over a wide area? Hardly. But that made little difference to those who were interested in anything that would be a mishap for the Frenchman. To spread such a story was apparently enjoyable.

The fact is that the sheep de Morès bought were ill suited for the Bad Lands, which he later admitted. They were the short-haired variety. Moreover, the people to whom he entrusted the animals promised to build shelters for them, but they failed to do so. Another factor which de Morès failed to consider was the lack of capable herders. Professionals are essential to tend flocks of sheep.

One of the Haupt brothers rode through the Bad Lands, viewing dead sheep by the hundreds. He reported that many were so old their teeth had been worn down; consequently, they couldn't graze properly. But they would probably have perished even if they had had good teeth. Unaccustomed to snow, they didn't paw down through it to get at the bunchgrass.

De Morès' foreman, worried about the rest of the sheep, wired the Marquis in New York, telling him about the disaster and recommending that the remainder of the flock be slaughtered for mutton. The suggestion made sense, but the Frenchman would have none of it. He wired back, with a certain arrogance, that he didn't want to be bothered with such details of his operation in Dakota Territory and that the surviving animals were not to be killed. What happened to them is not known, but de Morès seemingly felt that because of the initial success of his enterprise, he knew a great deal more about business in the Old West than his advisers and, apparently, the Haupts.

The Marquis was far removed, both physically and mentally, from the operation in Dakota. In those golden days of the 1880's, New York offered a wide variety of entertainment. The young couple was even more popular than they had been in 1882 when they first arrived from Europe. "The Cowboy from France," as de Morès was called in some circles, and his wife had acquired in the Old West a manner which gave them a recherché quality. They were entertained extensively. Between parties, concerts, and other affairs, the de Morèses busied themselves with shopping expeditions for the myriad of things unobtainable even in St. Paul or Minneapolis, where they did their buying in the West.

De Morès was prime copy for New York newspapers in the winter of 1883–84. He got a fine press. The *World* ran a story about him with a headline reading:

A BLUE BLOODED RANCHMAN
How a Nobleman with Energy Can
Succeed in America
The good the Marquis has done for Himself
and the Northwest—Making Money Among
Cowboys—A tribute to Henry Villard

Yes [he said to a *World* reporter], my life has not been lived upon a bed of roses since I cast my fortune with the citizens of this country. But don't ask me about my fights with the cow boys; they are all over now and I believe I can live in peace in the future. . . .

I own a good deal of land, and to encourage emigration I give each settler . . . forty acres of land broken in with crops sown upon it, so that he gets a start from the first year and has a crop as soon as he reaches there. In this way I benefit the poor and myself both. Several small towns which have sprung up since my arrival have given large tracts of land to me as a token of appreciation.

Yes indeed I like the life in the so-called wilderness. I take a great interest in the future of the West, and I ride over my ranches and personally superintend my men. I have had unusually good luck and have raised some fine cattle. *Before long some of my wealthy friends in France will come over to build tanneries, glue factories and horn works, and so establish interests that will tend toward a speedy development of the country* [italics supplied]. My neighbors are wealthy American ranchers, with interests as large if not larger than mine. We all work together and are on the best of terms. I have demonstrated that beef gets heavier in the winter than during the summer, when grass covers the prairies, and several large stockbreeders have been convinced that I am right.

The story incorporated de Morès' remarks about the many immigrants who had fine houses as a result of a single year's labor, having invested their energies and time through him. The piece also made the point that the Marquis was ready to invest a million dollars more than he had already put into his enterprises.

The Frenchman was very good copy for an excellent reason: he was bringing to the Old West a dash and style that were rare, and with them a conviction that the money he was investing would benefit not only himself, but all those who believed as he did.

IX

MEDORA IN 1884 AND 1885

When the de Morèses returned to Medora in 1884, they used the Northern Pacific line, but in contrast to the Marquis' initial foray into Dakota, they were riding in their own private car, *The Montana*, which the Frenchman had leased shortly after he arrived on the banks of the Little Missouri. In those days, private cars were not exactly common, yet for someone of means they represented little more than a small luxury. To de Morès, leasing *The Montana* was really no different from engaging all the sections of a *Wagons Lits* on the *Train Bleu* for the run from Paris to Nice. But the reaction of the Bad Landers was quite different. They thought the private car epitomized ostentation, and they held that this was another piece of evidence proving that the Marquis should be set apart from the rest of the people in Dakota Territory.

Despite criticism of *The Montana*, which surely reached the Marquis, the homecoming—and it should be called that—was pleasant. The de Morèses had become fond of the magnetic desolation of the Bad Lands. They were both amused and intrigued. This is emphasized by a sentence in a letter to me from Athenaïs de Vallombrosa, daughter of de Morès, who now lives in France. She was born in New York, went to Medora as a small child, then returned with her mother and brother in 1903. She wrote: "I can assure you that they [the Marquis and the Marquise] loved Dakota enormously."

One of the first items on the Frenchman's agenda was an appraisal of winter's effects on his cattle—he forgot about his sheep, at least for the moment. De Morès found they had fared quite well, despite the Arctic cold that had swept the Bad Lands. He lost only two animals, both to accidents rather than the elements. One reason for this happy state of affairs was that his cattle had been bred in the Bad Lands and could endure the climate. (Temperatures in the range of fifty degrees below zero still paralyze this part of the country at times.) Other ranchers whose herds had been brought into the area from afar suffered losses, in some cases severe. The results could have been much worse for everyone, including de Morès, had it not been for two factors: the competition for grass had been light because the range was relatively uncrowded, despite increasingly heavy cattle drives from the Southwest, and since winter snowfall had been modest, cattle could reach the stem-cured hay with ease.

That winter and the following one engendered a false sense of security in de Morès and others, among them Theodore Roosevelt. The blizzards of 1886–87 wiped out an appalling number of cattle and spelled ruin for many ranchers. Following that disastrous season, T. R. threw in his financial sponge, which had sopped up an inordinate amount of red ink.

But who should worry about such possible contretemps with fine weather now blessing the Bad Lands and prospects for the year ahead looking as bright as the wild flowers dotting the Bad Lands? Certainly not de Morès, and he was not alone.

The construction boom of the previous year resumed, with de Morès at the center of activity. He put up a block of brick structures in the middle of town, part of which he used for his new offices, the rest of the space being devoted to a billiard parlor, a restaurant, and a boardinghouse, with some room left for general storage. These buildings spelled continuity and substance for the frontier, usually characterized by clapboard and false-fronted stores.

The Marquise was interested in promoting education, and to that end she paid the wages of a teacher for the youngsters of the area. According to the local newspaper, the *Bad Lands Cow Boy*, a school was opened in the old cantonment; it was also billed as having occupied space in the church and in a building on the town's main street. (Another story has it that the teacher decided his earnings would be better if he were dispensing potables rather than knowledge; he opened a saloon and apparently did quite well.)

A hotel, another de Morès enterprise started in 1883, was completed. Its initial name matters little, but eventually it was called the Rough Riders, the name of Theodore Roosevelt's Spanish-American War outfit. (It has been refurbished and operates today under that name.)

Attracted by the building and general bustle of Medora, some solid citizens began to arrive, among them a doctor, a dentist, and a druggist, the latter known as a "pillroller" before the days of prefabricated potions and graduation to the title of pharmacist. Many came long distances, lured by what seemed to be highly promising prospects.

At the same time, migration from Little Missouri, which had begun the previous year, continued. The post office for that section of the Bad Lands had moved across the river to Medora in the fall of 1883, since Medora seemed assured of developing into the leading community in the area. Now the express stop for the Northern Pacific was also transferred to Medora. This, in a sense, was the *coup de grâce* for Little Missouri. Naturally, more saloonkeepers shuttled their establishments from Little Missouri to Medora, the place where people with parched throats were concentrated. It was a drinking town, and the press noted this. "Medora has grown into one of the thirstiest towns on the Northern Pacific," the *St. Louis Post-Dispatch* reported on June 29, 1884. Eventually, nearly a dozen bars operated in the Marquis' town, even though its entire population was short of three hundred adults in those days. (At least one estimate of the number of saloons goes as high as thirty.) Those statistics may be a bit shocking, but there was little entertainment anywhere in the vicinity. Although the booze was bad, it was in good supply, which generated plenty of "recreation."

With all of this going on, it is not surprising that Medora should draw undesirables, copies of those who had characterized Little Missouri. Their ranks were swelled in 1884 by many hearing the growing number of tales about the de Morès enterprises. Herman Hagedorn describes them in his admirable *Roosevelt in the Bad Lands*:

> The men who had drifted into Medora after the news was noised abroad that "a crazy Frenchman" was making ready to scatter millions there, were, many of them, outcasts of society, reckless, greedy, and conscienceless; fugitives from justice with criminal records, and gunmen who lived by crooked gambling and thievery of every sort. The best of those who had come that summer to seek adventure and fortune on the banks of the Little Missouri were men who cared little for their personal safety, courting danger wherever it beckoned, careless of life and limb, reticent of speech and swift of action, lighthearted and altogether human. They were the adventurous and unfettered spirits of hundreds of communities whom the restrictions of respectable society had galled. Here they were, elbowing each other in a little corner of sagebrush country where there was little to do and much whiskey to drink; and the hand of the law was light and far away.
>
> Somewhere, hundreds of miles to the south, there was a United States marshal; somewhere a hundred and fifty miles to the east there was a sheriff. Neither Medora nor Little Missouri had any representative of law whatsoever, no government or even a shadow of government. The feuds that arose were settled in the ancient manner of Cain.

What better environment for Jake Maunders, de Morès' "adviser," and his notorious accomplices, Bill Williams and Jesse Hogue, all thieves par excellence?

Williams had moved his saloon over from Little Missouri and was doing a fine business. When drunk, he lectured to the empty chairs in his establishment, just as he had done on the other side of the river. But his real love was rustling, and he was said to rank as one of the true masters of the running iron (the cattle thief's tool to forge brands).

Jess Hogue, another graduate of Little Missouri's school of scoundrels, was the "brains" of the illicitly operating trio. (Some gray matter, in addition to brawn, was required to bring the forces of evil into the sharpest focus for the highest return.) Central casting would probably have thought Hogue's natural features were overdrawn for the role he played in real life: he was swarthy, with glowering, ugly features dominated by a lantern jaw and an expression that forecast kinetic violence.

Whatever the three did—mainly rustling and other assorted thievery—usually bore the stamp of Maunders. That was enough to put all of them on the wrong side of the ledger in the community.

Why de Morès should have continued to have anything to do with such an unsavory character as Maunders is enigmatic, but he did. One explanation is that he may have thought he was buying protection from the bandits of the area, for Maunders certainly knew who they were. In fact, many of them were his cronies and accomplices. But among respectable people, such as the Eatons, A. C. Huidekoper, and Theodore Roosevelt, all pillars of the ranching community, the Maunders association could only tarnish the Marquis' luster.

On his return in 1884, one thing de Morès did not have to inquire about was his town, Medora. Its vigor seemed to forecast continued growth and prosperity. The village was permeated with optimism, much of which originated with the Marquis, and he constantly stirred in more enthusiasm.

Among the newcomers, there was little argument about de Morès. He was the benefactor, the father of the town, although he was then only in his twenties. But at the same time, vituperation from the less tolerant Bad Landers persisted. Lincoln Lang, son of the dour Scotsman, added to his previous jeremiads:

Prior to the coming of de Morès, it hadn't been so bad. Now, however, attracted by the scent of pickings emanating from his projected enterprises, human vultures were daily flocking to the feast. From all quarters they were making their appearance, prospective divekeepers, prostitutes, crooked gamblers, and gunmen. Already the devil was busy putting the skids under the place [Medora] in preparation for its nose-dive into the brimstone-befogged nether atmosphere common to frontier towns during their boom periods.

In spite of the rawhide-tough crowd and the general atmosphere of Medora, some people preferred conversation to drinking. Theodore Roosevelt was a leader among this element, and he gathered with a few others at the *Bad Lands Cow Boy* office to swap news and lies. It was there that he met Bill Jones, one of the area's most popular—some would have said infamous—men, whose choice of language in relating his exploits earned him the appellation "Foulmouthed Bill." Jones was an extraordinary fellow, even among the roughnecks, and even though he was given to violence, much of his exuberance was diverted to talk and good fun.

One day Jones was orating at his profane best in the *Cow Boy* office. T. R. was one of the crowd. When Jones had finished his scatological semantics, T. R. said: "Bill Jones, I can't tell why in the world I like you, for you're the nastiest-talking man I ever heard." Jones started to go for his gun. Then, according to Hagedorn, "a sheepish look crept around the enormous and altogether hideous mouth of Bill Jones. 'I don't belong to your outfit, Mr. Roosevelt,' he said, 'and I'm not beholden to you for anything. All the same I don't mind saying that mebbe I've been a little too free with my mouth.' " From that point on, the two were friends.

Bill Jones was a member of a trio that provided a welcome, of sorts, for passengers on the Northern Pacific who got off at Medora to stretch their legs while the engine was being readied for the next leg of the journey. Jones's partners were Bill Williams, the saloonkeeper, and Van Zander, a rich young Dutchman who was looking for adventure in the Old West. The three considered shooting over the tops of the railroad cars a first step, usually followed by firing through the windows of the coaches, which, of course, were occupied. Tiring of this procedure, one of them thought of a new wrinkle: he slithered under the dining car and fired through the floor, thereby effectively scattering food and diners in all directions.

Jones, whose shooting was as sweet as his language was sour, also paid particular attention to passengers strolling on the platform. One day an eastern dude wearing a derby at a jaunty angle got off the train. Taking only casual aim, Jones shot the hat off the stranger's head, then laughed uproariously, six-shooter still in hand. The terrified victim sprinted for the railroad-car door, but Jones insisted that he return and retrieve the derby on the grounds that such effete headgear desecrated Medora. Jones won.

Jones and his companions sometimes operated on the side of the river opposite Medora, for the reason that the train stop there was directly in front of the Pyramid Park Hotel. When the 4-4-0 wheezed to a halt, the passengers' attention was naturally drawn to the hotel, the only structure of any consequence in view. Shots would ring out. In a moment, two men would emerge carrying a body, which they would promptly stretch out in front of the hotel. Then they would hurry back inside. More shots. Another body would be lugged out and put beside the first. The process was repeated, with feminine screams piercing the air of the *Pacific Express* passenger cars. Then, with the train pulling out for the Montana border, the corpses would rise and repair to the nearest saloon to laugh and drink it up.

The fun was not confined to six-shooters. Since this was horse country, it was natural that the unusual in equine prowess be demonstrated. Races, wrangling, and roping contests abounded, and there were other events. In demonstrations of horsemanship, de Morès excelled, which is understandable in view of his training at Saumur and in the French cavalry. He delighted in telling an eastern visitor who thought he knew how to ride: "Just take a cup of coffee for breakfast and we shall have a little canter." An hour or so later, de Morès and guest would gallop in, the horses in a lather, the guest in a state of near-collapse, and the Marquis fresh and frisky as a colt.

Not to be outdone by his boss, Johnny Goodall liked nothing better than to ride his horse over the twelve-inch-wide rail of the bridge that spanned the Little Missouri. His destination, regardless of whether the exploit was carried out from west to east or vice versa, was the nearest watering spot—for himself; the horse could drink later.

Along with all this frivolity, there was the rough and tumble of the frontier, reminiscent of the lethal fights among the Mountain Men with knives and fists. To relieve men from combat, animals were employed from time to time. Bear-and-boar fights were common, but they didn't always work out as expected. The *Bad Lands Cow Boy* reported:

> Of all the dismal failures we ever saw, the bear and boar fight last Saturday was the worst. The two bears and a boar being put into a cattle car, the only sign of hostility between them was a sigh of satisfaction on the part of the boar as he nestled down in the soft fur of one of the bears, who had curled up into one of the corners and gone to sleep.

Medorans also had a pet bear who would do tricks for passengers coming through on the trains. But then he got away, and the report was that he was found fondly embracing a pig. Both de Morès and Roosevelt were amused by all these antics, but there is no record of their having participated.

De Morès, of course, was the center of attention in Medora. He was billed as dressing like a plainsman, a reasonably accurate description, although it must be said that he was something of a *Big Sky* Dick Summers *cum* Abercrombie & Fitch. (Photographs of the Marquis in his French army uniform depict him with a supercilious, arrogant expression; dressed to go hunting in Dakota Territory, he appears as a type no one would want to tangle with.) News correspondents from points east were intrigued by him. A *Detroit Free Press* reporter described the Marquis this way:

At the Little Missouri station . . . a few of the party were introduced to the Marquis de Morès, who has lately established a stock range in the "Bad Lands." He made a picturesque figure in the costume of a plainsman. To begin with, de Morès is tall, well knit and graceful. His face is ruddy brown with exposure with an amiable expression, and certain French characteristics made conspicuous by a black mustache and gleaming black eyes. His figure was set off to advantage by a leather hunting-coat with fringed seams and shirt. It had I know not how many pockets, but each one contained some essential—matches, cigars, tobacco, pistol cartridges, and a flask, a solar compass of considerable size, a field glass, a "Multum Parvo" knife, very large, with blades for every purpose, saws, corkscrews, gimlet etc. [He wore] a great white hat [*de quarante litre*] with a leather band. A blue flannel yachting shirt laced at the bosom with yellow silk cord, corduroy trousers, leggings [*sic*] of the same material as the coat, and stout shoes and California spurs completed de Morès's costume. Around his waist was a leather belt filled with gun cartridges; it also held two long barreled Colt's revolvers of heavy caliber, and a bowie knife which would meet inspection even in Arkansas. His gun was double barreled, made in Paris, a breech loader of plain but accurate finish, having a rubber shoulder piece at the butt to take up the shock of recoil. The arrangement of the locks permitted instantaneous firing.

De Morès was not dressing for a part or acting one; he was playing himself straight. He was a suave gentleman, but he was also a tough hombre—a paladin.

It is not surprising, then, that the Marquis should have exerted the most influence in Medora: he owned just about everything, which resulted in his being omnipresent, practically omnipotent, but not entirely omniscient. Herman Hagedorn said de Morès was something out of *Puss in Boots*, the children's story in which the Marquis de Carabas owned everything. (Hagedorn would not have led a proxy fight for de Morès.)

It would perhaps seem logical that with the growing importance of de Morès' enterprises, his diehard opposition would relent. But the early hostility toward the Marquis and the bitter resentment that seemed to solidify immediately following the twice-dismissed charge of murder did not abate. Indeed, these feelings grew.

The antagonistic forces de Morès faced were quickly recognized by a discerning correspondent of the *New York Times* who filed a dispatch from Miles City, Montana, in the summer of 1884. His story described de Morès as the cattle king of the region and then went on to say:

The enterprising young Frenchman was secure from interference and molestation of every kind so long as he went about his business in his own peculiar style without attaining success in any one of his undertakings. Just as soon, however, as it began to dawn upon the bewildered minds of the astonished natives round about that the foreigner was not so crazy after all, but that he was in reality about to make a fortune out of the Bad Lands and extinct volcanoes which they had considered worthless, there was a general uprising of "the terrors of the Bad Lands" *and other big men of the country* [italics supplied] to try to put a stop to the bold proceeding. The Marquis was not to be frightened. Although his opponents with a great deal of bluster appeared in force and presented inumerable 16 pound Spencer rifles and other deadly weapons to scare him out of his wits and drive him from the country, he received them with the choicest language and in the politest manner possible. He showed, however, about as many deadly weapons—all nicely silver mounted—as the other fellows had, and gave the impression that he was capable of defending his right and title to the land purchased by his own money. After one of two "terrors" had been killed [and] a couple more maimed, he was allowed to stick, and he has stuck there ever since. Medora is now a thriving, bustling little town of nearly 1,000 inhabitants . . . and is destined before long to become one of the greatest points along the whole line of the Northern Pacific Railroad for the shipping of dressed beeves to Chicago.

Most of the story was accurate, except for the population figure (overstated about fourfold) and the outlook for Medora (as accurate as a bullish forecast in a bear market).

X

THE *BAD LANDS COW BOY*

In late 1883, Arthur T. Packard, an enterprising and athletic 22-year-old newsman, compounded Horace Greeley's admonition and made a series of westward moves. His first stop was Bismarck, Dakota Territory, then a tough frontier town, now the capital of North Dakota. Today, Bismarck retains some of the ambiance of its territorial beginnings, but with suggestions of sophistication: its skyscraper capitol building is easily the most imposing structure for hundreds of miles around.

Packard became editor of the *Bismarck Tribune*, one of the best journals in the Territory and today a highly respected newspaper. His title did not mean that he managed and edited very much; he wrote almost every line in the publication, set up the advertisements, and literally fought for his freedom to express opinions in editorials on any issue he chose. Packard later moved west across the Missouri River to the *Mandan Pioneer*. But his vision aimed at much more action and reach: a paper of his own.

The ruckus raised by de Morès in building Medora attracted Packard's attention. Why not go there? He could enjoy a wide-open field in a booming settlement that was run (in the proper sense of that term) by the most colorful man on that part of the frontier, the Marquis de Morès. And so Packard founded the *Bad Lands Cow Boy* in Medora, its first issue gleefully bursting forth on February 7, 1884. He was owner, publisher, editor, and any other title one could think of, and he was unusual in the Territory on many counts, among them the fact that he had an

A.B. from the University of Michigan. Printer's ink coursed through his veins: his father had been a newspaper publisher.

Packard's first-night welcome to Medora and Little Missouri reflected the kind of places they were. Frank Vine was running the Pyramid Park Hotel, where Packard registered. He had met Packard in Mandan and now greeted him effusively, not just as a hotel guest, but as a friend. Packard was no patsy for anything in the Old West, but he was interested in local color. On that first night in the hotel, Vine pointed out a man at the other end of the bar as one of the most colorful cowboys in the area. Packard was intrigued. He riveted his attention on the man, who stood, with his back to the wall, smoking a roll-your-own cigarette and watching everything in the bar intently.

Packard began to write a letter, looking at the cowboy as he composed it. When he had finished, he went to the door of the hotel, thinking he would post the letter on the eastbound *Pacific Express*, which came through Medora at 3:00 A.M. When Packard opened the door, he met a blast of Arctic cold, so he decided to wait until the following day to mail his letter. As Herman Hagedorn relates it:

> The next afternoon he [Packard] was riding up the river to the Maltese Cross when he heard hoofs behind him. A minute later the object of his artistic efforts of the night before joined him and for an hour loped along at his side. He was not slow in discovering that the man was pumping him. It occurred to him that turn-about was fair play, and he told all the man wanted to know.
> "So you're a newspaper feller," remarked the man at length. "That's damn funny. But I guess it's so if you say so. You see," he added, "Frank Vine he said you was a deputy sheriff on the lookout for a horse thief."
> Packard felt the hair rise under his hat.
> "Where was you going last night when you started to go out?"
> "To the telegraph office."
> "Well, if you'd gone I'd have killed you."

The *Cow Boy* was a tabloid-size newspaper, breezy in style, completely uninhibited, and delightful to read. Its editor exemplified the best among frontier editors. His soaring enthusiasm, independence, humor, and confidence were mirrored in almost every story he wrote. Packard took no nonsense from anyone. He drew some of his strength from flinty, independent, and intelligent ancestors who probably would have been at home in Medora. He was not a William Allen White, but he was highly competent, courageous, and imbued with a strong sense of public service that he made felt not just in Medora but throughout the Bad Lands.

Packard began his first issue with a typical burst of direct talk, saying the *Cow Boy* was "not published for fun, but for $2 per year." He then went on with an introductory piece describing the kind of paper he intended to publish:

Unlike ninety-nine hundredths of the papers which have been started in the United States, we do not come to fill a long felt need. The cattle business here, though already of gigantic proportions, is still in its infancy . . . . We do not come to observe a great moral end. Another field would have been more congenial. We do not come as agent or tool of any man or set of men. There is a wide field for us to cover, and we intend to cover it. *We do come, however, to make some almighty dollars* [italics supplied].

There is nothing like honesty, and now that we have come out this plainly, our motives cannot be impeached. But to fulfill our mission we must publish a good paper. We will not be satisfied with less. Only when everyone will acknowledge that ours is the best cattle paper in the northwest will we be satisfied. Our beginning may be small, but not nearly so much so as that of many another paper which now stands at the head.

This, then, is next to our principal mission, to publish the best cattle paper in the northwest and to preach King Cattle to all men. For the present, our inside pages will be devoted almost exclusively to cattle and Bad Lands items. In politics we are Republican clear through to the backbone, and will continue to be so, as long as that party continues to merit the esteem of all fair-thinking men.

At first blush, this statement of political philosophy could have been interpreted as a form of obeisance to de Morès. It wasn't. Despite the Frenchman's aristocratic background, he was a liberal political thinker, a man who wanted to improve the lot of the poor. Indeed, de Morès became a rabid Socialist, but not a Marxist, when he returned to France, where he fought many political battles that would have placed him to the left of American Democrats.

The paucity of quotes on how Packard and de Morès got along is frustrating when one attempts to describe accurately the relationship between the two men. It is highly probable that the Marquis was delighted to know Packard and vice versa. Why? Where on the frontier could de Morès have met Packard's counterpart, or where could the young man from Michigan have known anyone like the Marquis? Nowhere.

Packard quickly became aware of what the populace might think of his relationship with de Morès. Above all, he wanted to assure his readers that he was not a trained seal:

> To make the matter perfectly plain, we wish to repeat what we said in our salutary. We are not the tool of nor are we beholden in any way to any man or set of men. Our whole outfit was purchased and our paper is edited and published by and in the interest of A. T. Packard. The Marquis de Morès is the heaviest advertiser as his interests are the largest here, and he will reap the greatest benefit through our publication. Beyond this, he has no interest whatever. We are fighting here for our own interests and wish it distinctly understood that we alone are personally responsible for every article that appears in our columns.

Not only was Packard incoercible, he was also endowed with great courage. He didn't wear a gun—unusual in Medora—but let anyone challenge him and he was formidable. His weapon? A type bar, a piece of steel about three feet long, three inches wide, and a quarter of an inch thick. Packard's prowess as a college batsman undoubtedly contributed to his ability to wield the type bar; he could knock the hell out of anyone. Although he was a peaceable man, he had to protect himself against those who visited the *Cow Boy* office to object about a story. This very thing happened after he printed a piece about a butcher (probably one of de Morès' men) who had used his knife on a Chinese. The butcher stormed in, knife in hand. He came off a bad second.

Packard's news sources were impeccable. During a time when the vigilantes were especially active in the Bad Lands, the editor learned of the impending lynching of two notorious cattle thieves. The hanging was to take place on a Thursday night, he heard. He normally went to press early Thursday morning in order to sell copies of his paper to passengers on the Northern Pacific train that stopped in Medora at noon, so he wrote the story of the hanging in past tense. When the *Pacific Express* stopped, he was there with a bundle of the *Cow Boy* under his arm. The first two passengers to descend from the train were the outlaws marked for lynching. Packard recognized them, of course; he sold his papers and left. The hanging story was confirmed that evening.

Packard covered the running story of the development of Medora and the Bad Lands. But he also related the items that traditionally have sold papers in small towns: social events, the people, and how to deal with the elements. In the last category, the *Cow Boy* pointed out:

A folded newspaper, covering the chest and shoulders under a coat will be found very comfortable in extreme cold weather, especially when riding. When about to take a long sleighride, make ready a piece of joist of any kind of hard wood, such as house builders use, the length of a sleigh seat and twice the thickness of a common brick; heat it on the stove or in the oven. It is surprising how very hot such a piece of wood will become without burning, and how long it will retain heat. On such a seat, and covered with a buffalo robe, I have known people to ride 70 miles, comfortably, and the wood to be quite warm at the journey's end. A similar piece for the feet, at the same time nicely tucked in from the wind, was delightful.

In addition to practical ways to cope with Bad Lands weather, Packard covered the paleontology of the area. He ran several stories about fossils and petrified pieces that had been picked up in the vicinity. The *Cow Boy* office promptly became a small museum for the rock pickers of the Bad Lands, with Packard cheering everyone on to hunt for more specimens.

Packard had other hints: "As the season approaches for the annual awakening to duty of the deadly massauger [massasauga], or prairie rattlesnake, whose bite is almost certain death, Mr. James Hannigan is about to confer a boon on the person bitten. The cure comes in liquid form in pint and half-pint bottles."

Frontier journalism was a cash business, and Packard the publisher was no exception to the rule that money in the box was essential. He noted in an early issue: "All will understand that the editor is not out here for his health, as it is remarkably fine in any locality, and that the printers are no millionaires in disguise who tender their services gratis on account of their consuming love for the editor." Packard would extend credit to a subscriber for three months, no longer, and if the cash was not forthcoming, delivery of the paper was stopped.

But Packard was also quite practical and flexible about the medium of exchange for a subscription. In a front-page story, he wrote: "If a subscriber should happen to be out of cash, furs of all kinds at the highest market price will be taken in payment. They are as good as money, and deer hides will be bought in this way for 25¢ a pound, from five to seven cents more than can possibly be realized for them in cash."

How competent was the *Cow Boy* in reporting the scene in Medora and the Bad Lands? Allowing for Packard's chamber-of-commerce attitude toward the area, it was highly competent. For example, he once observed that "Little Missouri is as peaceful as can be found on the Northern Pacific." In comparative terms, that may have been true, but legal statistics alone point out that Little Missouri and Medora enjoyed the dubious distinction of being very wild towns where little justice was rendered.

The editor went overboard frequently, but at his age and in the atmosphere of the Old West, who wouldn't have? Take Packard's view of the weather in Medora. "Last night was one of the most beautiful ever seen," he wrote, "even in the country. It did not seem cold at all. No one wore overcoats, but everyone was comfortable. Even to our citizens it will doubtless be the greatest surprise to learn that the thermometer all the evening was not higher than 28 degrees below. Not a breath of air was stirring, the moon shone beautifully from a perfectly clear sky and it was a positive pleasure to be out of doors." He went on to talk about 48-degrees-below-zero weather and how pleasant it was. This author, born in North Dakota and a resident there until in his twenties, will attest that pleasure is hardly the term to describe such meteorology.

Although an objective editor in many ways, Packard was at the same time one of the best press agents the Territory could have had. For instance, he once claimed that "the finest vegetables of all kinds grow in the greatest profusion. Small fruit does equally well, and doubtless large fruit would be a success." However, he related in a subsequent article that "the banana crop is ruined. For the first time in the history of man, snow fell here and the thermometer dropped nearly to the freezing point. The bananas were just ripening and the first fruit of the season would have been shipped Tuesday had not the storm come. The banana growers are rather discouraged with only their orange and lemon crops to fall back on, which seem not to have suffered severe damage."

The *Cow Boy* also reflected another facet of Packard's humor, which was sometimes morbid:

"Now," said drummer [salesman] number one, as the train pulled out of Pittsburgh, "I have a bottle of whiskey. I wish we had sugar and ice. Then we could have a toddy."

"I've some sugar," said drummer number two, unstrapping his valise.

"And my brother has some ice," said drummer number three. "He's in the baggage car. I'll step in and get some."

He did.

The travellers drank for some hours, and when about to compound a farewell drink, the drummer number three, who had made several trips to the baggage car for ice, returned empty-handed.

"Very sorry boys," he said, "but the baggage man says if I take any more ice off my brother he won't keep."

Packard took some lumps (but not without replying) from the older papers in the Territory, among them the *Bismarck Tribune*. The editor of that journal took a cock-the-snook attitude toward the *Cow Boy*:

The long looked-for paper from Little Missouri [not true; Medora was the *Cow Boy*'s home] has made its appearance and is bright and newsy, but a feeling of regret permeated the mind of everyone who sees it over the ill-sounding, horrible name chosen for it. The editor cannot be so stupidly blind as to be unaware of the fact that throughout the East the name "cowboy" is looked upon as a synonym for lawlessness and cussedness in its most active form, and the Bad Lands have ever been regarded as barren and desolate in the extreme. The name of the paper will be looked upon as an evidence of the ruling characteristics of the town in which it is published, and in eastern eyes it means all that is bad, lawless and desperate.

Packard unlimbered himself in reply:

The above is from the pen of Nasty Adams, the Prince of Smut, who is at present editor of the "Bismarck Tribune." For the opinion of an alleged paragrapher who constantly reviles the feelings which should be held as most sacred, we have an opinion far beneath contempt. The majority of his wit (?) is made up of low flings at women, and the rest is made up of abuse. He has made the "Tribune" popular with the class who enjoy such inuendoes at the fair name of women, but at the same time has made it totally unfit to be circulated in any pure household. We only publish the article as a thank-offering that we have not obtained his approval. That would be a far greater curse than we could bear.

Packard was also a health buff, and his enthusiasm for the restorative properties of the Bad Lands climate was boundless. "There is a wonderful amount of electricity in this atmosphere," he wrote. "The resistance shown in pulling a sheet of paper lengthwise off a stack is fully equivalent to pulling a pound weight. This prevalence of electricity is doubtless one cause of the great vitality of anyone who lives in this climate. It takes hard and continued labor to tire a man in this country, and then a rest of a few minutes is sufficient to completely restore his energies. No one feels that lassitude so common in the East."

The *Cow Boy* reflected the mores of its day in the Old West. In the February 21, 1884, issue were such items as: "The mother of Kid Wade, a Nebraska horse thief and outlaw, is in Yankton [now South Dakota] having been driven from home with her nine children by the hostility of her neighbors." And then there was a story which asserted that R. B. Kelly, "a well to do farmer living near White Lake, has been threatened with lynching by his neighbors on account of the brutal assault on his wife and several small children."

While the *Cow Boy* was a family newspaper, it took advertising and printed stories that perhaps raised some eyebrows and caused some tongue clucking. Here is the text of an ad:

Young men, middle aged men and all men who suffer from early indiscretions will find Allen's Brain Food the most powerful invigorant ever introduced; once restored by it there is no relapse. Try it; it never fails. $1; six for $5—At druggists or by mail from J. H. Allen—315 First Avenue New York City.

It is difficult at this point in time to run down anecdotes about goings-on in Medora and the way Packard handled them. It is possible that he relied upon a standard rule of many in his day: "If you get a good story in, run it from time to time." This may have been the case of the bear that was owned by Pennel & Roberts, one of the leading freight companies (horse-and-ox outfits) in the area. The story goes that the firm let bruin loose, but the people of Medora wanted it on hand, perhaps to entertain passengers on the *Pacific Express* when the train stopped. They set out to capture it, according to the *Cow Boy*, and succeeded with lassos. Packard's account of the affair, appearing in early 1884, ended this way: "When caught, it [the bear] held a pig in loving embrace, which was loosed only after considerable difficulty."

In an unsigned commentary on one occasion, Packard said:

"We have been offered $5 for the first copy of the 'Cow Boy' that was printed, but we can scarcely see it in that light. If it is worth $100 to anyone as a memento, it is worth twice that amount to us." Fortunately, Packard never sold the initial issue of the *Cow Boy*, and the file of subsequent issues is a memorial to an editor who produced outstanding examples of journalism in his time.

XI

DE MORÈS AND THEODORE ROOSEVELT

In the fall of 1883, another devotee of the outdoors and the vigorous life arrived in the Bad Lands: Theodore Roosevelt. He was greeted at the Pyramid Park Hotel in Little Missouri by Frank Vine, hardly a man to attract anyone to the Territory. Indeed, all Vine needed to become a complete caricature of revulsion was tobacco juice running from the corners of his mouth. T. R. was not discouraged. He seldom was—about anything.

Roosevelt had come to the Bad Lands to hunt. Like de Morès, he had heard about the game there and was itching to shoot some, especially a buffalo. Most of the great shaggies had been obliterated by the commercial hunters some years before, but there were still a few around.

Hunting guides abounded at the crossing of the Little Missouri and the Northern Pacific. (Happily, Jake Maunders, a guide celebrated for gypping his clients, could not be a candidate since he was working for de Morès.) T. R. drew a highly competent professional, and off they started for "the wild cow of the prairies," as some easterners liked to call the buffalo.

In addition to hunting, a major purpose of Roosevelt's coming to the Bad Lands was to recover from an illness. Despite his recent infirmity, he retained his stamina and seemingly generated strength from a burning determination to excel in any physical challenge.

The immediate exploit was grueling. T. R. and his guide rode their horses for three days and a good part of the same number of nights across rough terrain. They were often soaked by freezing rain and slept for only a few hours on the wet prairie. The two stalked a buffalo until even it was tired, and finally T. R. brought the beast down with his rifle. He was ecstatic. There were several places which for Roosevelt could be called home, one of them Gregor Lang's ranch. After shooting the buffalo, T. R. focused his interest on ranching. The business had many attractive elements: cowboys, the wild but beautiful scenery, riding, roping, shooting—and, of course, the prospect of making money. Roosevelt was a highly solvent blueblood, but he did not have a large fortune and he wanted to augment it. Although his New York financial underpinnings had been deeply rooted in blue-chip propositions, he still was fascinated by speculation; for anyone with such leanings, ranching was perfect. A few made millions out of it, but many, many more went broke. The game was, literally, trading in livestock on a thin margin.

Night after night Roosevelt talked with Lang about ranching, taking nothing but tea to fire his enthusiasm. T. R. wanted Lang to run a ranch for him. Lang demurred on the grounds that operating his own spread was enough. But Lang thought Sylvane Ferris and Bill Merrifield, two energetic Canadians, were men who might fill the bill. They agreed. The result was Roosevelt's Maltese Cross Ranch, named for his brand, south of Medora. Later, he bought another ranch, called the Elkhorn, north of Medora. Today, both make up the Theodore Roosevelt National Memorial Park.

Native Bad Landers (and adopted ones, too) looked suspiciously on Roosevelt when he first arrived. For one thing, he was an easterner. And he looked a bit frail, although he was quite the opposite. But perhaps more important, unreasonable as it may seem, was the fact that he wore glasses (they were steel rimmed, but the style would have made little, if any, difference). The glasses resulted in his being referred to as "that four-eyed son of a bitch." The epithet was affectionately shortened to "Old Four Eyes" after T. R. used his fists in a saloon to knock out a drunken cowboy who was threatening to shoot him unless he stood drinks for the house. (*Old Four Eyes* is a pageant now performed near Medora. It relates the story of T. R. in the Bad Lands and contains some material about de Morès.)

Roosevelt had ridden a great deal in the East, but now he was taking to the range in roundups and other forays that tried some of the toughest cowboys on the frontier: sixteen or more hours a day in the saddle, sleeping on the ground, then starting out again. Roosevelt kept up with the best, although his manner of speaking was hardly consonant with the jargon the cowpokes used. Being a rancher, he had some prerogatives, one of which was to order his men into action. On his first roundup, T. R. thought that his lead men were not sufficiently diligent in heading off some steers, so he shouted, "Hasten forward quickly there!" He was almost laughed off the range.

It was not long, however, before Roosevelt had ingratiated himself with most of the people of the Bad Lands. He was in. De Morès was out. Why? Mainly because T. R. was an American, native born, and although an easterner, he had proved that he could take care of himself on the range along with the best—and also use his fists. But so could de Morès. In fact, he was undoubtedly tougher, a better horseman, a superior shot with a variety of firearms, and highly skilled in fighting with knife, broadsword, and *épée*—but de Morès was French. Had he been Anglo-Saxon, things could have been different.

That de Morès and Roosevelt should meet was inevitable. Just how they came together has not been recorded, but it is easy to imagine their meeting by chance in Medora. They enjoyed each other's companionship, and T. R. dined often at the Marquis' place high on the bluff overlooking the Little Missouri (Roosevelt lived a spartan life in a cabin on his ranch). When de Morès and Roosevelt got together, conversation flowed freely, for both were interested in politics, books, horses, guns, the military, and the outdoors. It was almost foreordained that steel would strike flint when the two got together: Roosevelt, a liberal Republican, thought the Marquis's politics somewhat monarchic despite the fact that de Morès was actually an ardent Socialist.

The de Morès–Roosevelt arguments were not confined to Medora; the two saw each other during the winter in New York. Once in Manhattan, T. R.'s sister Bamie invited him to dinner. He asked if he could bring the de Morès couple. Bamie said yes, but added that she hoped he and the Marquis would not get into their usual heated argument.

Back in Dakota, de Morès' imperiousness generated a set-to with T. R. that could have been serious. The Marquis had sent his rangemen with about fifteen hundred head of cattle into a choice bottomland near the Maltese Cross Ranch, T. R.'s first home range. The Frenchman apparently thought he would keep the livestock there for some time, but T. R. held that this infringed his rights—the open range had indefinable boundaries, usually set by the location of the home place of the nearest rancher. Bill Merrifield, one of his men, went to the Marquis' foreman and told him he would have to move the cattle out of the area by the next morning. "And what if I don't?" de Morès' foreman asked. "We'll move them for you," was the reply.

Merrifield and another of T. R.'s men went to the Marquis, even though it was about three o'clock in the morning. De Morès listened to their complaint. He realized that unless he drove his cattle away, Roosevelt's men would do just that themselves through the simple method of starting a stampede. The Frenchman offered $1,500 to rent the bottomland for about three weeks.

Roosevelt's men listened with some deference, but also with the certain knowledge that their boss was right—and so were they, as his agents. Bill Merrifield said later that he could never have accepted the $1,500 offer, big as it may have seemed, for he knew that to do so would put him in the position of being bought.

De Morès agreed to move the cattle—and did.

By far the most serious clash between de Morès and Roosevelt occurred after the Marquis had been indicted the third time for the murder of Luffsey. De Morès thought T. R. had been against him in the first two trials and had something to do with his indictment for the third. On September 3, 1885, de Morès wrote:

My dear Roosevelt
    My principle is to take the bull by the horns. Joe Ferris [a storekeeper in Medora] is very active against me and has been instrumental in getting me indicted by furnishing money to witnesses and hunting them up. The papers also publish very stupid accounts of our quarelling—I sent the paper to New York. Is this done by your orders? I thought you my friend. If you are my enemy I want to know it. I am always on hand as you know, and between gentlemen it is easy to settle matters of that sort directly.
                                                    Yours very truly,
                                                            Morès

De Morès added in a postscript: "I hear people want to organize the county. I am opposed to it for one year at least."
    T. R. unlimbered his pen to say to de Morès:

Most emphatically I am not your enemy; if I were you would know it, for I would be an open one, and would not have asked you to my house nor gone to yours. As your final words however seem to imply a threat it is due to myself to say that the statement is not made through any fear of possible consequences to me; I too, as you, am always on hand, and ever ready to hold myself accountable in any way for anything I have said or done.
                                                    Yours very truly,
                                                    Theodore Roosevelt

Roosevelt talked to a friend about the possible duel. He noted that since he had been challenged, he would have the choice of weapons and would choose rifles. He was not particularly adept with a pistol (de Morès was), and he knew nothing about sword fighting (at which the Frenchman was most expert). But as things turned out, he should not have worried. No fight ensued, for although de Morès was never known to have backed down in any situation in which he believed he was right, he did not press the duel. He must have realized that he was wrong about T. R.'s intentions toward him. (He was wrong about Ferris' furnishing money to witnesses, too. Ferris was a storekeeper, but there being no bankers in Medora at the time, he acted as one.)

Precisely how Roosevelt regarded de Morès will always remain obscure, but he must have had some admiration for the Frenchman. Charles Droulers, the Marquis' biographer, thought so, for he wrote:

April 23, 1910 [this was fourteen years after de Morès' death], Roosevelt was solemnly received at the Sorbonne and I had the good fortune to mingle with the youth of the several schools who acclaimed the professor of energy and the man of action. He developed his ideas on the strenuous life, and in doing so he drew the portrait of a hero in whom I seemed to recognize his old friend de Morès:

"Mastery of himself, with power of self-restraint, the faculty of accepting individual responsibility and at the same time acting in unison with others, courage and resolution, there are the qualities by which people recognize the master," Roosevelt said.

"It is not the critic who counts. The credit belongs to the man who personally descends into the arena, who struggles valiantly, who makes mistakes, who tries and tries again, but who struggles with all his might in doing what he is doing, who knows great enthusiasms, great devotions, so fully that his place will never be at the side of those cool and timid souls who are ignorant of defeats, but of victory as well."

Droulers was probably right in believing that Roosevelt was talking about de Morès.

Why T. R. should have said these things about the Marquis so long after his death has never been explained. Could it have been that Roosevelt, viewing the situation in retrospect, felt he should have done something to dispel the ill feeling against de Morès in the Bad Lands? He had the means to do so, for he was very popular. Or did he believe that an activist such as he should have spoken out against the lynch threats that were so common after the Luffsey affair? Finally, did the man with the tentacular connections in Wall Street and the East think that he should have interceded when the beef trust ruined de Morès? It could have been all of these.

XII

LIFE IN THE BAD LANDS FOR THE DE MORÈSES

In the middle of 1884, the de Morès château was completed. Parts of it were habitable in 1883, but the finishing touches came the following year. The *Cow Boy* heralded the de Morèses' return to the Bad Lands, and what an arrival it was. A platoon of employees preceded or accompanied them: doctor, cook, butler, laundress, chambermaids, parlormaids, and assorted inside and outside servants. No one in Dakota had ever heard of—much less employed—so many people, known there as hired help.

All these hands were to put and keep things in order for the de Morès family. *Order* could be interpreted in several ways. For most people in the Territory, it meant providing the necessities of life. For the de Morèses, it could be defined as making it possible for them to enjoy most of the luxuries they had known in Paris, Cannes, and New York, tempered, of course, by exposure to some of the rigors of the frontier, with which they coped admirably, using their considerable resources of cash, intelligence, and adaptability.

The château epitomized what each wanted: an amalgamation of the simple ruggedness of the Old West, tinctured with the elegance of the Faubourg St. Germain. Its construction and furnishings followed that pattern. While the place was the plushest on that part of the frontier, it fitted perfectly in the setting—and does today.

To call the structure a château in the French sense of the term could be argued. It did not pretend to be a grandiose building, intricately fashioned from marble or lesser stone and surrounded by stately trees, fountains, manicured gardens, and lawns. But it was not competing with, say, Chenonceau or other châteaux in the Loire Valley, or any other region of France for that matter. Yet for the Territory of Dakota it was a château, and in that setting it was *sui generis*. Its seigneurial status stemmed from its many features, not the least of which was its location atop a high bluff where it smiled down benignly on the village de Morès had founded.

The Marquis' home, made of wood, was a long, low-slung, rambling structure two stories high containing twenty-six rooms and sprouting great chimneys. Painted French gray, with roof and shutters in red, it fronted to the south, with a wide veranda that gave those sitting on it an advantage in taking the sun. The place was fenced, but in a nonobtrusive way. Had the Marquis begun to sense the Bad Landers' antipathy to fences? Whatever, the fence was more a profuse collection of elk and deer antlers than a wooden obstruction—it was quite decorative.

The great living room of the château represented the best of the place: it was almost as spacious as the outdoors. Comfortable sofas and chairs centered around a huge fireplace, with openings on four sides, from which the glowing warmth of slowly burning logs spread in all directions. Some of the furniture was distinctly American and of robust character, made from cottonwood trees that grew near by along the streams and rivers. Set against these items, but with harmony, were exquisite European pieces turned out in rare woods. The floors were covered with fur rugs of the frontier, but Orientals (and perhaps some Aubussons) also figured prominently. Hunting trophies barnacled the walls and shared space with paintings, several from the hand of the Marquise; she had also made fire screens, small ones placed to shield the faces of women from the intense heat of the open fire. A piano had been shipped out from St. Paul and tuned on the spot (by whom? one wonders). The Marquise played quite well.

There was a library of sorts. De Morès was only mildly bookish—much less a bibliophile than T. R. His collection reflected his tastes: works on travel, social science, and economics. There was a paucity of philosophical and literary works.

The château's interior was neatly painted. Just how this was accomplished is difficult to imagine, for house painters in those days (and even later) were notoriously addicted to the bottle and plenty of bottles were available. The first-floor walls were papered, mainly in red, a favorite color of the Marquise. Here, partiality to the dining room was evident: lovely pieces of furniture abounded, and the china, much of it Sèvres and Limoges, numbered some 250 pieces, evidence of the volume of guests the de Morèses entertained.

The second story had bedrooms opening to the four points of the compass. The von Hoffmans always occupied the rooms facing south when they stayed there. They had a house in the town below, built by de Morès when he was having the other brick structures in Medora put up.

While the plumbing was rudimentary, the de Morèses did have bathtubs—rarities on the frontier. At least one oversize number (to accommodate the six-foot frame of the Marquis) was made to order by a tinsmith in St. Paul and cost $8.75. Other portable rubber tubs were bought at $7 each, but an order for inflatable ones at $9 was canceled; it is hard to envisage economy as the reason for this action.

The servants slept on the back side of the second floor in rooms no different, essentially, from those for the family and guests.

On the same floor, there was space for the de Morès children and their nurses. These quarters were furnished lavishly for such tots; the de Morèses were doting parents. (There were three children. Louis and Athenaïs, both born in New York, returned to North Dakota with their mother in 1903. Another son, Paul, was born in Paris.)

The cuisine at the château blended the best of the frontier with some of the Carême-like dishes prepared for the de Morèses by the best chefs in Europe. That they were gourmets is illustrated by the profusion of staples and kickshaws they either brought with them or commanded from such stores as Park and Tilford in New York. Some of these items were unobtainable in the Territory—truffles, for example; indeed, they were probably unheard of west of the Hudson, unless in Virginia City and San Francisco. (Just why the de Morèses should have bought a half-gallon of capers is somewhat mystifying; perhaps both were fond of *sauce aux câpres*, fine for fish, lamb, and some kinds of game.)

Along with all the standard items one would have ordered for a kitchen in those days, the family enjoyed a bounty from hunting expeditions, which they adored. Take game birds. Prairie chickens, relatives of the grouse, abounded. The young specimens, tested for age by resilience (or the lack of it) to thumb pressure on the back of the head, could be sautéed or deep fried, the same as domestic chickens. Their meat, dark and tender, was marvelously succulent. The older ones came off better when braised in a dutch oven with bits of wild onion, a lashing of broth, and a jigger of brandy or bourbon to finish off the sauce.

Wild ducks attracted the *fins becs* on the frontier, and the way to cook them could stir up a heated argument. Some vehemently held with the rare-cooking school: the bird thrust into a searingly hot oven for only five minutes. The result was rare duck, *saignant*, as de Morès would say, as a *châteaubriant bleu*, meaning practically raw in the middle. Others (then as now) hold that wild duck is best when roasted slowly, really braised, until the meat almost falls off the bones.

Venison and elk (maybe bear, too) were other game dishes to which the de Morèses treated themselves and guests. With the skill of the chefs of their staffs, the results rated as Lucullan.

What to drink? No hard stuff before meals, but, rather, an *apéritif*. Wine with the lunch or dinner, of course, but the Marquis didn't splurge on the rare numbers and vintages. For example, he chose Château Lagrange, 1875, at $24 a case, not a bad price, but not exactly cheap, either. That was, and is, a third-growth Bordeaux, and drinking it is a delight. But no family bills show his buying Châteaux Lafite, Latour, Margaux, or Haut-Brion, the ranking first four Bordeaux vintages, nor did he buy any of the fine second growths.

De Morès was fussy about champagne. He insisted on Mumm, and while there is no year indication on the bills, the odds are that he demanded the best vintages and got them.

He loved *fine champagne* brandy. The Marquis selected some in New York in 1884 that was bottled by Hennessy in 1880. It cost $5 a fifth, a surprisingly low price in view of the cost of the wines he was buying.

De Morès also took on some lesser potables (*vin rouge ordinaire*) that were served with such dishes as venison stew. All of these were stored in a wine cellar, probably the only one within hundreds of miles.

Vegetables? When the de Morèses arrived in the Bad Lands, most people ate the things they could gather outdoors: wild onions and other root vegetables and the fruit from plum, choke-cherry, and other trees. The profusion of sage provided one of the most fragrant herbs, and it was used not just in stuffing for fowl, but also with stews and egg dishes. De Morès thought the climate was ideal for vegetable culture and planted a miniature truck garden where edibles for his table could be grown.

The cost of running the château and the stables was recorded by the Marquise with the same care she employed in keeping track of household expenses when the family was living on Staten Island. Apparently, the Northern Pacific Refrigerator Car Company was either a source of drawing funds or a charging center, for the Marquis' books show bills paid to the company for running the house and stables. The monthly house account ranged from about $400 to $700, the stables with no middle figure but up to about $250, the higher amounts probably accounted for by the number of guests at the château.

Then, of course, the family had to pay for the use of *The Montana*, the private railroad car in which they rode from New York to Medora and points west. Considering the fact that the

Marquis was constantly going over the route, both eastbound and westbound, the bills were not too steep. In late 1885, for example, the de Morèses had the use of the car for nineteen days, of which four were running days, at $15 a day, and for an entire month in 1886 the charge for dining car services was only $123. It should be remembered, however, that the Frenchman carried his own chef and servants, and was therefore probably not drawing on the gustatory resources of the Northern Pacific.

The great room on the first floor of the château was frequently the scene of conviviality, for the de Morèses entertained a steady stream of the steamship and train set of the day. If ever there was a guest book, it does not exist today, but it is clear that in addition to Americans, many Europeans, including royalty, enjoyed the hospitality of the Frenchman and his wife. For the French guests, *le Far Ouest* was a delight, with overtones of comic opera but the characters in real life.

In addition to Theodore Roosevelt, the de Morèses had other neighbors who were invited to the château, among them Pierre Wibaux, the son of an industrialist in Roubaix, a grimy factory town in northern France. Wibaux, like de Morès, was in his mid-twenties, and the two shared other traits: handsome, strong, moustached faces; robust physiques; and a love of the outdoors. But there were dissimilarities: Wibaux was blond and poor, de Morès dark and rich.

The young Frenchman from the north arrived in the Bad Lands about the same time in 1883 as did de Morès. Wibaux went a little farther west—about thirty-five miles—and established himself along the banks of Beaver Creek, a tributary of the Little Missouri, in what is now Montana. (The place was first called Mingusville for Min and Gus, two frontier settlers, and finally Wibaux.) Wibaux's first dwelling was a cave he dug into the creekbank. He eventually owned some fifty thousand cattle, and the settlement whose nucleus was his collection of ranch buildings was named for him. This he deserved, for Wibaux lent to that part of the country the same kind of *élan* which de Morès epitomized.

Wibaux was just as spirited, argumentative, and courageous as de Morès. On one of his visits to the château, the two got into a gentlemanly although somewhat acerbic exchange of ideas, with the Marquise sitting quietly to the side and letting the flow of words swirl around her. The evening wore on and the argument continued, with each of the arguers fortifying his position with some of that excellent *fine champagne* brandy the Marquis served. The Marquise retired, thinking the two Frenchmen would continue their talk in the same friendly although slightly choleric vein.

Then a prolonged silence was broken with *"En garde!"* followed by steel clashing against steel. The Marquise knew the sound came from swords, and she was terrified by the knowledge that one weapon was being wielded by her husband, an *épéeist* who could easily kill his less skilled opponent. (That is exactly what had happened earlier in France and would occur there again about a decade later.) She quickly descended the stairs and, in the quiet but firm manner of an empress telling her ministers what to do, ordered the two to stop. They did.

There is no record of Gregor Lang's ever having come to the château; indeed, it seems that he avoided the Frenchman. It was a shame, for despite Lang's astringent outlook on life, he was well informed for a man of the frontier and he could have taken some of the sting from the attitude of the roughnecks in the Bad Lands if he and de Morès could have talked things out. De Morès tried, but to no avail.

Fine as the indoor life was, the de Morèses were attracted infinitely more by the endless scenery that beckoned on every side. Since both loved to ride, they were constantly in the saddle, exploring new parts of the fascinating country. They made a fine picture as they galloped across the prairies, the Marquis sitting his horse with professional precision, the Marquise riding sidesaddle, a picture of equestrian dignity and skill (she wore an eagle feather in a hat that covered her titian hair).

Hunting was paradise. The Bad Lands abounded with antelope, deer, beaver, bears, mountain sheep, mountain lions, wolves, coyotes, and jackrabbits. Prairie chickens and grouse almost had to be kicked out of the way. This delighted the couple and their guests.

De Morès loved guns and everything about them—he even had his own ammunition-loading equipment to adjust the charges he wanted for each particular purpose. He was an excellent shot, able to bring down prairie chickens on the wing with a rifle and pigeons in flight with a pistol. (To ensure that his employees at the abattoir would have a chance to go out into the Bad Lands and shoot their meals, he provided them with guns and ammunition free of charge.)

The Marquise was no slouch with firearms, either; in fact, the Marquis said she was a better shot than he, which was probably an exaggerated bit of polite description. But there was no doubt that the Marquise could shoot, as witness a story in the *Bismarck Tribune* of September 5, 1885:

SHE KILLED THREE BEARS

The Marquise, wife of the Marquis de Morès, has returned from her hunt in the Rocky Mountains where she killed two cinnamon bears and one large grizzly. The accomplished lady, who was a few years ago one of New York City's popular society belles, is now queen of the Rocky Mountains and the champion huntress of the great northwest.

The de Morèses could and did rough it on these hunting expeditions, but they did not believe in self-inflicted hardships, so the Marquis had a hunting wagon built. It was fashioned, in its own western way, after the headquarters vehicle Napoleon used when he set out for Moscow. Equipped to sleep two, it was an 1880 version of a modern-day trailer, pulled by horses and fitted with all the comforts that could be provided in such a conveyance, including folding beds, tables, china, silver, and linens. De

Morès brought along edibles and some wines that didn't lose their quality when bounced across the jumbled topography of the region in which he was hunting. It is sad to report that the hunting wagon didn't really serve its purpose, for it was not sufficiently sturdy to take the draws and ravines. It had to be abandoned.

The hunts were fascinating for the de Morèses, in part because the young couple employed one of the best professional hunters in the West: Vic Smith. Smith was a human hunting dog, able to find the kind of game his clients wanted, and he brought them within range with his uncanny sense of knowing what the various species would do. Antelope, for example, were curious as cats: a piece of cloth tied to a rifle cleaning rod would bring them sniffing and looking toward the hunter. Mountain sheep were most wary, but Smith knew how to approach them, too.

Smith, a crack shot, was often hired by de Morès, both for the Marquis' own hunting trips and those of his guests. Smith's fee ranged from $200 for a relatively short trip to somewhat more for a longer one. (The total cost for a de Morès shooting excursion into Montana would approximate $1,000, including Smith's services.) A man of the frontier, Smith did just about as he pleased, knowing that he could always shoot his living if it came to that. He also realized that many easterners would be attracted by the fine hunting in the Bad Lands and that he could therefore enjoy a fine income from an opulent clientele. He was honest, charged fees that could be justified, and was in every way quite the opposite of Jake Maunders, who cheated easterners every time he had a chance. The question which arises, of course, is this: If Maunders was such a skilled hunting guide, why didn't de Morès take him off his "advisory" job and send him with the hunting parties he organized?

Smith took no nonsense from anyone. On one occasion, the Marquis had a passel of Russian dukes as guests at the château. They wanted to hunt. De Morès was busy at the time, so he hired Vic Smith to take them out for a shooting spree in the Bad

Lands. Smith turned up herds of antelope three times. The Russians fired, raising puffs of dirt on the prairie; these were misses, and not very near ones at that. On the fourth encounter, Smith said nothing, but merely raised his piece, aimed, and fired, bringing down two antelope. The Russian noblemen were incensed. They berated Smith, saying: "If you were in our country and dared to shoot game in our presence, we would send you to Siberia." Smith lowered his rifle deliberately and spat out these words: "Well, this is not your country and you can go to hell. I'm going home."

De Morès became a somewhat jaded hunter. Fine shot that he was, just bringing down the wild beasts of the prairies and mountains was not enough. He wanted combat. The *Bismarck Tribune* noted:

> The Marquis and his talented wife are of a romantic turn of mind, and would go just as far to meet a beast of prey face to face as any trapper or mountaineer in the Rockies. As has been previously reported, the Marquis has killed many bears with a gun, and last fall the Marquise killed a big black bear and has since brought down some game.
>
> But this does not satisfy the wild cravings of the Marquis for the excitement and thrill of the chase and hunt, and he now wants to kill a grizzly bear with a knife.
>
> He started out for this purpose some time ago, but it is understood that he did not meet with the best of success and he will go into the mountains to stir up a hand to hand combat with the ferocious and somewhat muscular grizzly.
>
> It is his desire to meet one of these tyrants of the forest in such circumstances as will precipitate a conflict, and with glistening steel he hopes to win the fight. If the Marquis succeeds in this undertaking, he will put many of the old time trappers and frontiersmen to shame.

He didn't do it in just that way, but the Marquis accomplished the same thing near the château.

De Morès thought the fairest kind of encounter would be to meet the bear on neutral ground. To that end, he figured the field of combat should be a level place in a bottomland near the

Little Missouri. The Marquis set the stage this way: he put the freshly killed carcass of a horse along the riverbank, leaving plenty of room on all sides for the bear to approach; de Morès was seeking no advantage. He waited nearby, slightly crouched and on the alert, but not so close to the horse that the bear would smell him.

The evening wore on. Nothing happened. Then, just as the moon peeked over the buttes, a large bear lumbered into view, sniffing, looking, listening. The bear advanced. Seeing the carcass, it rose on its hind legs and ran toward the horse. De Morès rose. Attracted by the moving figure, the bear dropped to its four feet and charged. In the last few yards before reaching de Morès, it rose on its hind legs, sprinting toward the Frenchman with its front paws swinging.

The bear lunged with a snarl. It was the moment of truth for de Morès. The Marquis stepped slightly to left to give his right arm more leverage, then plunged an eight-inch hunting knife exactly into the vital part of the bear he had aimed for. He dropped it cold.

Some measure of the chance de Morès was taking is demonstrated by an encounter Wild Bill Hickok had with a female bear. In that instance, the animal was not baited but charged out of a thicket as Hickok rode by, apparently fearful that he was going to harm her cubs. Hickok's horse, startled by the bear, reared and threw him. The sow charged. Hickok drew and fired. An accurate shot, he put six .45 bullets in the animal. They didn't stop her. The mass of several hundred pounds, armed with claws as sharp as her vicious teeth and a bone-crushing swipe that could fell a horse, continued to charge Hickok. There was no time to reload, so he fought with his knife. The bear clawed, mauled, and bit him unmercifully. By chance, a rider soon came by: the dead bear was lying on top of Hickok, who was unconscious.

There were no more bear fights for the Marquis, but many more hunting expeditions into Montana and points west. When his private car passed through Bismarck, reporters noted that the rear platform was festooned with feathered game shot by the Frenchman and his wife.

Van Driesche—Mr. Willie, as the de Morès children called him—was also enjoying the Far West. He drove around Medora in a well-turned-out trap drawn by a fine-looking team of horses. He also took to riding broncos; the *Cow Boy* relates that he was thrown, but got up, game for more. He also ordered carrier pigeons from Bismarck and flew them when the weather was right. (The pigeons figured as a kind of subsidiary activity to the stagecoach operations of the Marquis.) Van Driesche seemed to be quite a good shot and enjoyed the hunting in which his employer engaged with such zest. And around Medora, Mr. Willie held civic jobs, including that of postmaster.

Despite the threats, the unpleasantness directed at de Morès, life in the Bad Lands represented a pleasant time—an interlude, as it turned out to be—and he and the Marquise were intrigued by all aspects of it.

XIII

DE MORÈS' BUSINESS AND THE BEEF TRUST

De Morès fared brilliantly in the first stages of his ranching–meat-packing business under the corporate name of the Northern Pacific Refrigerator Car Company. His competitive idea was sound: slaughter on the range and ship the finished product to consumers in the East. This would eliminate the charge for freighting the inedible parts of the animals and avoid the shrinkage they would suffer en route to meat centers, such as, say, Chicago.

The Marquis proved his contention by underselling the old-line meat dealers. The *Boston Leader and Herald* remarked that "it was a cold day among the slaughter houses in Chicago when he began." Moreover, de Morès had ample capital, the lack of which spelled the downfall of many enterprises in that era, and he was favored by an expanding market because of the multiplying American population.

De Morès estimated the prospects with keen business acumen. But he failed to take into account one overriding consideration that eventually brought him down: the collusive forces of the beef trust (it monopolized the meat business) and the railroads (the only form of transportation that could bring livestock from the range to slaughterhouses, mainly in the Middle West). Not only did the beef trust members conspire against a competitor in the market place, but with their leverage as prime customers of the railroads, they could demand preferential rates, often hidden as rebates. Then, too, the beef-rail combine exerted a synergistic power through interlocking ownerships, such as rail company officials' holding substantial interests in stockyards and packing-plant operations.

Before those piratical economic establishments forced de Morès to walk the plank into a sea of red ink, however, the people of the Bad Lands hailed him as a monetary messiah. In many ways, he was. No one else had thought of de Morès' venture, or if so, had never carried it out. He brought to ranchers and others in the western Dakota Territory something they had never dreamed of. This made the Frenchman prime copy for newspapers in the Territory, not only the *Cow Boy*, but also the *Bismarck Tribune* and the *Mandan Pioneer*, both of which recognized his exploits as events that would intrigue their readers. The coverage was excellent and, generally speaking, the reporting objective.

The *Cow Boy* was covering de Morès and his business as a running story, which, indeed, it was. This generated comment from readers, many of whom were beneficiaries of the revolution the Frenchman was creating in the meat business. De Morès must have been particularly gratified by a letter to the editor in the January 8, 1885, issue of the *Cow Boy*. It pointed out that he was making it possible for the local consumers of beef (in the Territories of Dakota and Montana) to buy at prices considerably lower than ever before:

Will you kindly allow a few facts in your valuable paper regarding the vast amount of good and general benefit that the Marquis has done for the general public and working people especially?

Heretofore, prices of meat were very high in this section of the country, and still are at the retail markets, simply because a few retail dealers in each town combined to make them so. In the opinion of many thinking men, beef should be as cheap here as in Chicago, if not cheaper, whereas cattle are raised by the thousands and shipped in hundreds of cars to eastern markets, paying high freightage, and slaughtered and sold there cheaper than people here at home could buy.

Now that the Northern Pacific Refrigerator Car Company has established storage and salesrooms in many prominent towns and accommodates the people with low prices, the enmity of the retail dealers is aroused against them, and they will not buy of them except where necessity compels it. . . .

Let thinking people consider the number of men that this company gives employment to, not only in the summer season, but in the dull winter, filling their ice houses and getting prepared for the spring trade. The company will, at some future day, reap the benefit of its good work by a liberal patronage of the people.

The letter was signed "Observer."

As for managerial ability, de Morès apparently had it. Droulers says the Frenchman organized his operation down to the last detail and that he delegated responsibility to his employees to the largest degree possible—indeed, he thrust responsibility on them. Then he made them perform. Each day, he came to his office in Medora armed with questions about the operation which he put to the men responsible for the various parts of the business. He quickly absorbed their answers, giving them new instruction where necessary. It may have been boastful to have said so himself, but de Morès apparently did have keen insight.

He was supremely sure of himself when he started out—witness the conversation with Howard Eaton, mentioned earlier, in which he said he was ready to take on the Armours and the Swifts at their own game. In that early talk with Eaton, he had also boasted about his probing mind and his ability to grasp a situation in a wink of the eye. But in extenuation, it should be recalled that de Morès was then in his early twenties, obviously keen of mind, and endowed with enormous energy. Why shouldn't he have bragged a bit?

In addition to running his abattoir, de Morès was also a rancher who had to look after his own livestock on the range, and this entailed his participation in the roundups.

In the initial days of his operation, it seemed that de Morès really did have the beef business taped, and of course there were queries about what made it run. He was not at all reluctant when asked to talk about it. The *Montana Stock and Mining*

Journal had one of its reporters interview him in November, 1884, about the economics of the ranching and slaughtering business, especially the capital required for one just starting out. De Morès' straightforward reply showed that he had carefully calculated the elements and the cash necessary for success. He told the *Journal* reporter:

> Gentlemen who have undertaken stock raising with five or ten or twenty-five thousand dollars have invariably become tired of it and quit in disgust. They set out with false figures, meet unforeseen conditions with which they cannot cope, and after using up their money are glad to get out as best they can.
>
> It costs as much for an outfit to herd 100 cattle as 1,000. A good foreman is indispensable and he needs three or four helpers.

A cautionary note de Morès may have struck in the interview was hardly borne out by his actions, for he was soon off and running with plans to establish himself in the states east of Dakota Territory. In an undated story, but probably in late 1884, an unidentified Duluth, Minnesota, paper had this to say:

A LARGE BOLD PACKING ESTABLISHMENT TO BE LOCATED HERE BY THE MARQUIS DE MORÈS— THE GROUND PURCHASED FOR IT

For some time past there has been figuring done by some parties here in the interests of the Marquis, who signified a willingness to open up on a large scale an arctic meat packing house, and yesterday morning his representative, G. S. Ober, arrived here to take the matter in hand. He was accompanied by John B. Sutphin and upon looking over the various sites to be had, they concluded to purchase the dock adjoining Granves & Company's warehouse, which they did, the price paid being $10,000.

In the absence of financial statements, it is virtually impossible to determine what the results of the Marquis' operations were, even though the final outcome was clear: a stunning loss. But in those days when disclosure of business financial matters was, at best, masked, the Frenchman was quite frank, even though he was whistling in the dark over competition. This is what he said a little less than two years after he had shipped his first carload of beef:

Today, June 1, 1885, the business stands in the following shape. Real estate and locations have been secured from Portland to Chicago. A thirty-years' contract has been made with the Northern Pacific Railroad. Cold storage and icing stations have been built at Helena, Billings, Miles City, Medora, Bismarck, Fargo, Brainerd, Duluth, Minneapolis, St. Paul, Portage and Chicago. [Note that he says "have been built," in contrast to the Duluth story quoted earlier.] A slaughterhouse, built and equipped in the most complete manner, and capable of shipping 150 beeves per day, stands at Medora. About 15,000 acres of land, controlling the different outlets and securing ample pasturage for the future, have been secured around the slaughterhouse.

The local business along the line of the Northern Pacific Railroad, and the sale of dressed beef in Chicago, will, this season, tax the house to its full capacity, making a shipment for 1885, at least 20,000 head of cattle, and daily sales of over $6,000.

The company has secured connections with Chicago over the Chicago, Milwaukee & St. Paul railway, which has furnished terminal facilities at Portage and Chicago. The company has also secured from the Northern Pacific Railroad, and from the Chicago, Milwaukee & St. Paul railway, the very best of refrigerator cars, using the Hamilton patent.

The company's re-icing system, composed of houses every 200 miles will allow them to put on the Chicago Market the very best of beef.

Arrangements have already been made with the Lake Superior and Lake Michigan Transportation Company to put refrigerators on their boats for supplying different lake points, and negotiations are now pending with a line of boats running to Buffalo for similar arrangements to reach the eastern markets by water. . . .

In addition to the aforesaid results we must add that an agreement to operate on joint account has been made between the Northern Pacific Refrigerator Car Company and the Crescent Creameries of Rochester, Minn. These creameries are celebrated for making the best brand of butter on the market, and their products will be sold exclusively through the houses of the Northern Pacific Refrigerator Car Company.

This was a rosy accounting, but de Morès was not the only

person in the Territory to think that his outlook—indeed, his performance—was fine. Take this *Weekly Yellowstone Journal and Live Stock Reporter* piece:

> The Niobrara Cattle Company have just completed the last delivery under their contract with the Marquis under which they have delivered to him since the beginning of July, cattle numbering 3,059 head.
>
> Last year, the Marquis bought and slaughtered at his abattoir about 30,000 head, it being the first year of active operation of the works. [It was] . . . an experimental year, but so well satisfied was he with the outcome that in April last, at the stock association meeting that was held here, he made the contract for 11,000 head. [The delivery is] nearly completed and it is a doubly gratifying fact that the cattlemen . . . have done better than they could have on the market [meaning Chicago].

The story goes on to point out that the Marquis was able to undersell competition in the East by about two cents a pound. This seems to be a minimum of what de Morès could do, and it shows that he had undoubtedly mounted tough competition against Armour, Swift, and others.

Meanwhile, things were going well on the range, both for de Morès and those who were doing business with him. It is difficult to separate fact from fiction in the Marquis' dealings with ranchers. Some wrote that the Frenchman was so inefficient that one seller herded his steers into de Morès' corrals, was paid, then turned them loose, rounded the animals up again, came back to the paying gate, and resold them. That this happened seems improbable, but it illustrates the kind of stories that were circulated about de Morès. Few people in the Bad Lands were for him. The ranchers were, but still, the small-bore, nibbling criticism of de Morès persisted.

The Marquis also had some trouble with Theodore Roosevelt on the price he was to pay for livestock. De Morès had agreed on a figure for several hundred head of steers, but when the animals were delivered the following day, he said he would pay something less. He gave as the reason a drop in prices at Chicago, hardly a valid excuse for changing a firm bid for anything, be it stocks, bonds, real estate, or livestock. This incident exacerbated the feeling between de Morès and T. R., but perhaps more important, it served to show that the Marquis didn't really understand the common verbal contracts that characterized business transactions in the United States.

De Morès had started his meat-packing operation with the apparent idea of confining himself to the wholesale market, but evidence indicates he had his eye on retailing fairly early in the game, even though he had really scared Chicago meat dealers when he first sold at wholesale there in 1883. The Marquis' initial move toward selling directly to the consumer occurred in St. Paul, Minnesota, where he established his first outlet. This led von Hoffman, a heavy investor in de Morès' enterprises, to say: "My God, de Morès has got that retail butcher's apron on me at last!"

There is little information to indicate whether the retail store in St. Paul succeeded or failed, but whatever the result, de Morès was determined to try his luck farther east, and he chose the logical spot, of course, in New York. There he organized the National Consumers Meat Company, capitalized at ten million dollars divided into shares worth ten dollars each, for which settlement could be made in installments payable in three months. The stockholders were to be the common people of New York, those who, in the words of de Morès and his colleagues, had been fleeced by the big meat packers. The National Consumers Meat Company was, in effect, a cooperative, and de Morès proposed to deliver his product "from the ranch to the table," as he advertised. This would eliminate the middleman and lower the price to the consumer.

The project was off to a flying start, with the Marquis calling a meeting at Manhattan College to explain the operation and solicit financial support. W. R. Grace, mayor of New York; Bryan Laurance, an influential merchant; and Eugene Kelly, an immensely rich banker, were among those who attended and pledged their support. Another important backer was Alex Patrick Ford, owner and editor of the *Irish World*. Ford had suggested a membership fee of ten dollars each in the company. Henry George, the labor leader, also was interested. Three stores were opened in New York, their fronts painted bright red (was it prophetic?).

The Frenchman described his difficulty in the beef business, and why he was retailing in Manhattan, to a *New York World* reporter. Under the headline "A Nobleman as a Butcher," the story occupied the better part of a column, with the first section describing his background in France and the Luffsey shooting in Dakota Territory. The Marquis was quoted as saying that he had "established the first slaughterhouse in the far West, with the object of supplying dressed beef to the Pacific Coast." (This was the first time the market in that part of the country had been indicated as a potential business target for the Frenchman, but, of course, he may well have had his eye on it from the beginning.) De Morès continued:

I encountered great opposition from Chicago men, who used to get live cattle from the West, kill them in Chicago and ship them as dressed beef back to the West.

The result of that competition was to bring us by degrees further and further East to St. Paul, then to Chicago, and finally, in July 1885, from Western Dakota to the seaboard, a distance of over 2,000 miles, a thing which had been called impracticable. Over 3,000 beeves were sold last year in New York, in perfect condition, but owing to the fact that we did not control any outlets, the returns were not what they ought to have been.

It all sounded fine and looked inviting on paper, but the ruthless beef trust, wouldn't give in.

It would be difficult to find more conclusive evidence concerning the power of the beef trust and its collaboration with the railroads than a story that appeared in the *New York Times* of July 1, 1883, in a very prominent place:

THE DRESSED BEEF RATE
COMMENT IN CHICAGO UPON
COMMISSIONER FINK'S DECISION

Chicago, June 30—Ever since the dressed beef business began to assume large proportions, the Eastern trunk lines interested in the various stock yards in this country have been at work trying to crush out the new industry because it threatened to diminish livestock shipments. ["The new industry" obviously referred to de Morès' then burgeoning enterprise, and a probing *Times* reporter sniffed out the situation.]

The present rate on dressed beef is 64 cents per 100 pounds, against 40 cents on livestock, making [the charge for] dressed beef 60 percent higher than livestock. The dressed beef shippers [read "de Morès"] claimed that the present rate is all the business could stand.

The Fink Commission [what commission Fink headed is not explained] recommended that the dressed beef rate be fixed on the basis of 77 cents per 100 pounds from Chicago to New York. As stated in the "Times" of Thursday, this is an increase of 20 percent over the rate heretofore charged and more than 90 percent of the cattle rate.

It was contended that the dressed beef rate would be raised to prohibitive figures, no matter what evidence would be obtained from the dressed beef people, because the managers of the trunk lines, including the arbitrator, Mr. Charles Francis Adams, are personally interested in the stock yards at Chicago, St. Louis and Kansas City and therefore would not allow the cattle business to be injured by the dressed beef business [italics supplied].

Commissioner Fink's recommendation has not been acted upon by the Joint Executive Committee, but there can be no doubt that it will be adopted at the next meeting.

There is no record revealing how the committee voted, but in the light of what subsequently happened to de Morès' operation, the odds are that Fink's thoughts on the matter were, in effect, a ukase.

Many newspapers recognized the unfair competition de Morès faced. Across the Territory from Medora, on the banks of the

Red River of the North, the *Fargo Argus* was noting the machinations of the Marquis' competition in New York:

> The efforts of the New York butchers to boycott the dressed beef of the West is significant as indicating the experiments in that direction promise to work important results. They show that there is an advantage in slaughtering cattle in the West and shipping the carcasses by refrigerator cars to the consumers, over the shipment of the live animals. The butchers are not able to compete with the western dressed beef, and are seeking some restrictive legislation from the New York legislature. But, as in the case of all new processes in business methods, if it has palpable merit it must prevail against all selfish opposition.

Fine words, but the "selfish opposition" believed in dollars, not words.

De Morès' stores in New York were staffed with highly competent butchers, the idea being to serve customers in the best possible manner. Again, the Marquis did well when he started out—too well, perhaps, for his initial success brought down the wrath of his competition, and in those days of untrammeled business enterprise, no holds were barred in bringing the Frenchman under the thumb of the beef establishment.

Take advertising, for example. The eastern beef men ran pictures of skinny cows, labeled "grass fed," against fat ones with a caption asserting the latter had been finished on corn and hence were fatter and better. De Morès countered with a declaration that "the meat furnished by this company comes direct from the ranches, uninjured by driving or long confinement in crowded cattle cars."

Then there was the matter of freight rates, which were figured off the bottom of the deck for de Morès. In that instance, too, there was no appeal.

Coupled with such machinations were the mechanical means of getting at de Morès. Ice was one. His refrigerated cars were cooled with great chunks of ice, sawed during the winter from fresh-water lakes and rivers and packed in sawdust in icehouses, where it could be kept for months on end. When the cars were en route from Dakota Territory to New York, the ice in them had to be replaced at specified stops. At first this posed no problem, but when the beef trust saw that de Morès was really a threat, the men who were to ice the cars in, say, Fargo, Dakota Territory, would just happen not to be on hand when the cars came through. The result, of course, was spoiled meat when it arrived at its destination. And who could prove whether this was by design or by accident? No one. It was not by chance, but preordained.

The beef trust and the railroads had another weapon they could use against de Morès: the charge that he had killed Luffsey. The threat of it was still very real, even though the Frenchman had been acquitted by two actions that passed for law in those days in the Territory. De Morès, advised by highly competent legal counsel, was shrewd enough to know that his enemies might go to court in an effort to bring him down. In an interview with a *New York Times* reporter, he said: "I think the charge has been kept hanging over me for the purpose of breaking up my business." He added: "If I could have been arrested and put in jail some months ago, it might have injured my business and perhaps put an end to my career." He was right, and even now it seems obvious that the meat packers in the Middle West, those farther to the east, and those on the eastern seaboard were determined to destroy his business. They did.

Meanwhile, de Morès conceived a plan that would put down the objection (phony as it was) that grass-fed beef was not equal to the corn-fed variety. He settled on barley, a crop that grew well in western Dakota Territory.

As late as April 2, 1886, some time after de Morès had actually given up his meat-packing business, the *Bismarck Tribune* was still behind him, plugging his idea about feeding. The *Tribune* noted that about two hundred beefs were consumed each day in New York and that de Morès thought he could supply about seven thousand head per year, which the paper claimed was the entire output for that part of the Territory. Ranchers in the area were lucky to have the Frenchman's facilities near by, the *Tribune* declared, for they could market throughout the year rather than just the sixty days during a normal selling period. "But the point most interesting to the people of the Missouri slope," it said, was "a bonanza to the farmers of the entire northwest," referring to "a new process of fattening cattle with barley." The *Tribune* was optimistic:

The Marquis will need 500,000 bushels of barley per year, which is several times more than the entire upper Missouri crop. Again, the "Tribune" is compelled to congratulate the people of the northwest upon the action of the Marquis in making Dakota his home. He is an aggressive, enterprising man, has the capital necessary to insure confidence in his projects, and is liberal in his dealings with the public.

In its March 28, 1886, issue, the *Tribune* ran a story about the Marquis' retail meat-selling operations in New York, noting that "the success of the new scheme of the Marquis de Morès to supply New York with fresh western beef means a reduction in the price and a decided improvement in the quality for the consumers. It is said that the dealers propose to boycott western beef in order to defeat the scheme. It will be in order for the consumers to boycott the dealers." But the end was in sight for de Morès in New York. He faced just as tough and unscrupulous competitors there as he had confronted in Chicago.

As late as 1902, the *New York World* published a long story describing the activities of the beef trust:

The packing firms of Armour, Swift, Hammond, Nelson Morris and Schwarzchild & Sulzberger are hand in hand, shoulder to shoulder in the greatest conspiracy to force up the price of the necessities of life the world has ever seen.

And with them in the plot to drive the people to pay higher prices for food or go hungry are certain railroads.

The railroads can easily create a false scarcity of livestock and produce in the markets, while they fill, almost to bursting, the great cold-storage warehouses. The rocket-like rise of prices that the combination of packers has compelled, now affects nearly every line of food products. Not only has the price of beef advanced unprecedentedly, but there have been advances in pork loins, sheep, lambs, poultry, eggs and butter as extraordinary as they are unnecessary.

The railroads in the pool with the packers make the supply scarce by a bit of jugglery.

In a related story, the *World* called the beef trust "defiant" in its resolve to raise prices and noted that "scores of butchers will close their shops" in protest. The trust then countered with the statement that "there will be still further advances before there is a decline."

These stories could well have been written at the time de Morès was trying to crack the beef markets, for the same set of circumstances applied then. De Morès was doomed by the beef trust.

The end finally came in the winter of 1885–86, although some operations were carried on at the abattoir in the late months of 1886. But de Morès must have seen the signs in 1885 and knew that he couldn't compete with Armour, Swift, and the others. In today's economy, with the antitrust laws in effect, he could probably succeed, but he was working in the nineteenth-century jungle of American business, where might was deemed to be right.

XIV

DE MORÈS' OTHER BUSINESS ENTERPRISES

French businessmen have been accused of being narrow minded, and for some very good reasons, such as their penchant for protective cartels, outdated labor relations, hidebound reluctance to embrace modern methods of production, and lack of imagination in grasping opportunities. None of these traits could be saddled on de Morès. Quite the contrary. If anything, the Frenchman was overenthusiastic, always ready to strike out on new ground, take long risks, and trust to his own judgment on the eventual profitability of a scheme. Not only was he several decades ahead of his time in meat packing, but he also envisaged other operations, some of which he mounted, that were completely outside the business of buying cattle and selling beef.

These subsidiary operations, despite the fact that some of them either failed or were not consummated, reflected de Morès' enterprise and his ability to judge a potential business opportunity (perhaps speculation would be more accurate) and to use the resources at hand. Take the salmon business, for example. When the Northern Pacific Railway knifed its lines through to the Pacific Coast, a new economic era opened in many fields, and de Morès was quick to see that the rolling stock of his Northern Pacific Refrigerator Car Company could be put to a use other than transporting beef.

In those days of the 1880's, a prelude to the gustatory Gay Nineties, West Coast salmon ranked as a great delicacy. (Bons vivants rated it with the superb Scotch and Nova Scotian varieties.) But most of the American product that reached the East

Coast was either smoked or canned, for the rail-freight time from the Pacific to the Atlantic was about twenty-one days. It was a simple matter to take the salmon with giant wheels that almost literally scooped them up from the Columbia River and other waters and fetched them up on the ground. Many canners and smokers did.

De Morès, a gastronome in his own right and a patron of New York's most recherché restaurants, was convinced that the fresh product would be snapped up in Manhattan. (Having been brought up on the distinctive and succulent *loup de mer* of the Mediterranean, the delicate Channel sole, and the *alose* from the Loire, the Marquis understood the attraction of the distinguished fish from the West Coast. He was right about its appeal to New Yorkers.) What did he do? He arranged to buy the catch of commercial fisheries near The Dalles, Oregon. Cleaned quickly at streamside, the salmon were packed in ice and put into one of the Marquis' refrigerator cars, which was then hitched to the *Pacific Express* of the Northern Pacific. Across the continent the cargo rumbled, the first cars garlanded with streamers announcing the progress of the fine Pacific Coast salmon to the gourmets of the East. The *Bad Lands Cow Boy* covered the story in glowing terms, heralding the Marquis' great business sense and noting that seven days after the fish were packed, they were delivered in New York.

De Morès made about one thousand dollars a car on the operation, and he was able to supply his customers in New York regularly. While this produced a relatively small income compared to the beef business, it did show what the Frenchman could do. And, of course, there was no fish trust to buck. (It is interesting to note, in view of the much vaunted American business acumen, that it was de Morès, a Frenchman, who took advantage of rapid transport to bring this choice and perishable food from the West to the East Coast.)

From stories in the *Cow Boy*, it appears that the Marquis had ideas about extracting the most from the slaughterhouse operation in many ways. He had said friends from France were thinking about putting up plants to utilize horns and other inedible parts of the animals for various purposes, but he himself had gone in for the manufacture of "butterine." There is no definition or description of the product, but it was apparently some kind of butter substitute made from animal fat.

Cattlemen have traditionally looked down upon dairy farmers, but not de Morès. He planned an extensive dairy operation, and with his refrigerated cars, it would seem to have been a natural adjunct to his beef business. The proposal, however, apparently went no farther than the idea stage.

Then there was the scheme of truck gardening, although that term was not used at the time. In de Morès' day, the Bad Lands were becoming arid, a result of the virtual extinction of the beaver by trappers, whose catch eventually became garments and hats. Beavers had kept large areas of the Bad Lands green as a result of their dams, which held the water of many streams in a series of reservoir-like ponds, a miniature version of the water conservation system of dams on the Missouri River today. But de Morès had the answer to aridity. He set aside a plot of some thirty to forty acres in the bottomland near the Little Missouri downstream from his château and ran an irrigation ditch to it from the river. He also installed a pump to get the water to his plants.

Never one to shrink from plunging into an operation with a vigorous application of funds, de Morès envisaged a substantial growth and sale of vegetables. Peter Henderson, seedsman, 35 Cortland Street, New York, sent a bill, dated November 12, 1883, for seeds, garden tools, and glass boxes (the latter to be made into hotboxes) totaling $365.54, a sizable sum in those days. The *Dickinson Press* told the story:

The Marquis de Morès has a novel enterprise under way, which he is confident will prove a success, it being a plan to raise 50,000 cabbages on his ranch at the Little Missouri, and have them ready for the market April 1. They will be raised under glass in some peculiar French manner, and when they have attained a certain size, will be transplanted into individual pots and forced rapidly by rich fertilizers, made from the offal of the slaughterhouse and for which preparation he owns the patent. Should the cabbages come out on time, he will try his hand on other kinds of vegetables and should he succeed, the citizens along the line [of the Northern Pacific] will have an opportunity to get as early vegetables as those who live in the sunny south.

That de Morès was serious about the project was demonstrated by his importing Monsieur Adolph Eyraud, from somewhere in France, and the Sigler brothers, expert truck gardeners from New Jersey, to run the enterprise. Drawing on his French background, the Marquis probably was thinking he would be able to bring *primeurs*, those succulent before-the-regular-season vegetables, to customers in the East, especially New York. There were also plans to raise grapes, and not just for jelly.

What happened to the truck garden is misted in time. In the spring of 1886, the Marquis was billed for seeds by Oscar H. Will at Bismarck. Whether these were for the vegetable garden or some other purpose is moot. In any event, there is no record of the gardening operation's ever reaching commercial proportions.

Wheat flourished in that part of the Territory east of Medora, so the Marquis bought some twenty thousand acres of land near Bismarck for raising grain. He then offered tracts to prospective farmers on these terms: free use of forty acres of cleared land without any charge for one year, which, weather permitting, assured the farmer of cash from a crop the first year he tilled the property.

De Morès had learned his lesson with sheep the first winter in the Bad Lands—running the short-haired variety had been a disaster—so he bought a large number of long-haired animals and put them out with ranchers on shares.

Someone discovered a rich vein of kaolin near by, and immediately the Marquis was using his sharply honed sense of the possible (with money and talent, of course), to build and operate a pottery works. The *Cow Boy* reported:

The Marquis is enthusiastic over the fact that the streak of whitish clay found about 20 feet above the largest lignite veins near here has turned out to be kaolin. This is the finest kind of pottery clay, the most costly ware being made from it. If it turns out as expected, the Marquis will put up large works, which will draw more money to Medora than the slaughtering business. We certainly hope there will be no disappointment in this new discovery.

The brick business was not directly a part of de Morès' operations: However, the Marquis was an important customer for the product. Bricks went into the construction of his packing plant, the block of business places he put up, the church that the Marquise financed, and the von Hoffman house. It is interesting to note the kiln's prominence in Medora. An advertisement in the *Cow Boy* reveals the exuberance of editor Arthur T. Packard and the brickmaker in announcing the opening of the operation:

BRICK!!
MADE AT THE
MEDORA BRICK KILN
AND
GUARANTEED BETTER
THAN ANY BRICK MADE IN DAKOTA, OR MONEY REFUNDED
ONLY $8 PER THOUSAND!
ADDRESS ALL ORDERS TO
PETER J. BOOK
MEDORA,
DAK.

The *Cow Boy*'s story of the new business ran on June 5, 1884, shortly after the advertisement:

The second kiln of brick, which will be ready for burning in a few days, is to contain over 200,000. A permanent kiln is to be erected immediately, thus saving much waste. Specimens of the brick at the "Cow Boy" office have been examined by many competent judges and unanimously pronounced equal to any brick made.

Aside from the cattle he bought and processed, de Morès was interested in other four-footed animals, horses, and he dealt at some depth in them, buying Indian ponies which the federal government had confiscated from Sitting Bull, Gall, Crow King, One Bull, Low Dog, and other Indians. By early 1884, the Marquis had a large enough herd to advertise for sale an "entire lot of stock horses consisting of 60 mares, about 15 two and three year olds, 20 yearling colts, 10 American mares and 3 stallions, one of which is a thoroughbred Clydesdale, one Norman and one Kentucky Messenger."

But de Morès' interests were broader than ranching and agriculture. He bought a substantial slice of the *Mandan Pioneer*, which was on a par with the *Bismarck Tribune*, one of the finest papers in the Territory. (The odds are that de Morès would have liked to own the *Cow Boy*, at least in part, but the bristling Packard wanted no part of such an arrangement, even though he was strongly pro de Morès.)

The Marquis also invested in a banking operation in the Territory, the Bismarck Loan and Trust Company. It was largely owned by Andrew W. and R. B. Mellon. In those days of unregulated financing, the Marquis could have made a handsome profit on his capital or lost everything, but there is no record of how he came out.

Apparently, de Morès thought gold might be found in the Bad Lands—perhaps not a bad supposition in view of the strikes that were being made to the west and south. Some kind of exploration was carried on, but nothing resulted from it. Unless most mining engineers are wrong, there was and is no gold in the Bad Lands.

XV

THE MEDORA-DEADWOOD STAGE LINE

Although de Morès erred about gold in the Medora area, its incidence could be described as almost abundant in the Black Hills of South Dakota, then a part of Dakota Territory. The Hills were some two hundred miles south of Medora, isolated from railroads and not served from the north by stage, express, or freight lines. In 1874, two prospectors, Horatio N. Ross and William McKay, rode through the Black Hills as a part of a U.S. Army exploratory expedition led by General George A. Custer. They struck it rich.

The Ross-McKay find exploded in a resounding gold boom, especially around what became the towns of Deadwood and Custer, where important strikes were made. Hundreds upon hundreds of gold-hungry people flocked to the Hills in search of an easy fortune. A few found it. Most did not. Some of those who didn't stayed on in other occupations.

Following the first strikes, the Black Hills were relatively isolated from the surrounding country. By 1880, two railroad lines, the Chicago and North Western and the Chicago, Milwaukee, St. Paul and Pacific, which were laying track toward Deadwood had been completed only to the Missouri River, about half the distance from the eastern border of the Territory to the Hills. They could go no farther because the western part of Dakota Territory, except for the Hills, was controlled by hostile Indians. By 1883, however, when de Morès was building his cattle empire, the Indians had been subdued, with the Sioux and the Gros Ventre on reservations, except for a few wandering bands. Even so, the only transportation into the Black Hills was by wagon train or stagecoach. Lines ran from Pierre (now the capital of South Dakota) and Chamberlain, the westernmost terminals of the North Western and Milwaukee railroads. Other lines fed into the Hills from Cheyenne, Wyoming Territory; Bismarck, Dakota Territory; and Sidney, Nebraska.

Looking at the map and letting his imagination soar, de Morès saw that a stage-express-freight line from Medora would have a distinct distance advantage over the existing lines, except for the one from Pierre. That didn't bother him—he was never afraid of straight-out competition. Moreover, the skein of trails that connected the established lines, if one could call them that, were impassable about half the year owing to mud, snow, swollen rivers, and the lack of bridges and grading.

Despite such impediments, mining machinery and merchandise had been freighted into the Hills by bull train; hordes of people seeking their fortunes arrived on horseback or in wagons and stagecoaches. This traffic continued briskly into the early 1880's, with mountainous piles of freight backed up on the Northern Pacific waiting to be hauled overland to the Black Hills. When that railroad crossed the Missouri River in 1879 and was pushing on to the West Coast, the idea of connecting the gold fields with some point on the Northern Pacific west of Bismarck became increasingly intriguing. The gold rush was reaching a feverish pitch, and it was clear to enterprising people that some town on the line was going to profit by establishing itself as the terminal point from the Hills to the Northern Pacific, which became transcontinental in 1883. What should that point be? De Morès knew the answer: Medora.

He faced tough competition, to be sure. The federal government, bent on westward expansion, had dispatched survey parties to pick a route between the Hills and the Northern Pacific. Belfield, near Medora, and Dickinson, about forty miles to the east, were the logical contenders. Dickinson had the advantage of being designated in early 1884 by the Northern Pacific as the forwarding point for Deadwood freight and express. But as Lewis F. Crawford has pointed out in *The Medora–Black Hills Stage Line*, "Dickinson . . . could only ask individuals engaging in the Black Hills trade to do their freighting from that point, while Medora had a man in the person of the Marquis de Morès who could establish his own line and invite the public to patronize it—without courting the sanction of anyone." That is precisely what he did in 1884, but there is strong evidence he was making plans in 1883, despite the fact that he was just then establishing his abattoir and having to dodge bullets, among other activities. The stage line was a de Morès operation through and through, although father-in-law von Hoffman had some money in the deal—enough, it seems, to criticize some of the operation, which he did.

The first step, of course, was to determine a route. De Morès, his French cartographic training again standing him in good stead, carefully studied a map of Dakota Territory (U.S. government surveyors had done a credible job of charting the country). He sketched out a course from Medora to Deadwood, taking advantage of the terrain that varied from the flat prairies and the jumbled topography of the Bad Lands to the mountainous Black Hills. He also had to figure on stretches of gumbo, a claylike substance which when wet turned into a glutinous, slippery mass that made passage on foot or horseback, wagon or stage, extremely difficult and sometimes impossible. (Even in the 1900's, motorists in the Bad Lands were warned of gumbo roads when rain was imminent, for traction, even with chains, would be dangerously impaired.)

How to see if the route on paper was right? Ride it. This was an assignment de Morès would not delegate. He carried it out himself, just as he and van Driesche had explored the Bad Lands along the Little Missouri when they first arrived in Dakota. The Frenchman had two companions on his ride, but that made little difference, for he would undoubtedly have ridden the course alone if it had seemed the thing to do.

They set out on a fine April day—at least it was fine in Medora, and April in the Bad Lands can be as *doux* as the *Côte d'Azur* which de Morès knew so well. Not far out of Medora, a vicious Arctic storm swept down on the three riders. Blinded by swirling snow, they had to dismount. (It must have been tough for the Frenchman to admit having to give up, even if only temporarily.) The men wrapped their heads in blankets—they would be sleeping out en route—and walked their horses in a circle to keep both themselves and their mounts from freezing. They won against the weather, and off they rode toward the gold-filled Black Hills. De Morès was in his element: well mounted; "armed like a battleship," someone said; and keenly anticipating the possible dangers ahead.

With his usual *éclat*, de Morès rode the entire route, 215 miles, sparing himself less than his mount and probably his companions. He traversed the distance in fifty-two hours, a remarkable feat. (Here was another example of the great physical prowess of the Marquis and his willingness to take on anything in the Old West, but except for a few enlightened people, mostly newspaper reporters and editors, his qualities were discounted in favor of criticism.)

De Morès made a great splash all around Deadwood, which was one of the roughest mining towns in the Territory, but populated also by those who recognized that their businesses needed the transportation seemingly promised by the Marquis. The *Black Hills Daily Pioneer*, just as much activist for that section of the Old West as the *Bad Lands Cow Boy* was for Medora, ran a story on April 19, 1884, noting that "Medora is almost in direct line with Deadwood" and extolling the idea of a transportation route between the two towns. It was quite natural, then, that in the next day's issue the paper should come out with a front-page piece that ran this way:

"OUR GUEST"
MARQUIS DE MORÈS PAYS A VISIT TO
THE HOMESTAKE MINES
AND MILLS
ACCOMPANIED BY A NUMBER OF PROMINENT
CITIZENS OF DEADWOOD
"IT IS A BIG THING," DECLARED THE DISTINGUISHED
GENTLEMAN OF THIS ENTERPRISE
THE COURTESIES OF SUPERINTENDENT GREGG
AND SECRETARY GREER, A COLLATION
WITH RESPONSES TO TOASTS,
AN IMPORTANT OCCASION
ALL AROUND THE BELT

As had been arranged by the committee appointed to receive the Marquis and entertain him while in the city, he was yesterday escorted through the flourishing cities of Lead and Central. At 10 o'clock the carriages were at Wentworth house and the Marquis in company with prominent gentlemen of the city started upon a well appreciated inspection tour. The party consisted of Frank B. Allen of Bismarck, attorney for the Marquis, Judge Corson, Alvin Fox, cashier of the Merchants National Bank, D. A. McPherson, cashier of the First National Bank, Thomas Jones and Joseph Pennell.

Pennell was one of the most influential and highly solvent freighters in the Territory, with huge herds of animals to draw the wagons he and his associates owned.

What followed in the story was the beginning of the chamber-of-commerce prose that proliferated all over the United States. Deadwood was Sinclair Lewis' *Main Street* with a mountainous background and peopled by those who elected to take their chances in the mines, or as prospectors, rather than settle down to the humdrum life of farmers and those who served them in Sauk Center, Minnesota. But the rhetoric was as bad in Deadwood as it would have been in towns with less glamor, and the *Pioneer* reflects this as it describes de Morès' triumphant entry into Deadwood and his stay there. Homestake Mining Company was just then in its beginnings, and that part of the Marquis' inspection trip to Deadwood was related this way:

There was nothing formal or undue in the meeting of the respected guest and the representatives of the largest mining enterprise of the world, but the cordiality of their greeting was as manifest as the culture of the gentleman is perfect. . . .

When the noted visitor expressed himself of the Homestake, he simply said, "It's a big thing."

Why did de Morès have so little to say? Reserve, perhaps, or maybe he was thinking about the mail contract he was to negotiate for the line.

His private talks in Deadwood, however, were another matter. He told his hosts that if he could have an exclusive option on the stage business, he would not only also establish a freight line, which was just as important to the Hills, but would also promote the construction of a railroad between Medora and Deadwood. (Soon after the Deadwood trip, he went before the board of directors of the Northern Pacific to present the idea of running a line from Medora to the Black Hills. He got nowhere.) The Marquis left Deadwood with the goodwill of the people he had seen and returned to Medora to face the practical matters of organizing his transportation enterprise.

De Morès was meticulous about the legality of whatever he did, and so the Medora Stage and Forwarding Company was incorporated in November, 1884; the Marquis put thirty thousand dollars into it. He held 290 shares in the company, and van Driesche and Frank B. Allen held the rest, five each. How von Hoffman figured in the deal is unexplained—perhaps he owned some of de Morès' shares.

After the initial reconnoitering on horseback, de Morès was convinced that his route to the Black Hills was right. Possessing a flair for the dramatic, he chose to slash through some of the most spectacular scenery in the Old West: the Bad Lands, the prairies, and the Black Hills. In those days, tourism as such was confined to the few rich people from the East and abroad who could afford it, so the traffic de Morès could expect was largely commercial. Yet even those riding the stagecoaches with only profit in mind could be expected to return home with tales of a picturesque, wild country.

Arthur T. Packard was ecstatic about the route de Morès had chosen, but he was equally critical of the possibility that one from Dickinson should compete. He wrote in the February 14, 1884, *Cow Boy*:

The route from here for almost the entire distance is as good a wagon road as could be desired, water and grass also being abundant. In the winter season almost a perfect route is furnished by the Little Missouri River. It will be news to many to know that Medora is not over three miles east of a line running directly north from Deadwood. The proposed route from Medora scarcely goes off this line, thus making this the nearest railroad point to Deadwood. [Packard pointed out the lack of obstacles on the route, especially gumbo.]

The Dickinson route, on the other hand [at best poor and impassable in some seasons] strikes gumbo from the start, and there is a great quantity all along their line. Their route then strikes the headwaters of the Heard, Cannonball, Grand and Moreau Rivers. These must be bridged or forded, but the ground is soft and everywhere abounds in gumbo. The route from Medora, however, goes above the headwaters of these rivers and is on the level divide between them and the Little Missouri.

It is estimated that at least 10,000,000 pounds of freight will be shipped over the road yearly. This will take hundreds of wagons and men, all with their headquarters here.

Packard estimated the new line would put twenty thousand dollars a month into circulation in Medora from wages alone and predicted that "this means successful business for a town of a thousand inhabitants. Taken in connection with the cattle and other industries, our rapid growth is certain."

Stagecoaches were not quite so easy to buy in 1884 as used cars are today, but since the transportation business was no sure bet and railroads were replacing stage lines, quite a lot of equipment could be bought from outfits going out of business all over the West. De Morès took advantage of this situation by picking up four Concord coaches, the Rolls Royce of horse-drawn conveyances, from the Gilmer and Salisbury Stage Company (it had folded an operation out of Sidney, Nebraska). He made a good buy, paying $300 each for coaches that had initially cost $1,500; they were in perfect condition. When brought to Medora, each was repainted and given a name: *Kittie*, *Medora*, *Dakota*, and *Deadwood*. De Morès also had "U.S. Mail" inscribed on the sides in gilt and black—wishful thinking.

At the same time, the Marquis bought complete sets of harness for the stage operation. These were much more rugged than those used for the usual kind of riding in a buggy behind a single horse or team.

Then there was the problem of horses. De Morès knew his mounts well; it would have been difficult for anyone in Dakota Territory to have bested him in any kind of deal involving riding horses. But animals for the stage were another matter, so de Morès sent one of his men to Montana to find the right kind of horses for the Medora-Deadwood run. Even an experienced horse buyer had to be extremely careful in those days, for the market was unruly, to say the least. One had to be prepared to deal with the most unscrupulous sort of men. It was, indeed, a case of *caveat emptor*.

When the Marquis' men went out to buy the animals, they knew that they could afford to pay only for broncos. Horses broken to the harness were not only scarce, but expensive. They bought 150 animals at one hundred dollars each.

It was at this point that von Hoffman first began to question the operation. "How many horses have you bought?" he asked the manager one day.

"A hundred and sixty-six."

"How many are you using on the stage line?"

"One hundred and sixty."

"What are you doing with the other six?"

"They are out on the line."

With a loud "harumph," von Hoffman replied: "Eating their heads off!"

The Wall Street banker must have had some money in the line and in other de Morès enterprises, but just how much is impossible to tell. The Old West was fertile ground for risk capital in those days, and Americans were not alone in selecting it as a place to try to parlay their fortunes. Europeans, especially the English, had huge stakes there, particularly in ranches and railroads. De Morès' talk of a 12 per cent return on capital in the cattle business may well have been right, given decent weather and market conditions, and the same could have applied to the stage line.

The Marquis needed a manager for the stagecoach venture, so he turned to Erasmus Deffebach, known in the Territory as "Rassy." One of his first jobs was to locate the way stations. These were spotted every ten to fifteen miles and equipped to take care of the stages and their passengers during brief stops to change horses and drivers and to let the passengers stretch their legs. At some of the stations, food and lodging were provided.

The passenger business was not the only aspect of the operation. Freight destined for the Black Hills continued to accumulate along the Northern Pacific, which meant an enormous business for anyone with the resources (mostly oxen, horses, and mules) to send wagons across the countryside from the Northern Pacific into the Black Hills. De Morès was ready to take on this business and did, contracting with the leading frontier freighters. Passenger traffic was the more glamorous of the two, however, and the Marquis bent his talents to satisfying the needs of travelers.

The initial run between Medora and Deadwood was made in late 1884, with one of the most skilled reinsmen on the box. Lloyd Roberts, an authentic frontiersman, rode shotgun—and he was not there merely for decoration. De Morès paid him fifty dollars for his services. The first trip surely ranks as a classic, for just about everything that could go wrong did.

The horses spotted along the route may have had some breaking, but many or most of them still resisted the harness. First, they had to be roped. Then they were thrown to the ground and blindfolded. Harnessing followed, accompanied by frenzied whinnying, flared nostrils, and slashing hooves. After an interval which the handlers thought and hoped would be somewhat peaceful, the harness was brought out.

Harnessing a bronco was a somewhat delicate operation, for if a horse felt anything more pressing than a natural weight, he was off and bucking. With the leather in place, the horses were then led, still blindfolded, to positions in front of the coach. This was a job of pushing and pulling—in fact, almost carrying the beasts. Herman Hagedorn describes what happened:

Noiselessly, one at a time the tugs were attached to the single tree, and carefully, as though they were dynamite, the reins were handed to the driver. At the Moreau Station, two thirds of the way to Deadwood, all six horses . . . were practically unbroken broncos. The driver was on his box with [Arthur T.] Packard at his side, as they prepared to start, and at the head of each horse stood one of the station hands.

"Ready?" asked the man at the head of the near leader.

"All set," answered the other helpers.

"Let 'er go!" called the driver.

The helpers jerked the blinds from the horses' eyes. The broncos jumped into their collars as a unit [but] they surged back, as they became suddenly conscious of the horrors they dreaded most— restraint. The off leader [the second horse from the front on the left-hand side as the driver faced the team] made a wild swerve to the right, backing toward the coach, and dragging the near leader and the near swing-horses from their feet. The off leader, unable to forge ahead, made a wild leap from the off swing horse, and fairly crushed him to earth with his feet, himself tripping on the harness and rolling at random in the welter, his snapping hooves flashing in every direction. The wheel team in the meantime was doing what Packard later described as a "vaudeville turn of its own." The near wheeler was bucking as though there were no other horse within a hundred miles; the off wheeler had broken his single-tree and was facing the coach, delivering kicks at the mélée behind him with whole hearted abandon and rigid impartiality.

After that first encounter, the horse wranglers pulled the off leader out of the tangle of horses, and one man sat on its head while the rest of the animals were put in place.

Then when all six of the steeds were in place, all in a highly agitated state, as was the reinsman, the signal went to Go! The horses did, the driver with trepidation, the horses with a will of the wild.

Off the stage thundered to Deadwood.

At the last stop before entering Deadwood, fresh horses were hitched to the stage so that the outfit could strut into town in grand style, the best reinsman on the Marquis' staff adding his bit. The townspeople cheered and the businessmen added to the din, for they now had a connection with a transcontinental railroad, the implication being that the link would soon be by rail.

Trade was brisk on the stage line, for the Black Hills gold strike continued to magnetize thousands of people eager to try their luck with shovel or pan. Ten or eleven passengers in each coach paid $21.50 to be jolted thirty-six hours between Medora and Deadwood.

De Morès faced competition, for there was no such thing as a franchise. Anyone with capital and equipment could go into business overnight, and some did. The opposition was brisk and resourceful, but de Morès again demonstrated that he had enough managerial skill to beat anyone who challenged him, provided there was no outside interference or influence.

Arthur T. Packard, a rabid fan of de Morès and his enterprises, kept up a drumfire of stories cheering everything the Marquis' stage was accomplishing. But he was also setting forth an important fact, namely, that the Frenchman had the edge on his competitors. On November 27, 1884, the *Cow Boy* reported the stage line's latest exploit:

Again the Medora stage smashed all records. The coach arrived here Tuesday night just 32 hours and 5 minutes out of Deadwood. This beats the best time in or out of Deadwood by any stage over any line by nearly four hours.

In that winter of 1884–85, with tough, cold, snowy conditions in the Black Hills and elsewhere, the de Morès line ran only a few hours behind schedule while its competition frequently measured tardiness in days.

The freight and express business also was booming, with the *Cow Boy* chronicling the number of horses, mules, and oxen used on the various outfits carrying supplies into the Black Hills, some of them coming out with gold bullion and other things.

De Morès was so sure of himself that he ordered construction of a freight depot in Medora early in the game. It was built before there was a firm indication he was going to have the volume of business he anticipated. A long shot? Perhaps. But it could be argued that with a warehouse, de Morès was in a better position to entice freighters to do business with him, particularly if outfits operating out of Dickinson and elsewhere had no warehouses.

Van Driesche, in addition to working on the Marquis' enterprises, had a venture of his own. The *Cow Boy* reported in its September 25, 1884, issue (before the stage went into operation) that "a new mode of communication is being introduced by William van Driesche, who has sixteen carrier pigeons which he is training to carry messages between this point and the Black Hills. William has made several experiments with them, taking them out to the stage stations, and they have invariably returned in remarkably short time. It is estimated that they can fly to the Hills in two or three hours, which is very good time indeed." What could have been a better adjunct to the stage line than carrier-pigeon service from Medora to points in the Black Hills and return?

De Morès was off and running with the stage line, but he had miscalculated one all-important element. The stagecoach business was widespread on the frontier, and the economics of its success had been clearly documented. The first essential for making money was a government mail contract. This would produce income to cover the costs of operation; profit would come from passenger fares and express charges on items such as gold dust and bullion, which could be substantial on a run from the Black Hills.

De Morès went to Washington, D.C., early in 1884 to negotiate a contract for carrying the mail between Medora and Deadwood. A *Chicago Daily Inter-Ocean* reporter interviewed him, but the story was about the beef business. Why de Morès didn't talk about the stage line and the mail contract remains a mystery.

Nor is there any record of the people in Washington with whom the Frenchman spoke. More the pity, because the fortunes of the stage line hinged on those conversations with Post Office Department officials and others. There is at least one indication, however, that de Morès merely applied for the contract and did no politicking to get it, which was apparently essential. This is a little hard to believe, for even though the Marquis had not been in business in France, he certainly had been exposed to intertwined government-business relations there. At the same time, it seems incredible that de Morès did not use some political muscle to secure the mail contract, for surely his father-in-law had political pull—and von Hoffman must have had some money in the operation.

The question of Theodore Roosevelt's influence impinges on my thoughts, and it is no more than that in the absence of documentation, which apparently does not exist. Since T. R. was such a political animal, it is quite possible that through his multifarious connections in Wall Street and Washington, the matter of a mail contract for the Frenchman could well have arisen. But a thorough search of all available evidence fails to show any connection between Roosevelt's influence and de Morès' bid for the mail contract.

What happened to Rassy's stewardship of the stage line is uncertain, but in any event he left. Then de Morès hired, of all people, Bill Williams, the saloonkeeper, to run the line. Williams' competence was confined to diluting bad alcohol and selling it as whiskey. When he didn't work out, the Frenchman turned to an equally improbable manager, Jess Hogue, Williams' crony, whose notoriety rested on various odorous and nefarious deals. Both choices were disastrous to the Marquis' operation.

Finally, de Morès went to the one man in Medora who, in his opinion, was beyond reproach in financial matters: Arthur T. Packard. He dashed into the *Cow Boy* office and said to the editor, with some feeling: "I want you to put on the stage line for me." Packard replied that he had never seen a stage line until the Marquis' came into operation, much less had he ever entertained the slightest idea of how to run one.

De Morès was not about to be put off by that kind of talk. Indeed, he insisted that Packard's nonprofessional qualifications mattered little. His comment probably reflected his feeling about many of his operations in the Bad Lands, for he said, undoubtedly referring to Williams and Hogue, that he was tired of being robbed and wanted someone he could trust to run the line.

Packard took over. From that time on, it was hard to differentiate between Packard the editor and Packard the manager. But then that was true of everything which happened in Medora. As I said before, Packard was a press agent for the Bad Lands, a good one.

The financial arrangement de Morès made with Packard was never disclosed, but indications are that Packard was to have a major interest, with the Marquis financing the operation. Just how much money, other than the initial capital, was involved is difficult to estimate, but the fact remains that Packard complained about the lack of cash and the reluctance (or inability) of de Morès to furnish it.

In the summer of 1885, passenger traffic on the line boomed, but then it faded, for two good reasons. First, placer operations in the Black Hills, which required large numbers of men, had been replaced by deep-vein mining, a process carried on with fewer hands. This not only stopped the inflow of miners to the Hills, but spurred those who were there to get out. And the getting was good, for a new strike had been made in the Coeur d'Alene area of Idaho Territory. It would have been possible, apparently, for the Marquis' stage line to have made money in this traffic, but because of the lack of working capital (the first indication of such a contretemps), de Morès couldn't take advantage of the situation.

De Morès, the constant optimist, figured he would get the mail contract. It may well be that he was led to believe this in his Washington conversations. Whatever the case, he had been so confident of the mail franchise that on February 21, 1884, he wired his men in Medora to go ahead with preparations for the operation, such as building the way stations. He also said in his telegram: "Mail route . . . o.k. Tell Pennell [the freight mogul] to organize three or four post offices at ranches on road to Deadwood and send applications directly." It is difficult to understand why a cautious man like the Marquis would proceed with such a major undertaking as a stagecoach line without having a mail contract in hand, particularly since the risks involved were so well known on the frontier.

The intrigue of business and politics in those days was Byzantine. The federal government was determined that the nation should expand to the West Coast, and the railroads were the means to that end; they were co-equal with the government in shaping America's destiny. It should be recalled that when de Morès established the stage line, he was competing vigorously against the beef trust and its allies—the railroads. The implication for de Morès' chances of winning the mail contract he so desperately needed was clear, but having started to run the line, he stayed with it during the winter of 1884–85. Even then, the end was in sight.

XVI

THE THIRD TRIAL

In view of the fact that de Morès was tried a third time for the killing of Luffsey, it is revealing that he should have told a *New York Herald* reporter on August 22, 1885, that "I was elected to the executive committee of the Dakota and Montana Cattle Men's Association, and upon my shoulders the task of keeping order and repressing horse stealing in my immediate vicinity fell. *Naturally, in so doing I made many enemies, and in six months I was shot at by unseen persons 18 times, thus beating George Washington's record at the defeat of Braddock by one*" [italics supplied].

De Morès told the reporter that to secure an indictment for murder was not difficult, and in the context of the Territory's legal system (if it could be called that), the Marquis was undoubtedly right. He blamed Dutch Wannegan for bringing the case up again, according to the *Herald*. He also thought Theodore Roosevelt was partly responsible for his legal troubles, noting that T. R. had hired Wannegan as a ranch hand. The Marquis was jumping to a conclusion; that Wannegan was working for Roosevelt didn't necessarily mean the future President of the United States was for his hired hand and against de Morès.

Regardless of who instigated the new legal move, de Morès was indicted in August, 1885, on the twice-dismissed charge of having killed Luffsey. The action is difficult to rationalize, especially in view of what has been called a traditional code of ethics for gunfights in the Old West. Nevertheless, the court acted through a grand jury sitting in Mandan.

The sleazy kind of justice that was being dispensed drew fire from de Morès, who filed with the court an affidavit in which he asserted: "This indictment . . . was not in the interest of justice, but to gratify spite, malice and avarice, nor was the same made at the instance of the public prosecutor of any party directly aggrieved." He was right.

The Marquis asked for a change of venue from the Second Judicial Subdivision to the First, which would move the trial from Mandan, on the west bank of the Missouri, to Bismarck, on the eastern side. He pleaded that he could not get a fair trial in Mandan because that city was populated by many people of Irish extraction who sympathized with Luffsey, also an Irishman. Moreover, he asserted, the lawless element in the Bad Lands, which fell under the jurisdiction of the Mandan court, wanted to force him to pay through the nose for legal protection. He also charged that some people didn't want a legitimate business like his established in the Bad Lands because it would impair their crooked activities.

The trial was set, and then the predictable happened: de Morès was approached with a proposition (by whom was not disclosed) to pay an undetermined sum (undoubtedly quite substantial) to have the indictment quashed. The predictable also happened: de Morès refused. He was quoted in news stories as saying he was not going to be blackmailed by anyone, which leads one to believe that somebody may have tried it before.

De Morès was in Medora when the indictment was handed down. He could, of course, have been taken into custody. Just what the circumstances were that precluded or prevented such action are unclear. Whatever, de Morès was smart enough to get out of the Territory. He took off for New York. This move may have saved his life in view of certain elements in the Bad Lands that hung over him like an evil spirit.

In Manhattan, he was again the object of newspaper stories, an understandable reaction from reporters and editors, for here was a man who was to be tried a third time for killing another man in what was considered a fair fight. Why weren't others retried under similar circumstances? There was plenty of shooting. Not only were empty cartridge cases littering the streets of Little Missouri and Medora, but there was the story of a man in Wibaux, Montana Territory, who was constructing part of a sidewalk with empty cartridge cases.

De Morès had no choice but to stand trial by jury, unless, of course, he elected to leave the country. That was no solution because in effect it would be an admission of guilt. His decision required courage, for he was laying his life on the line.

A *Times* front-page story on August 22, 1885, ran this way:

THE TITLED CATTLEMAN
THE MARQUIS DE MORÈS AS TO
HIS COMING TRIAL
PLENTY OF MONEY FOR HIS DEFENSE, BUT
NOT ONE CENT FOR BLACKMAIL—TO
START FOR HIS HOME TUESDAY

[De Morès was quoted as saying] I suppose the man who is pushing the case is Wannegan. He was one of my assailants. I have received no details, however. I have telegraphed my lawyer that I will leave New York on Tuesday morning on the limited express. I think the charge has been kept hanging over me for the purpose of breaking up my business. . . . If I could have been arrested and put in jail some months ago, it might have injured my business and perhaps put an end to my career. I determined that I would not be put in jail, to lie there perhaps for months waiting for a trial. Besides, a jail is not a safe place in that part of the country. [This was proved in a chilling way when de Morès did go back for trial.]

I was willing to be tried when all was ready. Now the court seems to be ready, and so will I be in a few days. I have plenty of money for defense, but not a dollar for blackmail. Most of the officers [apparently of the court] are my friends. I have nothing to fear from them and I don't fear the other sort, though I know, of course, they are my enemies. . . . The trial can't take long, and as I said, I do not fear the result.

In Dakota, Frank B. Allen was planning de Morès' defense with an intimate knowledge of the Marquis dating from their

165

first meeting at the Bismarck Land Office in 1883. Later, at the request of the Marquise, Allen wrote a long piece about de Morès. On January 3, 1903, the *New York Evening Post* published an article based on Allen's account. The section concerning the third trial is the best record one could ask for in the absence of a stenographic report:

When the Territorial court met in Mandan, it was evident that the Marquis would be indicted for murder in the first degree. His counsel decided that it would be better to have the trial take place because a charge of murder is never outlawed, and if by means of any influence an indictment was prevented, the same thing might have to be gone through with again and again. It was arranged with the District Attorney, however, that that officer should not object to a change of venue to Bismarck, and this was granted by the court, and Morès was duly delivered to the Sheriff of Burleigh County and provided with two rooms in the fine new penitentiary in Bismarck furnished by himself, where he passed twenty-seven days.

When de Morès returned to Dakota from New York, he was jailed at Mandan under precisely the circumstances he had predicted. The first night, a howling mob bent on lynching him stormed the log-cabin jail, shot through the windows, and attempted to burn the place down. Fortunately, the would-be lynchers were thwarted.

Despite this clear manifestation of hostility toward de Morès and the district attorney's agreement to a change in venue, there ensued a legal battle to have the trial moved across the river to Bismarck. Long, the prosecutor, obviously reneged.

Fortunately, the hearing on a change of venue came before a literate judge, which was not the case in the Marquis' first two encounters with what passed for justice in Dakota Territory. The man on the bench was W. H. Francis, who hailed from Newark, New Jersey, and who was, according to de Morès' counsel, an intelligent and impartial jurist.

Trouble at the hearing broke out almost immediately, for District Attorney Long plumbed the depths of invective in much the same way his counterpart had behaved during the second trial. But Judge Francis was a man of considerable substance who brooked no nonsense from anyone. The *Mandan Pioneer* of August 31, 1885, recounted the exchange between the two:

District Attorney Long in reply to the Marquis's request for a change of venue said:

"The motion is a somewhat novel proceeding in this part of Dakota, and I cannot let the arguments of counsel pass without replying to the insinuation and misrepresentations of the affidavits relative to the fair fame and name of the citizens of Mandan and Morton county. I have in my hand an affidavit of many citizens of Mandan and Morton county, stating that they are well acquainted with the feeling of the disposition and character of our settlement and civilization, and I desire to read it to the court partially for the purpose of answering the affidavits read in behalf of the defendant, the Marquis."

Mr. Long read the affidavit, and continued his remarks as follows: "From the affidavit read in this case in behalf of the defendant, asking for a change of venue, are we to assume that Mandan and Morton county are composed of a band of lawless brigands who disregard the law and have no respect for its mandates? Are we the lawless Bedouins of the desert on this side of the Missouri? The learned counsel would have us believe this. Is the gentleman in earnest? Does he really mean what he says? Are we to infer that the people of Mandan and Morton county are so far beneath the law and are so free to disregard the ordinary forms of justice that they can't give these defendants a fair and impartial hearing? Mandan and Morton county and their civilization compare favorably with Bismarck and Burleigh county. We are not a paradise of cowboys and wild Irishmen west of the Missouri. The charges in their affidavits and in behalf of this motion are an insult to this court and its officers, and I cannot believe that it is made in good faith. It seems to me to be the most gigantic burlesque that I ever seen in a court of justice. Then too, this change of venue is asked to be made to Bismarck. Bismarck! the synonym for all that is fair—the synonym for fair trials, honesty—"

Judge Francis: "This court is a resident of Bismarck."

Mr. Long: "I am aware of that fact. We all know full well the character of Bismarck. Bismarck is the home of more dishonesty, skullduggery, rascality, scoundrelism, fraud, perjury, subornation

of perjury, bribing of juries, corruption in public and private places than any other city of the same size on the face of the globe."
Judge Francis: "Not as bad as that. Let us keep to the motion."
Mr. Long: "In the name of the people of Mandan and Morton county, I resent the charges that have been made here, as false, and I hurl them back into the face of Bismarck as a falsehood. It is not true that the people of Mandan are prejudiced against de Morès. Twice he has been before justices in Mandan for this offence and twice he has been acquitted. Does that indicate prejudice? Does this indicate that we cannot give him a fair and impartial trial in Mandan? The people on this side of the river have always extended a generous hand to every capitalist and every settler who has come here. They feel proud of the large industry which this defendant has built up in the West Missouri country and it is to the people of the West Missouri country that he should look for aid and protection and not to Bismarck."

[Long continued his tirade, saying:] "The application for a change of venue has for its object three things: first to satisfy an envious rivalry of Bismarck; second, to delay justice; and third, if possible to defeat the law. These are the facts at the bottom of it all, and it is to say whether this court will lend the dignity of its official power to any scheme of this kind. They ask for a change of venue on account of a feeling of prejudice, and where to? To Jamestown? Fargo? Valley City? Grand Forks? Any point more than ten miles from Mandan? No! to Bismarck—a city within five miles of Mandan. Is it possible that there is so great a difference of feeling and prejudice between the two points? In the nature of things when an application for a change of venue is applied for, it should be to take the case far enough away to escape local prejudice. If it were made to Jamestown or Fargo, it might appear that there was some reasonable ground for the motion. I trust your honor will weigh this matter and refuse the motion for a change of venue."

Mr. Allen: "It would seem to me that it is apparent to the court that if prejudice did not exist against the defendant before the speech of the District Attorney, it must exist now."

The *Pioneer* reported that Judge Francis granted the change of venue.

Long's diatribe at the hearing drew fire in the eastern part of the Territory, notably from the *Jamestown Alert*, which said on September 12, 1885:

There is an irrepressible conflict raging and rankling between Mandan and Bismarck, which involves Judge Francis, on account of the change of venue asked by and granted to the Marquis de Morès. Some of the prominent citizens of Mandan construe it as an aspersion upon their sense of justice. It seems to the "Alert" that the people of Mandan worked themselves into a white heat over an affront that was entirely imaginary.

Attorney Long of Morton county [who is] working on the case travels about among the thieves and pickpockets on this side [the east bank] of the river with no other body guard than an air of arctic dignity and frigid superiority. The feature of the case, which attracts the attention of the country at large, is that the Marquis is the wealthiest and most noted man now on trial in the United States or the world. The history of the case does not need repetition.

With its usual sense of justice, the *Bismarck Tribune* rose to the occasion and championed proper jurisprudence with an editorial in its September 3 edition:

It is understood that in Mandan an indignation meeting has been held to denounce Bismarck in general, and Judge Francis in particular, for the change of venue in the Marquis's case. Mandan hoped to have the Marquis tried in that place; they sort of wanted to pick the lining of the Marquis's purse. As one Mandan party said, when he heard that the Marquis had been indicted, "Now is the time to feather our nests—we'll open up the purse of his royal nibs."

The *Tribune* closed with this line: "Mandan ought to muzzle its fool friends." But it didn't. Far from it.

On September 5, the *Tribune* reported that "an indignation meeting was held in Mandan and a number of citizens have signed a petition for the removal of Judge France because he granted a change of venue." Judge Francis answered the attack by saying:

All that is necessary is to satisfy the court that these defendants [de Morès' men were also indicted] could not have a fair and impartial trial in this subdivision, or that there is reason to believe such to be the case. From these affidavits, as well as other reasons coming within the general knowledge of the court since this term began, I am satisfied that this prayer—for that is what it is—should be granted.

Meanwhile, the *Tribune*, a hawk on the side of justice, was editorializing about Long:

The very fact that Mr. Long has championed the cause of the rabble in this matter shows him as unfit for the high position he occupies, and the sooner the people of Morton County and Mandan become aware of this fact, the better it will be for their standing as an order loving community. It is a sad commentary on justice and decency that a change of venue should raise the blood of a whole community and stir up almost a feeling of revolution.

Just before the trial began, Theodore Roosevelt visited de Morès in jail and found him quite unruffled over the outcome of the trial. It seems highly improbable that T. R. would have taken the trouble to call on the Marquis—Roosevelt was quite without guile—if he had really been responsible, even in part, for the court action being brought.

The trial began in Bismarck on September 12, 1885. From the start, the courtroom was jammed with spectators whose spurs and sidearms clanked against the benches as they took their seats and tensely followed the proceedings. Anti–de Morès forces, many from the Bad Lands, lined one side of the courtroom; the Marquis' servants and supporters were on the other. De Morès acted with great dignity during the trial. He refused to permit his wife to attend on the grounds that her presence could prejudice the jury in favor of him. He asked no quarter.

All the evidence from the first two trials was rehashed, but this time the prosecution pointed up the fact that de Morès had fought two duels in France before coming to the United States and that both were fatal to his opponents. Of course this bore no relation to the altercation that resulted in Luffsey's death or de Morès' responsibility for firing the fatal shot, but the jury had ears.

The district attorney got so far out of line in his prosecution that he was fined and jailed for contempt of court. Then the trial resumed, with de Morès ably represented by Frank B. Allen. The prosecution alleged that the defense enjoyed an advantage, because both Judge Francis and Allen came from Newark, New Jersey, and that Allen acted as a clerk to the judge (the two had arrived in the Territory at about the same time). No action was taken on the slur.

Among those who appeared for de Morès was A. C. Huidekoper. "Wannegan was the only man that could give evidence that could convict the Marquis," he wrote later; he presented no proof to back up the statement. He did, however, describe Wannegan as a drunk and a spendthrift, which is hardly compatible with his contention that Wannegan would have been a credible witness. Huidekoper also claimed the Marquis tried to bribe Wannegan by telling him a credit of some three to four thousand dollars would be established for him in a West Coast bank if Wannegan would go there. I find this very difficult to believe.

Following the final summations, the jury took only a few minutes to return a verdict: not guilty. The Frenchman's supporters in the courtroom cheered. His enemies griped. A friend, having heard lynch threats, slipped him a pistol when the trial ended. He stuffed it into his belt and strode from the courtroom. The *Bismarck Tribune* in its September 25, 1885, issue said:

> The Marquis has been vindicated by the verdict of 12 intelligent jurors. But one ballot was taken, and each read, "not guilty." This verdict will be universally approved by all who are in any way familiar with the circumstances surrounding the case. The promptness with which the jury acted in this matter shows the good sense of Bismarck citizens.

Operations at Medora had ground to a halt during the trial. Now de Morès received a telegram from his abattoir foreman: "When shall I advise my customers that we shall resume deliveries?" De Morès wrote a brief reply: "Will resume killing as soon as I can give it my personal attention." The Marquis' attorney, knowing the way in which private communications by wire were broadcast, suggested a revision in the wording to refer specifically to killing cattle.

De Morès was free. There was no chance, even in Dakota Territory, that he could be tried again. The *Weekly Yellowstone Journal and Live Stock Reporter* noted on September 26: "The Marquis was given an overwhelming reception on his return to Medora after acquittal at Bismarck. The cowboys were out in great force and vied with the citizens in expressing their unqualified satisfaction at the result of the trial." But the Lang crowd, and others who had opposed the Marquis from the day he came to the Bad Lands, hadn't changed their minds at all. Indeed, for them the jury's verdict was pure frustration. Their hostility continued unabated.

XVII

RUSTLING AND "THE STRANGLERS"

De Morès' operations centered on buying from ranchers in the northern sector of the Great Plains, cattle for slaughtering and horses for breeding purposes. He also owned large herds himself. At one time he had at least 6,000 cattle and an undisclosed but large number of horses. Some 150 cowpunchers worked the range to keep the animals in hand. The Marquis, then, was a victim of rustlers, just as were all the other ranchers in the Bad Lands. He was hit by thieves as often as they were. His horses were a particular target, for the man who rode with the best at Saumur chose excellent and highly valuable mounts.

All over the northern reaches of the Great Plains in the early 1880's, rustlers stole livestock with what can be classed as virtual impunity. The nearest law officer, except for a roving United States marshal out on an assignment, was stationed in Mandan, one hundred miles from Medora. Territorial statutes were constantly flouted by the outlaws. The six-gun was law, a very tough one that worked both ways: both cattle owners and rustlers used the equalizer with deadly accuracy.

An overriding circumstance contributing to the widespread rustling was the dismal fact that only a few ranchers stood up to the cattle and horse thieves. Many stockmen were intimidated, even to the extent of letting a thief come onto their ranges and demand a horse (or more) and giving up the plunder. In all fairness, however, it must be observed that the machinery of the law was so distantly removed from the Bad Lands that even if a case of rustling were reported to Bismarck or Mandan, getting satisfaction was difficult. Moreover, no one wanted to incur the enmity of the rustlers. Take the case of a rancher who was being stolen blind. One of his men was talking to a friend of the stockman. The friend asked why known rustlers were riding with the rancher's men on the roundup, then taking off with his cattle. The colloquy went something like this: "Turn one of those guys in? You're kidding. If I did, I'd be out on the prairie the next day with my toes up." That was Dakota Territory in the early 1880's.

At first, de Morès did little to stop the depredations that hit him and the smaller ranchers in the area. Eventually, he did act, but not until the thievery had become so widespread that it spelled the difference between profit and loss for operators with relatively modest herds. It is to the Frenchman's credit that Granville Stuart, a leading rancher just across the border in Montana Territory, wrote that "the Marquis de Morès, who was a warm personal friend of mine and with whom I had had some previous talks on the subject, was strongly in favor of a 'rustler's war' and openly accused me of 'backing water.' The Marquis was strongly backed by Theodore Roosevelt, who was also a member of the Montana Stock Grower's Association from Dakota." That must have been in late 1883, or early 1884, since Stuart himself led the fight against the rustlers in late July, 1884.

De Morès' early attitude toward the rustlers may have been influenced by the thought that their activities were not unusual in Dakota Territory and that nothing could be done about them. Although Jake Maunders, an ace livestock thief, worked for de Morès, it is possible that the Marquis was not aware of Maunders' moonlighting.

One reason Maunders and his ilk were able to carry on their illicit trade was the fact that there was no county organization in the area. Maunders had some influence among the riffraff and exerted it toward thwarting the establishment of a governmental organization in Billings County. His reason was simple: if a

county government were set up, he would be out of business—
the lawless sort, for that was all he knew.

Medorans, among them Packard, held a different view. Their
attitude was underlined by a piece in the *Dickinson Press*:

> Medora is clamoring for a county organization in Billings County.
> We hope they will get it. If there is a place along the line [meaning
> the Northern Pacific] that needs a criminal court and jail it is
> Medora. Four-fifths of the business before our justice of the peace
> comes from Billings County.

The *Press* article referred not just to the general lawlessness that
prevailed in Medora, but also to cattle rustling in the area.

De Morès suffered many losses from rustlers; indeed, it is easy
to picture him as a particularly lucrative target because he was
rich and a foreigner besides, although one must observe that the
rustlers were not discriminate in selecting their victims. The
rustling did begin to bother him, however, and on one occasion
when he was told that thieves had got away with some of his
finest horses, he saddled up quickly and rode out after them. He
didn't catch them, but at least he tried, which was more than
many (or most) ranchers did.

The extent of rustling in the Bad Lands was admirably described by Herman Hagedorn, who journeyed to North Dakota
in the second decade of the 1900's to gather material, much of it
through personal interviews, for his fine work *Roosevelt in the
Bad Lands*. He wrote:

> To an extraordinary extent these thieves possessed the Bad Lands.
> They were here, there, and everywhere, sinister, intangible shad-
> ows, weaving in and out of the bright-colored fabric of frontier life.
> They were in every saloon and in almost every ranch house. They
> rode on the round ups, they sat around the camp fires with cow-
> punchers. Some of the most capable ranchmen were in league with
> them, bankers east and west along the railroad were hand in glove
> with them. *A man scarcely dared denounce the thieves to his best
> friend for fear his friend might be one of them* [italics supplied].
> There were countless small bands which operated in western

Dakota, eastern Montana, and northwestern Wyoming, each loosely organized as a unit, yet all bound together in the tacit fellowship of outlawry. The most tangible bond among them was that they all bought each other's stolen horses, and were all directors of the same "underground railway." Together they constituted not a band, but a "system," that had its tentacles in every horse and cattle outfit in the Bad Lands.

The money involved in horse stealing amounted to a considerable sum in the 1880's; a good horse was worth at least one hundred dollars in the hard currency of those times. Cattle were another matter; depending on the market, a 1,200-pound steer brought approximately fifty-five dollars, a handsome profit to those who could get them for the taking. It is impossible to estimate the cost of depredations, but an annual figure of some 5 per cent of the total value of the livestock on the northern Great Plains seems to be rather well authenticated. That would mean a dollar loss running to seven digits.

Jake Maunders was a ringleader of rustling in the Medora area. He was not merely a director of operations, but a skilled rider, brand changer, informer to the thieves, and a man who could take over a herd of stolen livestock and deliver it to buyers almost anywhere on the Great Plains. Bad Lands traffic in stolen animals revolved on a north-south axis, with the Canadian border on the topside and the Black Hills, several hundred miles to the south, on the bottom. And Maunders knew the country like the back of his hand.

Notorious as he was, Maunders ranked as an amateur compared to a man named Axelby, who rated as the most skilled horse thief west of the Missouri River—and of course he was quite willing to operate on the east side of the Big Muddy. Thievery intrigued him. Dark and tough, Axelby immersed himself in wrongdoing, for he believed that anything he could take was legitimately his own. In common with most of the outlaws on the frontier, Axelby handled his mount well; he had to, for the long rides demanded skill and stamina.

Axelby had more than just the physical attributes necessary for a horse thief. He was also a rough-hewn strategist, an organizer who knew every draw and gully from the Black Hills to the Canadian border and the best ways to take his stolen herds over the terrain. Such knowledge was essential, for Axelby was a big operator, stealing from fifty to one hundred horses at a crack. To move that many animals, even though there was little law enforcement in the Bad Lands, demanded cooperation from a widespread network of people, aside from the horsemen who rode with him. Many of Axelby's spies were gamblers and saloonkeepers, but he was also allied with many of the settlers, whose ethics apparently were unquestioned and who could therefore supply him with valuable information. Canada was his primary market, but there were ranchers in the immediate area who were constantly looking for horses at bargain prices and got them from Axelby. By early 1884, he had become so notorious that newspapers in the East began to cover him, among them the *New York Sun*:

Mr. Axelby is said to be at the head of a trusty band as fearless and as lawless as himself. The Little Missouri and Powder River districts are the theater of his operations. An Indian is Mr. Axelby's detestation. He kills him at sight if he can. He considers that Indians have no right to own ponies and he takes their ponies whenever he can. Mr. Axelby has repeatedly announced his determination not to be taken alive. The men of the frontier say he bears a charmed life, and the hairbreadth 'scapes of which they have made him the hero are numerous and of the wildest stamp.

Despite the tribute the rustlers exacted from even the most reputable stockmen in the Bad Lands—some called it a form of insurance—a small, hard core of ranchers rebelled at being bled dry economically. One of these was Granville Stuart, who had a considerable spread in the valley of the Yellowstone River in Montana Territory. No stranger to dealing with outlaws, he had been one of the moving forces that stamped out the infamous Henry Plummer gang in the 1860's.

The Montana Stock Growers' Association, which also included ranchers in Dakota Territory, met in Miles City in April, 1884. One of the main topics of conversation was cattle and horse rustling, which by that time had assumed such menacing proportions that it threatened to put an end to ranching in the area. The lack of law enforcement spurred members of the association to take matters into their own hands, which meant they wanted to enlist enough honest cowboys to go out and string up the rustlers. Sentiment was strong. Stiffening their earlier attitude toward rustling, the stockmen wanted it stamped out and were ready to perform the task themselves.

A strong voice rose in dissent: that of Granville Stuart, president of the association. It wasn't that Stuart was against law and order, far from it. He had come across the country as a boy in 1849 and had grown into one of the most respected ranchers and statesmen of Montana Territory. Above reproach in every way, he commanded respect among the ranchers, who at this point were willing to take just about any kind of action.

Just as Stuart had told de Morès he opposed open war against the rustlers, he was against the kind of action now being proposed. He argued, as a skilled frontiersman, that a large-scale battle—and it would be just that—was doomed to failure. His reason: Experience had proved that once a large number of people were involved in such an action, the rustlers were certain to learn of it. Thus forewarned, they would hole up in fortified cabins where they had plenty of guns and ammunition. They were crack shots with rifles and revolvers. Stuart also predicted that some of those pursuing the thieves would be killed and the rustlers would still not be stamped out. Furthermore, he said, if the legality of the operation ever were to be questioned (highly doubtful, it would seem), the law could well end up on the side of the rustlers.

The arguments went back and forth, with Stuart remaining adamant in his position. Some of the older ranchers still wanted to go through with the scheme, and the younger enthusiasts accused Stuart of cowardice, which was certainly slanderous in view of his record of bravery and in the light of what subsequently happened. In the end, Stuart had his way. Aside from the impracticability of the proposed operation, Stuart didn't want the association to endorse lynch law, even though that is what it eventually carried out.

The meeting produced one particularly unfortunate result. Some of the ranchers, hoping to buy protection from the rustlers, told them about the vigilante proposal's defeat. The rustlers received the news with great joy, for the vote of the association meant they would not be bothered, for a time at least, so they bent their efforts toward unhampered thievery. But they failed to take into account the prime factor in the equation: Granville Stuart. With his granitic will and a deeply ingrained sense of justice, Stuart was convinced that the rustlers had to be put down.

Stuart was a canny operator. Drawing on the experience of the Plummer affair, he knew that three elements were essential to success in stamping out the range thieves: a small but highly select number of raiders, complete secrecy about their targets, and lightning speed in carrying out the missions. So in June, 1884, following the spring roundup, he invited to his ranch a small number (six has been given) of the top ranchers in eastern Montana and western Dakota. Not only did these men enjoy the respect of the people in the territories where they operated, they also had the courage to fight lawlessness. Herman Hagedorn wrote: "Less than ten men in the whole Northwest knew of the movement that was gradually taking form under the direction of the patriarchal fighting man from Fergus County; but the Marquis de Morès was one of those men. He told Roosevelt."

A young Englishman named Jameson was with T. R. when the Marquis told him about Stuart's plan. All three wanted to ride with the vigilantes—it was now clear what Stuart was organizing. This was just the kind of adventure they liked, for Stuart's plan called for a series of slashing blows against the rustlers.

The trio met Stuart in Glendive, Montana Territory, and

offered their services, which were promptly but politely declined. The leader of the vigilantes argued that the three were far too prominent and if word got around that they were members of the raiding party, the element of secrecy would be breached. Stuart also charged that the three didn't have the experience necessary for such an expedition and could well get themselves killed. "The three young argonauts pleaded, but the old pioneer was obdurate," Hagedorn wrote. "He did not want to have them along, and he said so with all the courtesy that was one of his graces and all the precision of phrase that a life in the wild country had given him. Roosevelt and the Englishman saw the justice of the veteran's contention and accepted the situation, but the Marquis was aggrieved."

That Roosevelt and Jameson accepted Stuart's decision without hurt feelings but that de Morès took umbrage is not surprising. Both T. R. and the Englishman understood the logic of Stuart's not wanting them on the raids. But in such matters de Morès, although obviously highly intelligent, frequently did not employ his brainpower to the end of practical conclusions. This may be excused on the grounds that he was a sort of knight-errant, a role he played in real life: he was ever combative and ready to put his life on the line, as he had done in Dakota Territory and would do in France, Indochina, and Africa. No doubt he was attracted to the Stuart operation by the soaring adventure it would provide. But at the same time, it must be remembered that de Morès was a highly religious man, one with a deep sense of justice, so he could have been thinking about the small ranchers who were close to being forced out of business by the thieves.

Turning down de Morès, Roosevelt, and Jameson did nothing to slow Stuart in his campaign against the rustlers. Like any good field commander—and that is what he was—he put a top-secret classification on his plans and enforced it.

Stuart's vigilantes—they were called "The Stranglers"—struck with a fury born of righteous indignation; the speed, secrecy,

L'ITINÉRAIRE DE L'EXPÉDITION MORÈS

Courtesy Librairie Plon

Map tracing de Morès' expedition in North Africa. The cross at El Ouatia marks the place where he was assassinated.

Deadwood, Dakota Territory, about the time the Marquis ran his stagecoach line there from Medora. The photograph at the left shows Main Street.

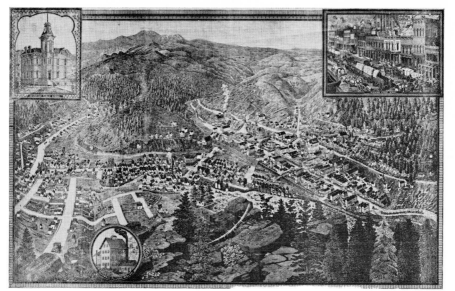

An artist's conception of Deadwood, Dakota Territory (now South Dakota), at the time de Morès ran his stagecoach line to that mining center. The artist probably took some liberties, but his general idea seems accurate.

Bismarck
~~Medora, Dak.~~, Sept 3. 1885.

My dear Roosevelt

My principle is to take the bull by the horns. Joe Ferris is very active against me and has been instrumental in getting me indicted by furnishing money to witnesses and hunting them up. The papers also publish very stupid accounts of our quarelling — I sent you the paper to N.Y. Is this done by your orders. I thought you my friend. If you are my enemy I want to know it. ~~~~ I am always on hand as you know. and between gentlemen it is easy to settle matters of that sort directly.

Your very truly

Mores

I hear the people want to organize the county I am opposed to it for one year more at least

Courtesy State Historical Society of North Dakota

The exchange of correspondence between the Marquis and Theodore Roosevelt that nearly ended in a duel. Note the dashing way in which de Morès signed his name; its near illegibility was characteristically French.

Most emphatically I am not your enemy; if I were you would know it, for I would be an open one, and would not have asked you to my house nor gone to yours. As your final words however seem to imply a threat it is due to myself to say that this statement is not made through any fear of possible consequences to me; I too, as you know, am always on hand, and ever ready to hold myself accountable in any way for anything I have said or done.

Yours very truly

Theodore Roosevelt

Courtesy State Historical Society of North Dakota

Rough draft of Roosevelt's reply.

The statue of the Marquis that his children had struck in Paris and erected in Medora, North Dakota, where it stands today. M. Antoine de Vallombrosa, grandson of the Marquis, stands beside it.

When the Marquise de Morès returned to Medora in 1903, she rode around the Bad Lands with her son Louis, top, and Athenaïs, her daughter.

A photograph of the Marquis, taken when he was an officer in the French army, used by the Marquise on a prayer card after his death.

and precision of their attacks would have done credit to a military operation. They started in Montana, masked figures thundering down on the camps where the rustlers lived. The trials (on the spot) were brief, the punishment meted out swiftly. Hagedorn describes the action:

> Out of the open country where Stuart's vigilantes were swooping on nest after nest of the thieves, riders came with stories that might well have sent shudders down the backs even of innocent men. The newspapers were filled with accounts of lifeless bodies left hanging from countless cottonwoods in the wake of the raiders, tales of battles in which the casualties were by no means all on one side, and snatches of humor that was terrible against the background of black tragedy.... Now that a determined man [Stuart] had shown the way, everybody wanted to have a part in the last great round up of the unruly.

The vigilantes skirted the Bad Lands on the north, then continued to the Missouri River in a broad sweep. This left the rustlers in Medora free. Some stories have it that Maunders was on the list of marked men but that he was not touched because he was still on de Morès' payroll. It is remarkable that he should have escaped, for he was precisely the kind of rapscallion Stuart would hit immediately. His connection with the Marquis must be the answer.

Stuart's raids broke the back of organized rustling in the Bad Lands, but a considerable amount of freelance stealing continued after The Stranglers had taken their grisly toll. Nor were the operations only in Dakota; they included Montana as well. The fact that Stuart's raiders didn't go through Medora may have accounted for some of the continued thievery in the area. Whatever the reason, de Morès was so concerned about the loss of his livestock that in the fall of 1884 he hired the Pinkerton Detective Agency to investigate rustling in an area bounded roughly by Bismarck on the east, Glendive on the west, Fort Buford on the north, and the Black Hills on the south. This was a formidable area to cover, especially since the only public transportation was the Northern Pacific east to west and de Morès' stage line between Medora and Deadwood.

The Pinkerton men were undaunted. Their prolix reports, detailing the drinking, gambling, and conversations with ladies of the night—all in order to run down the thieves—are footnotes to law enforcement in the Old West. Several rustlers were picked up, but it is impossible to determine whether the Marquis got his money's worth out of the agency. However, had he not hired Pinkerton, things could have been worse.

Even after de Morès left the Territory, vigilantes were still running down rustlers in the Bad Lands, and there are stories of their perpetrating crimes rather than just trying to eliminate thieves. None of them attained the stature of Granville Stuart. He goes down in history as a fearless man of the Old West who, when necessary, took the law into his own hands.

XVIII

THE COLLAPSE

The success of Granville Stuart's vigilantes in suppressing rustlers in the Bad Lands of Dakota Territory and contiguous areas in Montana had a salutary effect on the outlook of honest people in the region. They forecast that nothing but good would result. The citizens of Medora felt this way, and although the cattle thieves there had not been cleaned out, Medorans looked forward to the further development of the town into something profitable and permanent. Unfortunately, they were wrong.

So was de Morès. The imminent collapse of his enterprises, the main one being the packing plant, was evident to most observers in late 1885. De Morès himself may have seen it, too, but he went on whistling in the dark. So did Packard, to the point where he was offering his stock of wagons (a sideline to the publishing business) at knocked-down prices.

Always accessible to newsmen, the Marquis was interviewed in St. Paul, Minnesota, in December, 1885, and the story ran soon after on the front page of the *Bismarck Tribune*:

> The Marquis de Morès is here, en route to France to spend the winter. He says his business is in no way embarrassed, and that he will return and resume the direction of his dressed beef and cold storage industry on the Northern Pacific in the spring.

The *Tribune* followed up with an editorial four days later:

> The Marquis de Morès has gone to New York, and expects to visit France before he returns to Medora in February. He denies all reports of financial troubles. He has a steady income from an estate

that cannot be encumbered. Financial embarrassment is an absolute impossibility. He has done much toward the development of Western Dakota, and proposes to continue the various enterprises he is now engaged in. He will, however, concentrate his enterprises in Medora.

De Morès' concentration was actually on trying to extricate himself, as gracefully as possible, from a hopeless situation.

One of the first public rumblings of the downfall came in the *New York Tribune*:

A cable dispatch from Paris, received in this city, a day or two ago, relates an interesting piece of gossip which deals with the affairs of two men well known in this country. Although no names were given in the dispatch, those who read between the lines would have no difficulty in identifying the persons referred to as Louis A. von Hoffman, the banker of No. 50 Wall Street, and his son-in-law, the Marquis de Morès, the young Aragonese nobleman who is known in this country through his connection with the cattle ranch business in Dakota and the scheme to furnish Eastern consumers with meats brought directly from the feeding ground of the cattle in the far West.

The story told is to the effect that there has been a serious disagreement between Mr. von Hoffman and his son-in-law over the latter's investments in the meat business, which is said to have proved unprofitable, and that the banker has decided to withdraw the financial support which he has hitherto given the Marquis in his ventures.

The *Tribune* checked the dispatch with an unidentified friend of de Morès in New York who confirmed the fact that von Hoffman and the Marquis had clashed but refused to say anything more because it might embarrass the Marquis. The odds are that the story was right, but it is understandable that neither de Morès nor von Hoffman would say anything publicly.

The Frenchman never gave up formally, except for closing out the stagecoach line. However, he did pay off the Haupt brothers, St. Paul businessmen who had invested in the Northern Pacific Refrigerator Car Company. In the absence of conclusive documentation, it is impossible to determine de Morès' liability toward Haupts. But one gets the impression that they were stock-holders, not creditors, and therefore the Marquis was not bound to reimburse them for the money they had put into the company. This line of reasoning is reinforced by a statement from de Morès' grandson, who says that everyone involved in the Marquis' operations was paid off.

It is clear that de Morès lost money, and so did von Hoffman. Between the two, a million dollars or so was dropped. It is impossible to pinpoint the amount, but obviously it was large; just two items, the construction costs of the abattoir (some $200,000 to $300,000) and the household account (the de Morès family denied itself nothing), show that a lot of money was sunk in Dakota. A *New York World* story had the Marquis spending $1,000 a day during his stay in America, which may be true, but it is impossible to calculate a total from that daily estimate.

When de Morès left the Territory for Europe in December, 1885, he must not have had any real plan of returning in an effort to revive his business operations. Nevertheless, he came through Dakota in 1887 on an around-the-world trip and told a *Bismarck Tribune* reporter in a trainside interview that "he had no intention of removing his business interests from Dakota." According to the paper, the Marquis added: "I like Dakota and have come to stay."

Why de Morès should have said such things is enigmatic, for he usually talked straight to the press. It must have been clear to him that the beef trust had beaten him and could do so again. Nor could the stagecoach line ever be revived. Moreover, he had wired Johnny Goodall, his former range foreman, to refrain from taking any permanent job. De Morès said he had a spot for Goodall running a construction job in the Orient—he didn't, as things turned out.

As if de Morès were not having enough trouble with his business, stories began to circulate about his relations with the Marquise, and of course they quickly got into print. The canard was that the Marquise was suing for divorce and that the Marquis was going to India for a year-long tiger hunt in order to absent himself from the proceedings. This would obviate his testifying, so the story went, and thus make for a less messy affair.

The *Bismarck Tribune* carried all of this. Then, four days after breaking the first so-called account of the marital rift, the *Tribune* ran a front-page report saying that the Marquise was going to India with her husband. An employee of the Marquis was supposed to have been the source of this piece, which also related that the two de Morèses would return to France via the United States (which they did), with a stop in Medora (which was not the case). The *Tribune* continued with a statement that the story of the supposed rift was a "racy bit of newspaper gossip." By whom, of course, the journal did not remark, but it was, quite obviously, the *Tribune*'s own doing.

In addition to the gossip, it must be said that the Marquis' business was completely misunderstood in quarters where there should have been some comprehension. As late as 1967, a prominent North Dakotan remarked that de Morès' failure stemmed from the fact that he was trying to sell freshly dressed beef at points distant from Medora although there were no refrigerator cars in those days. It should be recalled that the Marquis' main enterprise was named for the refrigerator cars it used and that it would have been impossible to ship fresh meat more than a few miles unless it were iced.

Looking at the meat-packing business with a cold eye, anyone could have seen in 1885 that the figures on the balance sheet and operating statement spelled doom. De Morès must have read them that way, and if he didn't, the odds certainly are that von Hoffman's flinty banker's eye caught the signs of impending disaster.

The Frenchman was not one to run, but in addition to the financial aspects of the situation, there was the matter of continuing hostility toward him. Some of it was generated by people in small communities who resented the publicity Medora was getting because of the Marquis and his enterprises. But more decisive was the attitude of the Lang crowd, which remained as implacably spiteful as ever.

In the spring of 1885, the stage line was clearly destined for oblivion; de Morès either didn't have the working capital necessary to continue operations or he didn't see the efficacy of putting more money into the business. Johnny Goodall told the Marquis that if he were going to discontinue the line, he would have to say so publicly, since service between Medora and Deadwood had been advertised. De Morès replied that he didn't know anything about American laws but that if notification were essential, then it should be made.

De Morès never formally announced the closing of the abattoir. That was unnecessary; it was always locked up in winter, and when this was done in late 1886, the operation ceased forever.

The Marquis said nothing about his defeat before he got back to France, and then not until he was about to go to Africa. In the early 1890's, he talked at length to Charles Droulers, author of *Le Marquis de Morès*, about many subjects, among them the Dakota operation. The Marquis set forth his interpretation of the basic reasons why the meat-packing business had failed. Droulers does not quote de Morès directly but says the Frenchman and other "cattlemen had to meet the merciless demands [*fourches caudines*] of the commission men," meaning the meat dealers or middlemen, the principal ones being those de Morès had first encountered in Chicago.

(Droulers may have thought of the term *fourches caudines* himself or he may have been quoting de Morès, who could have borrowed the term from his military background. The Caudine Forks are two defiles that form a pass high in the Apennine Mountains of southern Italy. It was there in 321 B.C. that a Roman army was lured by an enemy, the Samnites, and being unable to maneuver out of the narrow gorges, was forced to surrender.)

Droulers goes on to say that the middlemen, "for the most part Jews, united, allied and powerful, determined, at their pleasure, whether the price [of meat] should be high or low, while the growers, scattered over an immense territory, far from each other, with no united commercial organization among themselves, were helpless. It was impossible for them to dispute the prices offered by the 'Black Band,' for to take unsold cattle back to the West meant more heavy charges, loss of weight and death of many steers." De Morès shipped dressed beef, but he was subject to precisely the same pressures from commission men as those who sold live animals. It is pertinent to note that the Marquis believed most of the middlemen were Jews, and perhaps they were. His rabid anti-Semitism in France will be discussed later.

The withering of Medora's boom-time growth, like that of anything else starting with great promise, was dolorous. When the glittering prospects for the success of de Morès' enterprises faded, Medora began to atrophy. Except for a few dozen people, the town literally moved away: houses and other structures (the wooden ones that could be uprooted) were put on flatcars and freighted to other settlements. The *Cow Boy's* stories about what was happening to Medora in 1886 formed a running obituary. Their funereal tone sharply contrasted with the swelling enthusiasm that studded articles about the town when de Morès was building it.

One of the most bitter observations about the demise of Medora came from Lincoln Lang, who shared his father's hatred for anything de Morès touched—Lang *père* had turned down the Frenchman's pleas for friendship when he first arrived in the Bad Lands. Here are young Lang's words about the decline of Medora:

Marking the end of the old era and the beginning of the new, with the passing of the hard winter [1886–87] de Morès and his ill-starred enterprise quickly faded away. Medora's packing house, its Black Hills stage line, its spectacular newspaper, the "Bad Lands Cow Boy," were dead.

Gone all but one or two of its numerous stores and saloons. Gone its State Capitol aspirations [the first mention of this in all the documents about the town] its civic pride, its Chinaman and its boiled collars. Gone, about all of its population who had anything left to get away with, together with their lares et penates, in many cases inclusive of the houses themselves, shipped away on flat cars. It was worse than a busted cowtown. Worse, because its general inaccessibility from the surrounding country would always militate against it, a condition which had long ago rendered it necessary for us up-river ranchers to transfer our trade to Mingusville [now Wibaux] just over the line in Montana. At best, Medora never had anything to recommend it as a town site. Reduced now to a mere hamlet, so it would remain to the end of the chapter.

Lang adds that the solid people of the town remained, and this may well be true. The town is still there.

One of the *Cow Boy's* last stories related that Jake Maunders had put some buildings—he must have owned them—on flatcars and moved them to Dickinson, where he apparently lived out his days, never paying for any of his crimes.

Although that was the end of Medora as de Morès knew it, the Marquis' dreams of an empire did not fade. Back in France, he was quoted as saying:

It is necessary for me to make some money, for I cannot let my house fall. Unfortunately, for five hundred years we have been soldiers. It is hard to change the old instincts of the race. I am profoundly worried by these financial losses; I blame myself for believing that I was stronger and better than the others—but, patience! Every lane has its turning. A man without ambition is good for nothing. There must be an aim in life, always higher. I am 28 years old. I am strong as a horse. I want to play a real part. I am ready to start again.

And then he said:

Life has never meant very much to me.

That may well have been true, but he was always ready to live it to the utmost—and to challenge fate.

XIX

PARIS AND THE ORIENT

When, in 1887, de Morès found himself back in Paris, the ambience for him was jejune compared with the hypertonic life he had been leading in the Old West. Familiar surroundings and old friends didn't compensate for the pleasures of a personal empire: no ranch to savor in a seigneurial way, no great herds of animals to look after, no struggle with the beef business (or the beef trust), no challenge from the myriad enterprises he had dreamed of when he founded Medora.

He tried the country and found it just as stifling as Paris. Indeed, in some ways it was worse, for there the mainstream of French life flowed in only a tributary way. He was bored stiff.

The Marquis considered moves that could put him back into some commercial enterprise. For a man in the early thirties with aristocratic (read "influential") connections throughout the nation, it should have been easy to find a responsible position. But he didn't want that. He craved action.

His father, the Duc de Vallombrosa, from whom he had inherited much of his adventuresome spirit, had hunted big game in India some years earlier. He had found the country fascinating and, in true de Morès tradition, had also been intrigued with shooting wild animals, which were so plentiful that they menaced the people and domesticated animals. Vallombrosa *père* recommended a tiger hunt in India for his son's ennui, a suggestion that was snapped up with traplike speed. Not only was the Marquis eager to go, but so was the Marquise, for well traveled as she was on the Continent, she didn't know the Far East. And neither she nor her husband had ever had an opportunity to shoot the kind of big game that prowled the jungles there.

It seemed, then, that hunting tigers would offer a perfect counterpoise for the kind of therapy that the Marquis was taking in France, which was not working. The pursuit of wild beasts, in fact, would permit the Marquis to expend some of his restless energy.

In those days, a trip to India was an adventure in itself, one enjoyed by only a few people other than those who were going there to work (such as the British governing staffs and armed forces) and a few journalists and writers (Kipling, for example). De Morès wanted to be sure that he would have skilled and congenial hunting companions, men who were as much at ease in the jungle as in a salon. The choice was easy. He merely picked some relatives, Prince Henri d'Orléans and the Duc d'Orléans, who, in common with most aristocrats in France in those days, were ardent huntsmen. They jumped at the chance to go along.

Outfitting himself and his companions for the field was no problem for de Morès, what with his Algerian military experience and the innumerable hunting expeditions he had organized in Dakota and the Rockies. Tropical gear was obtained, including hammocks for outdoor sleeping and a collection of firearms that would have been adequate for a small revolution. Formal attire was also packed, for in the days of the maharajas Indian levees could be quite fashionable, not to mention the pukka social gatherings of the caste-conscious British.

The de Morèses arrived in Calcutta with eyes on the hinterland, but before they could get into the bush, they were given many a bash—by Lord Dufferin, the viceroy of India, and other leading British and Indian notables. The two were just as popular in Calcutta as they had been in New York, and their Dakota Territory interlude had given them a glamorous, wild touch.

Soon de Morès was slashing through the jungle, but not before arguing vigorously and victoriously with the British and the Indians over what territory was and was not safe. Safety was about the last thing he was thinking about. He wanted to hunt from the back of an elephant, but local advisers said the animals just couldn't make it through the tangled undergrowth in the rough country the Marquis proposed to penetrate. That was no bar to de Morès. He and his party slogged on foot through the jungle in a part of India that was literally infested with some of the most dangerous predatory animals on earth. At night, they swung hammocks, carefully placing them some distance apart so that an attacking animal would endanger only one man and the others would have a chance to rescue the victim and shoot the beast without endangering the lives of their companions.

Although this was de Morès' first trip to the jungle, he adapted to conditions as if he had been there all his life. Later, the Prince d'Orléans said de Morès was charming all the while and that had it not been for the Marquis' expertise, the party would never have been able to reach its destination and return. He was a born organizer and leader.

De Morès and his friends bagged several tigers, a dangerous bit of hunting for men on foot, but the Marquis was not satisfied. He was after even more dangerous game. "I want very much to kill a rhino to show the English that we can manage this on our own without their help," he said. He did.

The Duc d'Orléans, an ardent nimrod, was delighted with the hunt, but he itched for country even more exciting and dangerous where game would be plentiful and of greater variety. That spelled Nepal. Again the Frenchmen were off, this time with a reinforced party consisting of the original three plus the Marquise, the Duc de Montrose, Colonel Parseval, M. de Boissy, and Docteur Forsythe (just where these added starters came from has not been disclosed). This time, the arms and ammunition supply was even more formidable; indeed, it was described as a veritable arsenal.

Elephants transported the party and served as shooting platforms. The Marquise had an opportunity to duplicate the marksmanship she had displayed on hunts in the Bad Lands and

Montana. She stood her ground with the big cats of India, bagging her share of tigers from the back of an elephant, her doll-like figure contrasting with the huge beast she rode and the animals she shot. The Marquis killed four tigers and so many other animals of the high Nepalese country that he lost count of them.

Although mighty with sword and gun, de Morès was laggard with the pen. He wrote little to his family (except later on his ill-fated African trip) and recorded only a few of his exploits and impressions, and then with a minimum of words. But he did leave some thoughts in writing about Hyderabad (could it have been because of the Croesus-like wealth of the nizam?). And he wrote that the French had retained Pondicherry and Chandernagore just to annoy the British—those tiny geographical specks like miniscule fleas on the hide of the British lion.

The tiger hunt in India proved a delightful interlude, one that helped de Morès make the transition to becoming a European again, even though it took place on another continent. The expedition had little to do directly with what subsequently happened to the Frenchman, but the trip back to France did, for in that spring of 1888, some of the Marquis' shipboard companions turned out to be classmates from St. Cyr and Saumur. De Morès was delighted to see his old friends again, to exchange reminiscences, and to learn about the adventures of those who had stayed in the service. The young military officers aboard—they were then about thirty years old—had been fighting in Tonkin (now North Vietnam), which had been a French protectorate since 1884. The French had been in what became known as Indochina since the early 1860's, fighting sporadically as parts of the country were brought under their control. This did not involve the natives of the area so much as it did the bands of brigands, a mercenary force called the Pirates of the Black Flag. In an earlier era they had infested the southern part of China, mainly Yunnan Province, later were employed by the Annamites, and now were on their own.

The stakes in Tonkin were high and the French knew it. The province was rich in rice, silk, sugar, pepper, oil, cotton, tobacco, timber, and fruit, while underground, deposits of copper, iron, coal, and antimony beckoned. Moreover, the northeastern border of Tonkin backed up against the Chinese province of Yunnan; the trade-hungry French saw in that geographical juxtaposition an excellent way to infiltrate a very rich market in a part of China that was landlocked and hence isolated from the rest of the world.

With St. Cyrian professionalism, de Morès' colleagues had gone about their mission of rooting out and destroying the lawless Black Flag bands that roamed the land, murdering the people and plundering their villages. (They were the counterparts, in many ways, of the Viet Cong, except for an apparent lack of political aims.) The French officers were learning some truths about fighting in that part of the world which their descendants were to rediscover in the post–World War II Indochinese debacle that ended at Dien Bien Phu: to dislodge the enemy required a frightful toll in lives and money. In several years of fighting, de Morès was told, the French had lost 30,000 killed or dead of disease and the monetary cost had been 300,000,000 francs (about $60,000,000). That was a stiff price to pay, but the French said they had liberated a people, the Indochinese, from a chronic brigandage which had inflicted an infinity of pain and death. The fight was not over, as de Morès was to see at first hand, for the Pirates of the Black Flag were still holding out in some places and descending on villages to take their grisly toll.

The Marquis' classmates told him they were severely hampered by the lack of that one element so essential to all successful military operations: adequate supply lines which even the units farthest from Hanoi and Haiphong could depend on for ammunition, food, and other essentials. River transport was fairly efficient and the streams in good number, but they didn't always flow in the direction the traffic had to go. Overland routes were seldom more than trails and impassable quite frequently. It was evident that railroad lines were badly needed. Even a single line to serve part of Tonkin, especially that portion which fringed the Chinese border, would help.

De Morès' interest in the problem sharpened when he looked at a map. He saw the possibility of a line that would start from Lang Son, some seventy miles northeast of Hanoi, and run southeast to the China Sea. Three other lines would lace the northern part of Tonkin.

The Marquis knew the undisputed military value of such a line. He knew, too, that once the fighting stopped, it would be endowed with great commercial promise, for it would traverse rich country that could easily be tapped. In addition, of course, the Chinese trade factor bulked large. The British had astutely recognized its potential and were trying to push a rail line through from Burma to Yunnan. In effect, the French and British would be racing each other to get their rails down, their goal being the rich trade that could easily be generated with Yunnan. De Morès could hardly wait to get back to Paris and present his plan to the French government.

In Paris, the Marquis' cousin de La Feronays introduced him to M. Goblet, the French minister of foreign affairs. De Morès wasted no time. Outlining on a map the route of the rail line he proposed, he said: "I think I am able to build a railroad without any subvention or government guarantee, a railroad that would join the Chinese frontier to the sea by Tonkin. I don't share your political views, but politics stops at the frontier. Therefore, you can use me or not." Although Goblet thought de Morès had an excellent plan, he believed it to be outside his jurisdiction and therefore referred the Marquis to M. de la Porte, undersecretary of state for colonies, with whom de Morès conferred.

Following these presentations, de Morès went before M. Floquet, president of the Council of Ministers, on August 15, 1888, and set forth his plan, stressing the fact that he was asking for no money and that the French government would benefit from the railroad, not just immediately, but also over the long haul. He emphasized the great commercial benefits, especially those dealing with China.

De Morès made other entreaties, and while some of the government officials agreed in principle, they hesitated to grant him the concession he wanted. It was really a rather simple matter of letting him build the railroad and granting him in return certain commercial rights along the right-of-way, much the same as American railroads had been treated in the United States.

Many other presentations were made and met with at least approval, if not enthusiasm, by most government officials—except one, the undersecretary of the navy. There is no explanation of his objection, nor is he identified in Droulers' work, but it appears that he was Jean Constans, former governor-general of Indochina whose tenure there was eventually attacked by de Morès as scandalous.

De Morès finally realized that he was not going to get the franchise. This impasse could have been accounted for by the congenital stuffiness and myopia of French officialdom, or it may have been that Constans' influence was greater than his post as undersecretary of the navy would indicate (he was said to have been instrumental in the Republican election victory in 1880). Whatever, the Marquis did not give up on his project, even though he could not get the franchise; he finally wrung out of the ministers and functionaries a promise that they would facilitate an on-the-ground study of the proposal by him and others he might choose to take along.

The Marquis was to be accredited to the French colonial officials in Hanoi, who were to see that he was helped in other ways, such as being furnished with personnel. With first-hand knowledge of the project, he would then produce a more definitive blueprint of the *chemins de fer* that would help the French win the war in Tonkin, open up the country for commercial exploitation, and tap the rich Chinese trade that was languishing for lack of an outlet to the sea.

De Morès hadn't achieved all that he had hoped for from the

French government. Nevertheless, he was pleased with the opening gambit and the knowledge that no one else had taken any initiative toward establishing rail service in Tonkin. He was also sure of backing from the French army—remember, Pétain had been a classmate at St. Cyr. And other officer friends who had fought in Tonkin were all for the dashing young entrepreneur who wanted to provide an essential element for winning the war. De Morès was confident that once he was on the scene, he would have no trouble securing the cooperation of the French. He was right. But he couldn't have known how a small-bore minister in Paris could influence the outcome of his proposal.

Some accounts have de Morès flitting about Paris, trying to induce his friends to put up money for the project. Droulers, who bordered on being a hagiographer of de Morès, does not confirm this, and he should have known. One thing is certain: the Marquis was jubilant over the prospect of the trip to Indochina for a number of reasons, not the least of which was that it could pay off handsomely and thus make it possible to recoup his Dakota losses.

This time the Marquise would not be going. De Morès picked a skilled engineer, M. Thorel, as a technician. And the man who rode the *Pacific Express* with the Marquis to the Bad Lands of Dakota Territory, William van Driesche, was to be at his side during the expedition.

XX

RECONNAISSANCE AND INTRIGUE
IN FRENCH INDOCHINA

De Morès had plenty of homework to do before setting out for Tonkin. He took care of it in his usual methodical fashion. One can picture him in the Bibliothèque Nationale poring over books, maps, reports, and other sources or combing Paris for experts on Indochina. The Marquis' thoroughgoing research paid off; when he reached Tonkin, he was ready to spring into action.

In October, 1888, de Morès, van Driesche, and technician Thorel went to Marseilles for embarkation. The Marquis was delighted to be back on the Mediterranean again, for it was the home of his ancestors and he loved it. The trio enjoyed a short layover before sailing. In contrast to the drizzle and frowning skies of Paris, a bright sun smiled on Marseilles. De Morès and his companions strolled the narrow, picturesque streets of the old city, especially the docks, listening to accents right out of Marius, watching ships warp their way to the piers, and breathing sea air that was a rich mélange of naval stores, fish, and garlic, so pungent that it seemed almost palpable. And of course they reveled in the cuisine: aromatic bowls of *bouillabaisse à la Marseillaise* and its companion fish stew, *la bourride*, and other piscatorial delights, such as *loup de mer* and *rouget*, accompanied by that garlic-dominated sauce, *aïlloli*, and washed down with delightful Tavel *rosé*.

De Morès and his colleagues sailed from Marseilles on October 21, 1888, on the *Calédonien* and landed in Hong Kong a month later. They remained there until November 29, the time being spent studying the operations of the port. The reason? The rail

198

line the Marquis proposed to build from Lang Son would termi-
nate at the Gulf of Tonkin, where dock facilities would have to
be provided; Hong Kong could offer some practical tutelage.

The four-day trip to Haiphong was made in a small, ram-
shackle freighter, but the conveyance made little difference to
de Morès. He was now getting close to his destination.

The first thing to strike de Morès when he got ashore and
began talking to people was that the administrative machinery of
Indochina was unbelievably snarled because of the conflicts between the French army and navy, between the resident-general
and the military, and finally among the various ministries in Paris
that had responsibilities in Indochina. To complicate matters
further, the minister of colonies considered Indochina as French,
while the minister of foreign affairs held that it was a foreign
country. Compounding the paralysis this intramural fighting
engendered was the fact that Jean Constans, who had been
resident-general of the colony for six months preceding the incumbent, had left a legacy of disorder and confusion. The
various actions had crippled the pacification of Indochina.

The chief French civilian officer in the colony was Resident-
General M. Richaud. Quite the opposite of Constans, he was a
capable self-made man who came from an old and distinguished
naval family. His integrity and devotion to the nation were
matched by superb administrative ability. He was in the process
of straightening out the mess he had inherited when de Morès
arrived. The Marquis and Richaud took to each other immediately, and cordiality marked relations between the two men for the
duration of de Morès' sojourn in Indochina.

The Marquis stayed in Haiphong for a few days, spent in
pleasant and profitable calls on the military, after which he went
to Hanoi, then, as now, the capital of the surrounding area.
There he paid his respects to the military governor and explained
his mission to army and civilian authorities. He was cordially received and his project was endorsed, particularly by the army
officers who were with the governor when de Morès called.

They did everything they could to help him: maps, information, letters permitting the Marquis to draw supplies from military posts en route to Lang Son, some seventy miles northeast of Hanoi. Wasting no time, de Morès was off on December 18 with eight ponies and thirty coolies, who, when paired off, carried eighty-eight pounds of gear slung on a bamboo pole. The wage rate for coolies was seven and a half sous a day; de Morès paid them ten, which raised their daily salary to the equivalent of about two cents. De Morès rode at the head of the column and Thorel, the engineer, in the middle. Van Driesche brought up the rear.

Three days out on the jungle trail at a small fort near Kep, de Morès learned that a tiger had killed several Annamites in the area the night before and had prowled around the military post's sentinel. From that point on, the three Frenchmen took turns standing guard at night, not just because of tigers, but also to prevent the coolies from running away. Van Driesche took the third trick, and when the stars began to fade, he fed the horses and brewed tea or coffee. The party was en route before dawn and continued to push on during the day, constantly soaked by what Droulers described as "C'est horrible crachin," the drizzle. De Morès paid no attention to it. Indeed, it was said that "anyone who travels with de Morès must understand how to have contempt for fatigue and sickness, cold and heat, hunger and thirst, and have muscles of steel and unflinching nerves."

After climbing through mountainous country, the group arrived in Lang Son six days after leaving Hanoi, a rate of about thirteen miles a day. This was a brisk pace considering the terrain, weather, and load for the coolies, but remember that the indefatigable de Morès headed the column.

The Marquis was welcomed by the commanding officer and his staff at the army post in Lang Son on December 24, which the French celebrate as the *réveillon*, a gay Christmas Eve party beginning at midnight when a Lucullan feast is served with choice vintages. It continues until dawn, as the name of the celebration signifies. Even though far from home, the fighting men from France were determined to have their *réveillon*. De Morès and his two men were invited. It was delightful in many ways, not the least of which was that the Marquis ran into more classmates from St. Cyr. While the young Frenchmen enjoyed themselves as Niagaras of champagne hissed into their glasses, the talk naturally turned to de Morès' project. He won new supporters for his idea.

De Morès' map studies strongly indicated Lang Son as the logical inland starting point for a railroad to the Gulf of Tonkin. Now that he was on the scene and could talk to army officers stationed there, he was convinced. He saw Lang Son as a natural military post, a base for surveillance of the near-by Chinese frontier and for military operations. It also provided a natural site for political operations, essential because of relations with Chinese military and civilian authorities.

The Marquis was surprised to learn that the French army post at Lang Son was being supplied, mainly with food, by Chinese soldiers, proof enough for him that the Chinese were far more interested in making money than war. This was confirmed a few days after his arrival when a Chinese came across the frontier— no trouble with such passage in those days—and offered him nine thousand coolies as construction laborers (news of De Morès' mission had apparently leaked out) for an undisclosed price.

In a somewhat atypical habit, de Morès was committing some of his observations to writing. The notebook in which he set them down has survived. It is clear from what he wrote that he was looking farther than the rail lines he hoped to lay, for he set forth some basic principles on the French position in Tonkin in 1888. They remained valid throughout the French occupation of Indochina. The Marquis wrote:

The colonization of Tonkin will not be accomplished with rifles, but with public works.

We must take the position of being associates of the people of Tonkin.

There will be piratical elements in Tonkin until the day when we get them on our side. Let us use them for public works.

It is easy to imagine the animadversions such thoughts must have provoked at the Quai d'Orsay and in the French business community.

De Morès established cordial relations with the Chinese in Yunnan Province; they were living and operating as associations or communities in which mutual help was one of the conditions. He told them he was "neither a soldier nor a tutor" and that he "came to build railroads. These . . . will attract commerce. Will you let me pass?" The question shows he envisaged the rail line's entering Yunnan Province. This was logical, for if any meaningful volume of commerce were to develop in China and move to the sea from Lang Son, a dependable, all-weather means of transport would be essential. That spelled railroad.

De Morès spent several days in personal reconnaissance of the area, confirming studies that had emphasized the richness of the country in natural resources and some manufacturing. He was interested, but distressed, to find 220,000 pounds of rice rotting at one place because there was no way to get it to the sea or to such cities as Hanoi or Haiphong. Obviously, a railroad was sorely needed.

On January 7, 1889, de Morès and his party left Lang Son to explore the proposed railroad route from there to the sea. The Marquis had read his map well, for he struck out to the southeast, following a course that corresponds almost exactly with that of Route 4, a main highway in North Vietnam today. Could the French, who built the road, have used his reconnaissance for laying out Route 4? Probably.

A day out of Lang Son, the party traversed a beautiful countryside dotted with emerald pools and heavily wooded with ancient trees. Partridge and pheasant abounded, and soon fine specimens were turning golden over the fire, a welcome addition to the food supply.

Up through a mountain pass the column wound, then descended to a valley with stifling heat and humidity, but the Marquis drove on relentlessly. Then the ravages of the Black Flag brigands showed their ugly scars: village after village pillaged and burned, the men murdered, women and children kidnaped. It was an 1889 preview of modern-day Viet Cong terror in South Vietnam.

The Frenchmen pushed on, but now de Morès ordered that no tents be raised at night. Everyone slept in the open, with a fire going constantly to keep away the tigers which, in the words of one writer, swarmed over the area.

Four and a half days out of Lang Son, de Morès and his men reached the Bay of Tonkin at Tien Yen, a march of about sixty miles, or slightly more than thirteen miles a day. De Morès' on-the-ground inspection had proved that the route he selected, with only two mountain passes to traverse, was feasible.

De Morès was off immediately for Haiphong and then Hanoi, where he quickly got in touch with M. Richaud, the resident-general. Richaud, delighted with the results of the reconnaissance, demonstrated his enthusiasm for the rail project by providing de Morès with all the technical help he would need, including two engineers, so that work could go forward, starting with a dock at Tien Yen.

In characteristic fashion, de Morès forged ahead, even though he had no authorization, formal or otherwise, from the French government, either in Paris or Tonkin. Soon he had 250 Tonkinese constructing the docks under the supervision of four Europeans. (This was the kind of job de Morès had in mind when he wired Johnny Goodall not to look for a permanent job in Dakota.) De Morès was taking a chance, for he was spending his own money at the rate of 1,000 francs a day ($200 in the currency of the time). He obviously thought it was a good risk.

In February, 1889, the colonial administration in French Indo-china sent an engineer, M. Lion, to examine the progress de Morès was making. He spent eight days at the site and reported that the enterprise was feasible and that two of the materials essential for the work, wood and ballast, abounded in the vicinity. He congratulated the Marquis for getting the project under way.

Lion's inspection was followed by another, carried out by a consultative commission appointed by M. Richaud. By virtue of his position, Richaud had the power to grant the kind of concession de Morès needed for railroad right-of-way, but apparently he had to be backed by the opinion of technicians. (Had this not been the case, de Morès, by all odds, would have had Richaud's permission to go ahead.)

The engineer who was to prepare the report for the commission had borrowed a sizable sum from the Banque de l'Indochine before he left Paris. He was now in financial difficulty and went to de Morès, asking him to pay the bank 25,000 francs, or about $5,000. De Morès said no. It was an obvious bribe. Otherwise, why would the engineer have said, "If the concession is not signed before the 28th of February, it never will be"?

Meanwhile, in Paris, the musical-chairs game of the Third Republic was being played again. M. Floquet, who had looked with favor on de Morès' proposal, was deposed as prime minister and succeeded by M. Tirard. That in itself could not have been necessarily bad for de Morès, but one ministerial appointment in the new government was disastrous: Jean Constans, who as undersecretary of the navy had opposed de Morès' plan, was given the all-powerful post of minister of the interior. The Marquis simply had no luck.

Remember, Constans had preceded Richaud as resident-general of Indochina and Richaud had discovered that not only had his predecessor left things in an unholy mess, he had also conducted some extremely questionable activities, such as granting a trading concession to certain Chinese interests. All of this—and more, too—Richaud had documented. He had Constans dead to rights, and Constans probably knew, through the various sources under his control, just what Richaud was up to.

Constans then began his intrigue, using, among other devices, the *soi disant* fact that in Chinese political circles there was great worry about a railroad that would drain off commerce from Yunnan to Tonkin. This was absurd, for there was no rail line in Yunnan that could move goods anywhere; besides, the British were trying to push one through from Burma and were meeting no Chinese objections.

No doubt Constans was out to destroy Richaud, and in the process he shot down de Morès, too. First, he took the power to grant the railroad concession out of Richaud's hands and lodged it in Paris. Then he ordered the favorable report of M. Lion buried and another commission appointed that would render a negative finding. Finally, de Morès was officially "invited" to return to France and, as a sop to his pocketbook and pride, was given the vague promise of some sort of grant. Understandably, the Marquis was extremely upset by this turn of events. He stopped all work on the docks and ordered the laborers paid off and dismissed, a painful act for him to carry out. On March 5, he was back in France, having come via Japan and the United States, stopping briefly in Medora.

Richaud, who took no nonsense from anyone but underestimated Constans, cabled the minister of colonies in Paris on June 10 about the misdeeds of Constans. This he followed with a detailed written report in which he spelled out the difficulties he experienced because of the maladministration he had been left to clean up. He was fired by return mail—Constans had invoked his considerable influence—and ordered to return to France immediately. He was promised a post in the administration of the minister of finance.

He embarked on the *Calédonien*, armed with documentation on all of Constans' activities. He was also in perfect health.

A few mornings later, Richaud was found dead in his cabin, as was his cabin boy. Their bodies were sewn into bags and buried at sea. The official report was that both had died of cholera, but when the *Calédonien* docked at Marseilles and was put in quarantine, nothing indicated even a suspicion of the disease; there was not a case among passengers or crew. A French government official came aboard and confiscated all of Richaud's papers and put them under seal. That was the end of Richaud and his attempt to bring Constans to justice. But de Morès was not about to forget the minister of interior, and this led to some fiery incidents in France.

XXI

FRANCE–POLITICS–DUELS

When de Morès returned to France in the spring of 1889, he focused his attention on settling accounts with Jean Constans: for sabotaging the railroad project, for malfeasance as resident-general of Indochina, and for forcing Richaud out of office and to his death. It was not simply a case of vengeance, but the automatic reaction of a Frenchman who was imbued with a deep-seated sense of justice, honor, and devotion to the proper conduct of men and government, which the Marquis firmly believed had been breached. He was right.

De Morès was challenging not only an extremely wiley and unscrupulous adversary in Constans, but also the Third Republic's political system, in which intrigue and under-the-table dealings were as natural as breathing. Moreover, the political landscape was cluttered with aspirants for power. Among them was the white-bearded General Boulanger, who hoped to ride his black horse up the steps of the Élysée Palace and take over the government of France. He almost did. De Morès became a Boulangist.

Constans opposed Boulanger and claimed credit for bringing him down, although all he did was issue a warrant for the general's arrest, at which point Boulanger fled. This may have increased Constans' power and standing, but that made no difference to de Morès. He took on the man.

The Marquis had plenty of ammunition. It was public knowledge that before entering politics, Constans had a shady past, including theft from a business associate in Barcelona. A remark he made after euchring his way into the Turkish ambassadorship revealed the level of morality and legality it was his custom to observe. He said: "I am stronger than the Sultan. I'll assassinate him myself."

Through a prominent member of the Chamber of Deputies, de Morès instigated an investigation of Constans. It died aborning, despite backing from powerful men such as Georges Clemenceau, the Tiger of France; even the president of the Council refused to support the inquiry. Whether this legislative whitewash of Constans was perpetrated through fear of reprisal by him or was mere politics has never been determined. It was obviously a defeat for de Morès.

But the Marquis had Richaud's dossier on Constans. He now used the facts in a letter to *Le Matin*, a leading Paris daily that was neither more nor less venal than other French newspapers of the time. De Morès wrote that Richaud's investigation proved Constans had lost 440,000 francs (about $88,000) in French government funds through an arrangement with Chinese business interests in Saigon and near-by Cholon whereby they went tax free in return for an apparent personal payoff. De Morès also charged that Constans had willfully falsified military reports in order to deceive the French government. The Marquis went on to say that when he was in China, he was ashamed, as a Frenchman, to be represented in Indochina by such an unscrupulous man. He said Constans gravely compromised the interests of France in its treaty with China concerning, first, the commerce in salt; second, the enclave at Paklung (in Laos); and third, the delineation of the frontier between China and French Indochina. He also charged Constans with dishonoring his office as a French representative to China with his personal buying and selling operations.

Constans refused at first to reply and later said very little of substance. That the elections were coming up was one reason, but undoubtedly the minister of the interior felt secure in his position: he was inside the government in control of the police powers from Paris to the smallest village; de Morès was on the outside.

De Morès carried his fight against Constans to the elections in 1889. The minister was running from Toulouse, where he was opposed by M. Susini, a Boulangist. De Morès went down to support Susini and in the process came close to getting into serious trouble. At a political rally there, Constans had his followers surround de Morès in a menacing way. The Marquis, seeing the danger to his life, pulled a gun. He was immediately arrested. Just at that moment, one of Constans' men drew a *canne à épée* (a sword concealed in a scabbard that looks like an ordinary walking cane). He thrust it at de Morès, missed him, and hit a policeman. De Morès told the judge who heard his case that he was lucky to have had the gun; otherwise he would have been assassinated, which probably was a sound judgment. He got off with a small fine. There is no record of the arrest of the man who pulled the sword, but of course he was a Constans man.

The elections were held. Despite de Morès' well-documented and damaging evidence of Constans' malodorous past, the public paid no attention and returned the scoundrel to office.

The Indochinese and Constans affairs embittered de Morès, and if he harbored any illusions about the Third Republic, they faded. At the same time, these unfortunate defeats fired two of the Marquis' beliefs: socialism and anti-Semitism.

That he should have embraced these doctrines was not surprising, considering his background. Many aristocrats were disgusted with the way the French nation was being run. They held that the destiny of the country rested in the hands of middle class dolts, with whom the aristocracy had much less rapport than with the common man, the worker. There was, indeed, a close bond between the top and bottom rungs of the social ladder. It should be recalled that the Marquis' mother had said to him: "My birth confers no privileges on me; it gives me great responsibilities." She was obviously referring to those less fortunate than she. Remember also that the Marquis' New York City meat-retailing operation was called the National Consumers Meat Company, and when he set forth his ranch-to-table philosophy, he began his manifesto with the words "to the consumers and workers." He had compassion for the common man, but he was no Marxist.

While there is no available record of the Marquis' having said in the United States that he blamed the Jews for the failure of his beef business, he was voluble on the subject when he returned to France. He said he was convinced that not only were the big packers fighting him, but the Jewish meat dealers were also in league against him.

Anti-Semitism had long been rife in France, especially among the upper classes. Take the army, for example. Most of the top officers were graduates of St. Cyr, and the student body there consisted almost entirely of Catholic aristocrats. (It should be noted that these aspiring cadets developed into fine officers with two outstanding traits: they were devoted to serving the nation and their probity was beyond reproach.) Another reason for de Morès' growing anti-Semitism was the fact that his Indo-chinese railroad project had been torpedoed by a Jew, the engineer who tried to bribe him for the equivalent of five thousand dollars in return for which he allegedly would have delivered a favorable report. And finally, the Marquis proved that the butchers who were selling rotten meat to the French military post at Verdun were Jewish.

De Morès spent a part of the autumn of 1889 in England and returned to Paris early in 1890. Although he was still rankled by the Constans affair, the Marquis put the matter aside and immediately addressed himself to politics. Fired with a passion to serve the state and its people, especially the common man, he was convinced that his goal could be reached only through socialism.

The Marquis plunged into his political work with the same vigor and selflessness that characterized everything he did. Nothing else mattered. He gave all of his time, dismissed the prospect of some kind of profitable employment, and spent his own money to further his political aims. Even the tranquility of his family life was sacrificed; the Marquise, usually a happy person, was reduced to a state of constant anguish, for de Morès was playing a dangerous game, so much so that he was usually armed. For her, the days in the Bad Lands when the local hired guns were after the Marquis were being re-enacted in Paris.

Naturally, de Morès' aristocratic friends read him out of the lodge. When he went to the exclusive Jockey Club, wagging heads turned away from what may have been the object of one of the early uses of the pejorative phrase "a traitor to his own class." De Morès was outwardly tough, but he was a sensitive man, so the snubs and criticism undoubtedly bothered him. Yet he said nothing about the slighting remarks that were passed, and he was buoyed by the fact that some of his old and titled friends stood by him.

His father was another matter. One can picture the rising choler of the Duc de Vallombrosa as he saw his son embrace and promote a philosophy so alien to his own. He publicly disowned the Marquis, which was perhaps the most distressing of all the reactions de Morès had to live with. (Previously, it should be noted, the two had become involved in legal skirmishes over money in business deals; later, the Duc brought a court action to have his son's property placed in the hands of a trustee. The outcome was murky.)

Despite all of these reverberations in family and social circles, de Morès slashed on into the French political thicket as relentlessly as if he were leading a cavalry charge. Indeed, the Marquis treated his self-assigned task with the same devotion to purpose he gave to his army missions in Algiers. Nothing blunted his determination to serve.

Regardless of one's social position in France at the time, a sensitive person would have deplored the lot of those at the bottom of the economic heap. And heap it was, for salaries were miniscule (workers lived in miserable hovels) and union power was yet to bring the workers' demands effectively to bear on management. Moreover, the laws favored the all-pervasive cartels, whose public-be-damned philosophy included first of all the workers in the factories.

Nor was the state of agriculture much better, except that those who lived on the land could always grow a large part of what they needed to eat. Agriculture was hard hit by what would today be called a profit squeeze, and those pinched the hardest were owners of large châteaux, farms, vineyards, and woodlands. De Morès saw many of his titled friends forced to the wall, their estates put on the block and snapped up by the financiers, mainly Jewish and, in his view, unscrupulous.

The Marquis had nothing against the Jews because of their religion—he respected their beliefs. But he deplored their tentacular power. He saw political leverage as the only way to break what de Morès believed was the hold that the Jews had on France, especially because of their control of the important banks. (The Rothschilds were ready to hold an umbrella over European governments caught in financial storms.)

In reading up on anti-Semitism, de Morès discovered that one of the most violent works on the subject was *La France juive,* published in 1885. The author, Edouard Drumont, was a skilled propagandist and excoriated the Jews, blaming them for all the ills France suffered. Pleased to find his ideas confirmed, de Morès arranged to meet the author, who, although a Christian, looked like a caricature of a Jew. They became friends and collaborators.

One of the first results of de Morès' meeting with Drumont was an invitation to participate in a political rally in Neuilly, which bears the same relationship to Paris as the Connecticut Gold Coast does to Manhattan. The event, held in January, 1890, was designed to sustain a Boulangist deputy of the National Assembly who had recently been elected on a platform which included the slogan "War on the Jews!"

De Morès appeared on the speaker's platform dressed in a well-cut black suit, boutonniered with a gardenia. The Marquis was not the only *de* in the room. The audience included the Duc d'Uzes, the Duc de Luyens, the Comte de Dion, the Prince Poniatowski, the Marquis de Breteuil, the Prince de Tarente, and the Marquis de Payronnet.

In an impassioned speech, de Morès called on his fellow aristocrats to join with him "in fighting again side by side as in the times when nobility and plebians mixed their blood on the field of battle to constitute a French fatherland which the Jew is in the process of destroying." He said he was willing to die fighting against "the feudal financial policies followed by all governmental forces." Then, calling for social reforms, he asserted that "the rich, the aristocrats, are ready to make all sacrifices toward relieving the lot of the people. They want nothing in exchange but a bit of friendship."

The speech revealed the personal magnetism de Morès exuded when he was talking about something in which he believed fervently. It had deeply touched the audience, especially the working class. And it generated a wave of de Morès popularity in Paris and the surrounding towns.

The address also infuriated the Jews, especially Camille Dreyfus, a member of the Chamber of Deputies, who enjoyed a reputation of note among the most skilled duelists in France. He wrote an article for *La Nation* headlined "The Daughters of Jews and the Sons of Knights" and vented his feelings:

I wish to say a thing about the meeting at Neuilly. A certain Marquis de Morès gave vent to the cry of Gaul for the Gauls. Now it happens that this fullblooded Gaul has a Spanish title, is the son of the Duc de Vallombrosa, an Italian title that rhymes with bankruptcy, and if we are rightly informed, he married a Miss [von] Hoffman of New York who is neither a Christian nor a Gaul. [A list of men who married wealthy women followed.] This enumeration is sufficient to prove that noble gentlemen of the noble Faubourg know what they are about in their misalliances, especially when they take them, in the words of Shakespeare, naked. But that is a question between themselves and their consciences. But at least they should show some decency. They take the daughters and the money, but they don't wipe the boots which were paid for with a dowry or a father's gray hairs. That is the behavior of fancy men.

Dreyfus either didn't know about de Morès' hypersensitivity or he didn't value his life, for the Marquis' reaction to an insult was as certain as acid on litmus: a challenge to a duel. He sent his seconds, the Comte de Dion and M. Feuillant, who were met by Dreyfus', Messrs. Lockroy and Pichon. The terms: pistols at twenty paces, six shots on a countdown of three for each round. The place: Comines, a small village just across the Belgian border. This locale would avoid flouting the French law banning duels, which was breached frequently and usually with impunity, and it would also avert the gaping audience such an encounter would surely draw in France.

On January 31, 1890, the *New York World* ran a short piece on the impending duel—New Yorkers were always ready for more news about the Marquis. In Paris, news of the impending confrontation spread like a choice bit of gossip. And in what must rank as a great journalistic scoop, a Paris correspondent of the *New York Herald* covered the affair as an eyewitness, his incognito consisting of a plaid, British-style traveling cap, an English paperback novel, and a tightly closed mouth. He also photographed the duel with a small, well-concealed camera. His story appeared on February 3:

The much talked of duel between the Marquis de Morès and M. Camille Dreyfus was fought this morning on the outskirts of the little town of Comines, just beyond the French frontier.

At the word of command M. Dreyfus fired and missed. The Marquis aimed more deliberately and sent a ball into the arm of his opponent just above the elbow joint. The wound is painful, but not serious. Had it not been for the fact that M. Dreyfus dropped his arm immediately on firing, it is very probable that he would have been mortally wounded. M. Dreyfus, in a feverish condition, with his arm bandaged and greatly swollen, is now lying at Lille, where he remains until the doctors allow him to return to Paris. The Marquis de Morès, accompanied by his seconds, reached Paris this evening in time for dinner.

Besides the principals, nine men witnessed the duel—two seconds, one on each side; two doctors, a French officer (a friend of the Marquis de Morès) and M. Va Eslande (owner of the property where the fight took place) and myself. No other newsman was present.

The duel in many respects was a remarkable one. It was occasioned by an article written several days ago by M. Dreyfus in "La Nation," which the latter considered insulting. . . .

The conditions of the duel were that if neither was wounded after the first round, a second should be fired, and after that a third if necessary. As both men are expert shots, many of their friends looked forward to the result with serious apprehension. For years the Marquis de Morès has been accustomed, on his immense cattle ranch in Montana [*sic*], to the constant use of the revolver. It was his boast that no thief had ever stolen one of his horses or steers and lived.

M. Dreyfus has long enjoyed the reputation among Parisian journalists of being the one whom it was particularly inadvisable to challenge. He rarely missed his man.

About seven o'clock Saturday evening, a tall, handsome man, enveloped in an ample ulster, stood near the ticket office at the Gare du Nord, apparently intent on reading a paper. He was really waiting for his seconds. It was the Marquis de Morès, just about to start on a journey from which he might never return alive. Presently two others approached, also enveloped in ulsters. The taller and larger of the two was the Comte de Dion and the other was M. le Capitaine Feuillant, recently prominent as one of Boulanger's staunch supporters. These were the Marquis' seconds. After whispered conversation, during which glances were shot from time to time in the direction of a similar group not far distant, the party moved toward the train.

M. Dreyfus and His Friends

A second group followed. A pale faced, medium sized man walked in front, accompanied by M. Lockroy, ex-Minister of Public Instruction; M. Pichon and Dr. Malecot. The pale faced man was M. Camille Dreyfus. They took their places in the express which presently rolled away for Lille.

The Marquis and his party at once established themselves in the dining car for the next hours, eating, drinking, laughing and having a glorious good time. Then they withdrew to their compartment

215

and were succeeded by their opponents who also dined, though less joyously.

The train reached Lille at 11 o'clock and all hands prepared to enjoy a good night's sleep, if a good night's sleep were possible under the circumstances. Strict orders were left for a general awakening at seven o'clock next morning with hot water, barbers, mutton chops, eggs, coffee, etc. The bedrooms were frigid. The hot water came too late. The barbers overslept themselves altogether, and the morning meal was not enjoyable.

Reaching the Dueling Ground

An hour's run from Lille brought us over the Belgian frontier, and at Comines all alighted. I had the pleasure of riding a brief distance in the same carriage with M. Dreyfus and his friends, who apparently mistook me for an English tourist, probably because I wore a plaid travelling cap and was reading an English novel. They talked freely of the duel, but there seemed to be an atmosphere of gloom in the railway carriage, which made it pleasant to get out again into the fresh morning air.

At last the scene of action was reached; the carriage came to a halt and the occupants alighted. Walking across a few hundred yards of ploughed ground brought the party to a stone cottage, where preparations had been made to care for the wounded, if wounded there should be.

Meeting of the Fores

Here for the first time, the two enemies met. There was a grand lifting of hats all around and a profusion of solemn bows, but not a word was spoken.

Without losing time, the four seconds proceeded to business. The ex-Minister Lockroy drew forth a five franc piece and sent it spinning into the air.

"Heads!" cried M. Feuillant, but a tail came. This gave M. Dreyfus the choice of position. Up went the coin again and the Captain won the choice of arms. At the third toss the Captain won the privilege of giving the word of command. The next thing was to measure a distance of twenty metres, which was done by the Comte de Dion, who unrolled a tape measure with the dexterity of a man accustomed to this sort of thing. Indeed, the Comte has fought no end of duels and has never been touched.

They Take Their Places

M. Dreyfus placed himself at the end of the line near the road, marking the exact spot with a cane. The handle of this cane, curiously enough, was a death's head carved in ivory. The Marquis de Morès placed himself opposite. Both wore white gloves, silk hats and afternoon dress. Neither combatant had any advantage from position. The sun, which was exactly between them, was low on the horizon. The pistols, furnished by the Marquis, having been taken from a sealed box in which they had left the makers, were tried carefully by the Comte de Dion, who discharged them several times in the air. Then, the weapons having been loaded in an approved manner in the presence of all the seconds, M. Feuillant handed an uncocked pistol to M. Dreyfus, while M. Lockroy performed a similar service for the Marquis.

Going Through the Motions

Each principal having given his word of honor that there was no sort of armor concealed beneath his clothes, M. Feuillant explained that his associate, the Comte de Dion, would first go through the act of giving command and then really do so. The Captain lifted his hat and held it in his right hand in a position prescribed by duel etiquette.

"*Allons, M. le Comte,*" said he; whereupon the Comte raised his hat in a similar manner, and drawing a gold stop watch, called out distinctly, "Fire! One, two, three," each count being marked by the beat of a second.

During this trial performance the two principals held their pistols in their right hands, with the muzzle upward, according to directions received from the Captain, but now the command was about to be given in earnest.

The Exciting Moment

Again lifting his hat with the same courteous sweep, M. Feuillant cried: "Cock your pistols, gentlemen!" Then with a bow to the Comte, he added: "*À vous M. le Comte.*"

The Comte waited a few moments. Then seeing that both weapons were cocked he said, "Are you ready gentlemen?"

"Yes," answered M. Dreyfus.

"Yes," answered the Marquis.

"Fire! One, two, three."

In the preliminary proceedings Captain Feuillant had cautioned both men to aim deliberately before firing, but M. Dreyfus did not choose to follow this advice. Hardly had the first word been uttered when the report of his pistol sounded through the quiet morning air. A glance at the Marquis showed that he was uninjured. One could fancy M. Dreyfus giving a hurried start as he saw his aim had missed, and as he also saw his enemy's arm rising slowly to the deadly horizontal. As the word "two" sounded the Marquis touched the hair trigger and the leaden ball, twelve millimetres in diameter, sped straight toward the breast of his adversary, but the adversary's arm meantime having fallen, received the ball that would otherwise have penetrated to some vital organ. Even at the distance where I stood one could easily see the shock caused by the impact of the bullet.

He Had Enough

"I am hit!" called M. Dreyfus, as the seconds came running toward him. With that he threw his pistol to the ground and walked toward the cottage, where the doctors promptly did their work. I saw them both after it was over, and received their assurance that the wound, while painful, would not prove serious. Both doctors said that but for the intervening arm, the worst might easily have happened.

While all this was going on, I stood a few dozen yards away, watching every detail and from time to time taking instantaneous photographs with the aid of a detective camera stowed beneath my waistcoat. These photographs will be reproduced in the "Paris Herald" within a few days.

Ten minutes after the duel was over the whole party was on its way back to the station where telegrams were sent to anxious friends in Paris and elsewhere.

Good News for His Wife

Among those who must have been most rejoiced by the news that the Marquis de Morès had escaped uninjured was the young Marquise, formerly Miss von Hoffman, of New York. . . . By the way she is said to be as sure a shot as her husband. On one occasion . . . she killed three grizzly bears. More recently . . . she shot three tigers from the back of an elephant.

As his wife has been ill for several weeks, the Marquis had taken the strictest precautions to keep her in ignorance of the duel.

M. Lockroy Surprised

On my way back to Paris, I had a pleasant talk with M. Lockroy, who expressed himself profoundly astonished to find that the in-offensive Englishman with the plaid travelling cap and novel was a correspondent of the "Herald." He took it all, however, in good part, and even went so far as to compliment the paper on its enterprise.

The time during the journey home passed pleasantly enough in the compartment where the Marquis and his friends were seated.

The Captain's Reminiscences

Captain Feuillant, who is what the French call a "vieux loup" at dueling, related a number of his experiences with sword and pistol. He has fought no less than forty-three times. The Comte and he had a friendly argument as to the relative advantages of the two weapons, but came to no conclusion. Both gentlemen congratulated the Marquis on the precision of his aim and were in their turn complimented by him on the manner in which they had discharged their duties as seconds.

M. Dreyfus, tossing about uneasily in bed at Lille, was meantime thanking Providence for the inspiration that made him lower his arm.

Shortly after the encounter, Dreyfus apologized for the insulting article about de Morès and the incident was closed.

This was only the beginning of de Morès' delivering and accepting challenges to duel. Despite the Spanish blood that ran hot in his veins, he was not a killer like the gunslingers of the Old West. For de Morès, dueling was simply a matter of settling a point of honor. (He once slightly wounded an inept opponent, refusing to injure him further, much less kill him, either of which he could have done with ease.)

The Marquis was now diverting his energies to politics; he decided to run for office in the Paris municipal elections of 1890. In France, a politician need not live in the district from which he seeks election, either in national or local contests. De Morès chose to stand on the ballot, not from a bourgeois quarter, but from Des Epinettes, a section in the scruffy Seventeenth Arrondissement (ward) of Paris, huddled up to the factory town of St. Ouen and populated largely by people of modest means, many of them railroad workers, retirees, and small merchants.

Immediately upon announcing his candidacy, de Morès was

copy for the press. *Le Figaro*, then, as now, a leading Paris daily, interviewed the Marquis about his seeking office as a socialist. He was ready with a reply. "You must distrust the words that are sometimes attributed to me," he said. "I do not propose at all to fight a desperate war against all the rich, and I do not have the extreme program attributed to me." He explained that he interpreted socialism as meaning that there could be no right without corresponding duty and "that it is the duty of society to help the producer obtain the greatest return possible from his work." His view of law was this: "I believe ... that the expression of the will of the people is the law."

The interview continued, with de Morès treating the reporter with his usual politesse—one reason he got such a good press in the United States and generally fared well in France, except for the government-controlled sheets masquerading as newspapers. He explained his point of view on the state of affairs in France, saying the nation was approaching a revolution. One cause, he believed, was the antiquated political and administrative machinery of France, which was no longer working effectively for the good of all Frenchmen. De Morès asserted that the country simply could not live under the centralized, despotic code Napoleon had created in order to divide the natural grouping of forces in the nation and thus make it easy to concentrate power in his hands:

At the top of these centralized institutions, there is the possibility of exploiting a financial or official position, and there we find a race which, in a France divided, is united. I name the Jews.

In the Socialist campaign in which I am engaged today, the main obstacle is the Jews. That is why I am attacking them.

The present laws must be changed, for they are dangerous arms in Jewish hands, since, instead of serving society, they serve to squeeze it.

Up to this time the skill of the kings of exploitation has been to safeguard their anonymity and screen their operations behind a legitimate institution. Thus the feeling of proprietorship embedded in the hearts of the French, as evidenced by their savings, has served to hide for a long time the exploiters' speculative fortunes, the origins of which are not justified.

De Morès' socialism could not be equated with Marxism such as that espoused by the extreme French leftists Paul Lafargue (he married Karl Marx's daughter) and Jules Guesde. Charles Droulers observed that de Morès "profoundly respected religion, the fatherland, family and individual ownership of property, all the things reviled and condemned by the pontiffs of collectivism." When he expounded his political philosophy, de Morès' religion shone through:

I ask God to help me find the thunderous words to make understood the danger of a sleeping nation, in order to prepare its spirit for the task of tomorrow.

I implore each Frenchman to ask himself at night: What shall I do if war breaks out? What aid, by my personal action, can I bring to the defense of the country?

In March, 1890, de Morès set up his campaign headquarters in the rue Sainte Anne near the Place de l'Opéra and somewhat distant from his would-be constituents. Strangely enough, he chose a seedy building for his operations: the ground floor had once served as an office for a dentist, who had stuffed the door cracks, apparently in an effort to contain the cries of his patients, which gave the place a conspiratorial air.

The office attracted malcontents of all shades: royalists, Boulangists, socialists, and anarchists, not to mention members of a union of employees who had been fired from their jobs and others who came merely to exploit the generosity and confidence of the Marquis. There were, of course, some serious supporters of de Morès.

Of all the groups, the police were the most numerous. In Droulers' words, they "stank up the place with their infestation." Some of them were uniformed policemen, others were undercover agents, and both classes were under the command of the Paris prefect of police. Some of the *flics* sniffed around the building for evidence that would incriminate the Marquis as a subversive person. In the cluttered basement they found old newspapers with passages marked in blue pencil, which they carted off as incriminating evidence. The secret police even infiltrated de Morès' political staff, some of them, in disguise, acting as his most trusted lieutenants. It is not difficult to picture the long arm of Constans in this snooping and harassment, for a mere suggestion or hint from him as minister of the interior to the Paris prefect of police would be interpreted as a command.

The Marquis was opposed in the election by Paul Brousse, the incumbent. Although a former convict, he was extremely popular, for he was constantly going about his district doing favors for the people. And in this election he had some fiscal matters going for him: the Paris budget was rising, and he campaigned on a promise to keep it down, an appealing issue for those of limited means and a generally conservative outlook.

De Morès campaigned vigorously, stressing his socialistic views, the carrying out of which he claimed would do more for the people in Des Epinettes than the current system. He also plumped for demolition of the fortifications that saddled Paris with useless, antiquated structures. In their place he proposed that low-cost housing be built. He argued for strong labor unions that could wield influence with management. He urged socialization of transportation, distribution, and credit. He also espoused a plan whereby a laborer would capitalize his earning power, thus permitting him to borrow from the state a part of what he would be worth as a worker over his lifetime. It would seem that he should have been the landslide choice of the electorate to which he was appealing, but Brousse won in the April 27 balloting.

De Morès was not downhearted. Quite the contrary. With tongue in cheek, he wrote to his would-be constituents: "The first of May will be the fête of labor, and I make you the following proposition: I invite all of you, on that day, to come and lunch with me at the Champs-de-Mars. Each of you will receive a bludgeon, and at the end of that bludgeon there will be a basket containing bread, sausage, a litre of wine and a pastry. We shall lunch joyously and we shall show that we are neither pillagers or arsonists." Droulers wrote that this humorous leg pulling by de Morès was taken as tragic by Constans. "One could not talk about sausage in his [Constans'] presence without bringing up the disagreeable memory of his unscrupulousness as administrator of the society 'La Ville de Lyon.'" (*Saucisson de Lyon* is one of the most well-known sausages in France, but the name of the society Droulers cites is obscure.)

Even before the Marquis' joking letter was written, the government was wringing its hands over the possibility of the May Day labor demonstrations' getting out of hand. To preclude any untoward events, Constans was given unlimited powers to cope with the situation. As a preventative, his first move was to arrest a dozen anarchists at random, then alert garrisons in Paris and neighboring villages. He deployed troops in Paris in such numbers as had not been seen since the Commune. Meetings and funerals were banned.

Next, de Morès was arrested and hustled off to jail. There he was searched, his wallet and briefcase were taken, and he was thrown into a cell, charged on three counts: arousing a mob to violence; inciting murder, pillage, and arson; and instigating disobedience by troops to military officers' orders. Of the three charges, the third was the most ridiculous and fantastic (a dedicated reserve officer, a graduate of St. Cyr, provoking a mutiny?) and the most serious (punishable by a severe penalty).

Constans' below-the-belt revenge had not ended. De Morès' residence and his rue Sainte Anne office were searched. Nothing to support the charges was found in either place. Infuriated, the police put de Morès in handcuffs. "This is abominable," de Morès told a visitor to his cell. "Handcuffs on me, an officer of the dragoons, ready to break my head for the fatherland!"

The day following his arrest, Paris newspapers, except those edited by puppets of the government, correctly declared that de

Morès' apprehension represented Constans' personal vengeance, wreaked on the Marquis because of the Richaud affair.

De Morès was released on May 4 and on June 4 appeared before a judge who harangued him on every conceivable aspect of his life, including his personal fortune, which he put at 800,000 francs ($160,000). The judge said nothing about the charge of corrupting the army and little, apparently, about the other counts. De Morès was defended brilliantly by Maître Demange, the lawyer who later defended Dreyfus—and the Marquis, too—in another action. Despite the phony charges, de Morès was sentenced to three months in jail, the maximum sentence that could be meted out.

De Morès wrote to his wife, asking for all his books on social questions and a volume of Macaulay's essays. He read voluminously in his cell and planned the political action he would take when released. The more he read and thought, the more convinced he became that socialism was the answer to France's problems.

Released from prison in September, de Morès resumed his attack on the Jews in November, opening with a conference entitled "The Bank of France and the Rothschilds."

(The famous banking family was hardly popular after a recent incident at the château of one member at Boulogne-sur-Seine. "Two poor devils," as Droulers describes them, came onto the estate to pick magnolia leaves, which had some value in pharmacy. A guard shot and killed one, who had a wife and children, and garroted the other. Rothschild was not prosecuted, of course, but the man who had been garroted was: he drew four months in jail.)

De Morès attacked the Rothschilds, saying the nation could never attain its goals as long as they wielded power as economic monopolists and controlled the reservoir of credit. The Marquis also accused them of juggling the metallic backing of French currency, citing figures to support his case.

The verbal arrows hit sensitive spots. At the sound of the

Marquis' name, it was reported, one of the most august of the Rothschilds would fly into an uncontrollable rage, pound the table with his cane, and shout: "If the French government doesn't protect me against that man, I shall explode, everything will explode!" To this de Morès replied in the public press: "Well then! Rothschild, thy head against mine and we shall have it out together!"

Following this brush with the Paris bankers, de Morès took to the hinterlands of northern France and elsewhere, preaching his doctrine of socialism with varying degrees of success. When he returned to Paris, he again took up with Drumont and his *La Libre Parole*, a newspaper founded by the brilliant anti-Semite and editor. Soon swords were flashing in duels, with Drumont holding his own on the field against the Jews who challenged him and de Morès establishing a reputation as one of the most famous and dangerous duelists in France.

One of the first of these encounters was reported by the *New York Herald* in March, 1892. Who challenged whom was not disclosed, but the incident grew out of what is described as a "political discussion" between Frederick Isaac and de Morès. A sword duel was fought on an island in the Seine. It ended abruptly when de Morès wounded Isaac, whose seconds terminated the match.

Then *La Libre Parole* ran a series of articles about Jews in the army officer corps. They were signed by one of the editors, Comte Paul de Lamase. A Jewish officer, Captain Cremieu-Foa, challenged Drumont, editor of the paper; both were wounded in a sword encounter in the Forest of St. Germain. Cremieu-Foa then challenged de Lamase, who accepted (de Morès was one of his seconds) with the provision that the terms of the duel not be publicly disclosed. This was to spare de Lamase's wife and children worry over the outcome, for Cremieu-Foa was rated as one of the best duelists in the army. The duel was fought, no one was hit, but the secrecy was breached beforehand.

De Morès blamed the disclosure on one of Cremieu-Foa's

seconds, Captain Armand Mayer, a professor at the distinguished École Politechnique who was so expert with the *épée* that he taught the art of its use there. De Morès' charge led to Mayer's challenging him to a duel with swords, to be fought at ten o'clock in the morning of June 23 in a covered structure on the Île de la Grande Jatte in the Seine, slightly west of Paris. This was actually a circuitous way for Mayer to settle accounts with de Morès for the Marquis' having supported Drumont in many ways, not the least of which was testifying on his behalf at a trial.

The terms of the duel were carefully spelled out, which was often the case when the opponents were evenly matched or, more important, if death were not the objective of either contestant. Droulers said the conditions "showed the keen desire that they [the seconds] had, not to give the affair a serious shape." For example, the contest could be stopped only by the intervention of the seconds, and any ground gained in a single reprise by one of the duelists must not be held by the man who gained it. Also, there was to be no close-quarter fighting, and the contest was to end when one of the combatants was wounded in a way that would place him in a position inferior to that of his adversary.

The duel got under way, both swordsmen starting out briskly. Then Mayer attacked de Morès with a low thrust. The Marquis, who had a remarkably strong wrist, parried Mayer's *épée* with his weapon, and as Mayer continued to lunge, de Morès' *épée* pierced Mayer's right armpit, went through the upper part of his lung, and stopped at his spinal column. Mayer threw down his weapon and cried to the doctors in attendance, "I am hit!" But he didn't fall and showed no sign of fainting. De Morès, greatly moved, rushed to him and said, "Captain Mayer, will you permit me to shake your hand?" Mayer extended his, and they shook hands. The wounded man was taken to a room near by and given first aid. The wound bled very little. Then he fainted. He was moved to a near-by hospital, where he died at five o'clock the same day.

The event was given prominent notice in the Paris papers, of course, and in the *New York Herald*, where New Yorkers saw a story under the headline "Marquis de Morès Kills His Man." The account, by Jacques S. Cere, told of the duel and Mayer's death:

> I cannot say what will be the result of this duel. According to some, every Jewish officer in the army intends to challenge the Marquis. According to others, de Morès will be arrested tomorrow.
>
> The last supposition is the less probable, but he will certainly be brought before a jury. The punishment is from two to five years imprisonment. In any case it will be necessary for a series of duels to finish the matter.
>
> It looks as if we had returned to the times of religious wars, for between Captain Mayer and the Marquis de Morès there was no other subject of dispute. It is a shame that such a duel should be possible in our country. The two adversaries deserved a better fate.

In an interview the following day (at a hideaway in the country), de Morès told a *New York Herald* correspondent: "Well, as to the unfortunate Mayer duel, I wish to state that all efforts were made to arrange this fight as gentlemen should as can be seen by the *procès verbaux* [report of the seconds on conditions of the encounter] published in the press. Captain Mayer was a dangerous fencer. He was in perfect health, with a long reach, and with arm and leg accustomed to exercise in a *salle d'armes* and in full condition. He had expressed the intention of killing me."

"And you tried to kill him?" the correspondent asked.

"No," replied the Marquis, "but when you have the naked point of a sword in front of you, you fight. The moment I felt I had struck him I held my hand, but it was too late." Droulers, describing the fatal point in the fight, wrote that *"Mayer, emporté par son élan, vient s'enferrer."* This means that Mayer, carried forward by his sally, ran himself through on de Morès' *épée*, although, of course, de Morès did make the thrust.) The *Herald* report said de Morès was deeply grieved at the outcome of the duel, and one must respect what he said, for it is clear that de Morès was no killer by design.

It was predictable that Mayer's friends would try to avenge his death. The first to do so was Captain Cremieu-Foa. In the interview with correspondent Cere in the country, de Morès said he knew about the challenge and explained his position:

> I will not be drawn into any trap, for I have not the same protectors as Cremieu-Foa; I do not fight as he does with the authorization of his military chiefs surrounded by friends coolly discussing the situation.
>
> I have come here to obtain quiet. I consider I have to look at the situation in the calmest possible mood, and I will remain here until the case has been before the courts. I refuse to be drawn into another duel until the question of the result of this one is settled.
>
> Captain Cremieu has been rushing about since five o'clock in the morning, banging at the door of my town residence with his sword and leaving cards and papers saying he is seeking the Marquis de Morès. But he knows perfectly well that I have to answer before a court of justice for the result of yesterday's fight. Now, I do not intend to go into court with the result of two duels on my hands. When I have cleared myself of the last, then I shall be ready to give M. Cremieu all the satisfaction he wants.

The French army apparently felt it would rather have a live, but thwarted, officer on its rolls, for the *Herald* said in its June 30 issue that Captain Cremieu had "been ordered on a special mission to Tunis."

On June 25, two days after the fatal encounter, a warrant was issued for de Morès' arrest, the assignment being given to M. Goron, chief of the Sûreté, which would be somewhat comparable to the U.S. Secret Service or the Federal Bureau of Investigation, or a combination of the two. Constans controlled the Sûreté.

Goron writes in his memoirs that he was led by spies to the house where de Morès was staying. When he knocked at the door, the Marquis himself opened it, shook hands with him, and introduced him to his friends, Guerin and de Lamase. This discourse then took place:

Goron: "Leave quickly I told the two [friends of de Morès]

and go to your homes. One [the police] is in the process of searching your respective domiciles. As for you, Monsieur de Morès, you know what brings me here?"

De Morès: "*Parbleu*, you come to arrest me . . . but without police, eh?"

Goron: "No assuredly not, I am alone with my secretary, completely without ceremony."

Then, the chief of the Sûreté wrote, "we went down, and entering a carriage with the top down, we parted, chatting as if we were going to a cabaret for dinner."

Goron said de Morès had "an irresistible fascination," relating that when they reached his office in the Quai des Orfèvres on the Île de la Cité, the Marquis started to indoctrinate his agents with de Morèsian political beliefs. "In two hours the *sorcier* had them in his pocket," he wrote. "In another day they would be repeating what he said!"

The injustice of de Morès' imprisonment was demonstrated in the outcome of a saber duel fought a few days earlier by two noncommissioned officers of the cavalry. One was killed, but his opponent was neither arrested nor tried.

De Morès appeared before a judge on August 29, which resulted in an interrogation as detailed as that following his arrest for the May 1 incident. (More of Constans' doing?) Maître Demange pleaded his case beautifully—and fortunately, it was a jury trial. De Morès was acquitted.

In 1893, de Morès joined Georges Clemenceau's enemies in an attempt to defeat the Tiger of France in his bid for re-election to the Chamber of Deputies. It was a dirty affair in which Clemenceau's opponents used forged papers. Angered by this, Clemenceau made de Morès admit that he had borrowed money from Cornelius Herz, a Jew who was mixed up in the scandal of financing the ill-fated Panama Canal venture. The loan was made through Drumont, and its disclosure so riled him that he denounced de Morès. The two come close to a duel—lucky for Drumont that it was only close.

The Herz loan damaged de Morès' standing, although he still had followers he had organized among elements which shared his feelings about socialism and anti-Semitism. Some sources claim de Morès' adherents were Paris toughs who were in the movement for the fun of having a leader with a title, one who wanted to make his efforts as public as possible. Reflecting the style of dress in Dakota, de Morès and his supporters wore cowboy shirts and ten-gallon hats. The Marquis' detractors ridiculed the "uniform," but de Morès was determined to have a distinctive organization, even though nothing came of it in the long run.

By the early 1890's, the star of the Marquis' socialistic, anti-Semitic movement was setting. He had no discernible political future, and he didn't want to settle down to the humdrum life of business. He looked for a place to carry on his beliefs, recoup his fortune, and at the same time establish himself as a public figure. North Africa, then under French domination, seemed to be the spot, so he set his sights on it. He had good reason, too, for the British and French were skirmishing over who should control the vast reaches of the Dark Continent.

XXII

AFRICA—THE ASSASSINATION

It is not surprising that North Africa and the Sahara should magnetize de Morès: both could rightly claim status as wild frontiers, more dangerous in many ways than the Old West.

In the late nineteenth century, France's dominions in Africa occupied an area—much larger than the homeland—about two-thirds the size of Europe. The steaming jungles along the equator were part of the realm, and so were the upper-tier countries that bordered on the Mediterranean. Residents-general held sway in Algeria, Morocco, and Tunisia, but outside the cities their influence was wafted away on sand-laden winds. Across the desert, the French maintained an uneasy peace, principally through the Foreign Legion, whose members fought under the Tricolor but frequently and mainly for their own self-imposed amnesia. The enemy: fierce tribes that pledged no allegiance and bowed to no one.

De Morès knew that many distinguished French explorers, adventurers, and freebooters had been attracted to this land of inhospitable space and people. The roster of those who didn't return after setting out from what passed for civilization was long, but this did not discourage others from following and meeting a similar fate. Indeed, the disappearances seemed to heighten interest in the Sahara and endow it with a mysticism which to some was irresistible. De Morès regarded it that way. The Marquis saw Africa as a place designed for his practical purposes. The Sahara was the key to his plan.

The first consideration was the international politics involved:

if de Morès could persuade the Islamic tribes to join the French with their forces, he would thwart the British, whose aim was similar. Such a coup would obviously put him in a strong political position. The second inducement was money. The exploitation of African resources was only beginning, and the further reaping of profits would depend to a large extent on the peaceful co-operation of the indigenous people. Anyone on the scene would find himself in an enviable entrepreneurial stance. De Morès was eager to fill that role, not only to recoup his losses in Dakota and make up for the drain on his resources since he had returned to France, but also to enrich his estate for the benefit of his wife and children.

How to implement this dual-purpose project in a practical way was the problem. Again de Morès consulted his maps, plotting his strategy with boldness: go south from Algeria toward Ghadames and Ghāt (on the Libyan-Algerian border); then east to Al Kufrah, almost on the Egyptian frontier; then south again to the Sudan to join forces with the Mahdi, the fanatical Moslem leader. After that, Tchad was the next objective. This was a trek of substantially more than two thousand miles through territory guarded by natural features and inhabited by tribes ready to sacrifice their lives before submitting to anyone.

Muslem support was essential to consolidating tribal loyalties. A start in that direction came from an old African hand, Prince Ludovic de Polignac, a retired French army colonel. Whether Polignac and de Morès had met before is obscure, but there was a natural bond between the two: the French army and aristocratic underpinnings. The Prince, who was in Algiers, wrote de Morès: "I shall be happy to see you here in Algeria. It is the sphere of great activity. There is here at hand the most powerful lever in the world—Islamism. . . . There is much to do and not a moment to lose." De Morès lost none. He landed at Algiers in December, 1893, and went straight to Polignac.

The Prince had a thin, creased face, with strength and character demonstrated in his jutting chin and hawklike nose. His head was topped by bushy white hair that matched his pencil-thin moustache. Energetic and alert despite his seventy years, he greeted de Morès effusively and paternally (the Marquis was then thirty-five years old).

From the balcony of his house, the Prince pointed out the place where de Morès' grandfather, the Duc des Cars, then a lieutenant general in the French army, had defeated enemy forces and thus paved the way for the conquest of Algeria, in which Polignac's father had played an important role. The view and the memories of the glorious days when France was carving out her empire in Africa moved the Prince to say: "Sixty years have passed, and here we, descendants of those men, find ourselves again on the same ground to defend their work menaced by the English and the Jews. Against that coalition, we must take the Muslims as allies."

In 1859, then Captain Polignac was assigned to open negotiations with the Islamic Touaregs. After long diplomatic skirmishing, the talks culminated in the Treaty of Ghadames in 1862, which guaranteed the French free passage through the desert over trails that the Touaregs had guarded since their beginning. But when the French emperor launched his disastrous Mexican expedition and needed the friendship of the British, he forgot about Africa, the Touaregs, and the treaty.

Polignac fought in the War of 1870, then retired and went back to Algeria. There he brooded about France and how the nation suffered from the actions of the British, Freemasonry, and the big banks controlled by the Jews. He had therefore carried on the same campaign in the Algerian press to which de Morès had addressed himself personally in France. It was natural, then, that the aging Polignac should want to pass his Algerian baton to de Morès, and in effect, this is precisely what he did. He also offered de Morès his advice, based on some forty years of experience in Algeria. One of his first suggestions was that de Morès collaborate with the Arabs; he pointed out that although they were "from the same nest," they hated the Jews. Polignac then said to the Marquis: "If you dream of doing great things in Africa, start by knowing Algeria."

One of the first things de Morès discovered was that the common people in Algeria were, in his opinion, being set upon by the Jews, just as their counterparts were being oppressed in France (or so he believed). He also observed that the autochthonous Algerians had joined in common cause with the French *colons*, immigrants from France who were also called, somewhat ingloriously, *pieds noirs*. De Morès' arrival in Algeria signaled the beginning of an overt anti-Semitic movement. He did everything possible to help it along.

In February, 1894, the Marquis undertook throughout Algeria a violent campaign designed to arouse the people to work for their just demands. He spoke before large and enthusiastic crowds, denouncing the British for their actions against the French government in Africa and calling for an alliance between France, Spain, and Islam. "Give the Arabs land, justice and the Koran," de Morès said in one address, "and march with them, with Algeria as the base, in the peaceful conquest of Africa." In reply, the audience shouted, "*À bas les Juifs! Vive de Morès!*" The Marquis was mobbed by admirers when he left the podium. It was the same in other appearances, but especially in Constantine.

For ten years, Constantine had suffered as the fief of a man named Thompson, an oily representative to the Chamber of Deputies. Thompson was a copy of Constans and a son-in-law of Captain Cremieu-Foa, the Jewish army officer who had precipitated the Mayer–de Morès duel. Hot but sputtering feelings against him were fueled by de Morès' anti-Semitic speeches, which singed Thompson's sensibilities. In the Chamber of Deputies, he said there would be no Jewish problem in Algeria "if it were not for the points dragged out by de Morès." The Marquis fired off a telegram to Thompson, saying that he would obviously not be permitted to reply in the Chamber and challenging the deputy to a duel. Thompson's seconds considered a duel unnecessary and would not accept the challenge—an underhanded, rather than open, fight would entail less risk for Thompson.

De Morès and Polignac also encountered stiff opposition from resident French military officials in Biskra, but this didn't prevent their winning support from the native population. The imposing figure of de Morès always attracted attention on trips, and Biskra was no exception. The *New York Herald* reported after de Morès' death that the Marquis had conversed with a Dr. Henri Faure (not further identified) at the Royal Hotel in Biskra. De Morès was quoted as saying: "It is not in Paris that the deadly danger to which France is exposed can be understood. Everything is ready for the slaughter, and unless God intervenes, all is over. This desperate state of affairs is, it appears, due to an alliance between African Jews and the English, who are advancing their aims with giant strides according to a long-prepared and deeply elaborated plan." De Morès added that his goal in Africa was to put an end to such a scheme.

By early 1895, the Marquis had finished his reconnaissance of South Algeria. He returned to France, but only to prepare for a much longer stay in Africa. He was convinced that he had a mission there, and he intended to carry it out.

In Paris, de Morès continued his talks with Colonel Polignac, who had come to spend the summer there. Polignac introduced his young friend to several old African hands, among them some distinguished explorers who knew the continent well. Ferdinand de Béhagle was one of them. He had spent much time in Africa and was convinced that French interests could be promoted there only in collaboration with the Arabs. De Béhagle emphasized this point in telling de Morès that two of the most important African leaders were Rabah, the Negro who had taken Tchad, and the Mahdi, then in control of the Sudan. (De Béhagle later visited Rabah to help him organize his small kingdom. After he arrived, Rabah saw a column of French soldiers marching toward his camp. Thinking de Béhagle had betrayed him, which was not true, Rabah hanged him.)

Colonel Polignac told de Morès that if he were going through with his African scheme, he should "begin by devoting six months to the study of the Arabic tongue, and [do] that in the Souf [an area in Algeria stretching south from the Mediterranean]. You will get to know the region whose people will never cease to be the friends of the Touaregs." Then, in response to a stirring poem the Colonel read, de Morès replied: "Life is but a battle and a passage. Life is worth while only through action! Too bad if that action is fatal!" Did he have a premonition?

At the end of 1895, de Morès returned to Algeria and immediately set out for the Souf in order to establish relationships with the desert tribes there in anticipation of his journey to the Mahdi. His first stop was Constantine, where he met General de La Roque, who commanded the area for the French army. He was cordially received, which was encouraging, for the general was in charge of a sector that was, in effect, the port of entry to the Sahara.

De Morès didn't expose his plans entirely, but explained to the general that he proposed to undertake a commercial expedition in the direction of Ghadames, some 450 miles south of the Mediterranean coast, under the protection of the Touaregs. (This was the first indication de Morès was masking his primary mission: winning over the Islamic tribes.) The general pointed out that the desert people had been stricken by famine and that de Morès would therefore be well advised to postpone his trip. The Marquis countered by saying that because of the tribesmen's serious circumstances, they could interpret his presence as one of sympathy for their plight and he could thus win their confidence.

Whatever, de Morès set out with five men, three horses, and three camels. By pushing his caravan about fifty miles a day over terrain hardly suited for that speed, he arrived at El Oued in the

Souf, about 250 miles from the Mediterranean, in five days. En route, he stopped to see a number of desert chieftains; generally speaking, his reception was good.

The French had a military post at El Oued, and of course de Morès visited the officers there, telling them of his intentions and discussing particularly his plan of using the Touaregs as his guides and protectors. The officers took a dim view of the Touaregs. They thought the tribe deceitful and dangerous, but de Morès would hear nothing of this. (He was banking on Prince Polignac's high opinion of the Touaregs.) The Marquis asked the officers to find for him a native who could go to Ghadames and Ghāt, some five hundred and nine hundred miles, respectively, from the coast. The mission was to price Sudanese merchandise there and also lay out a route to Al Kufrah, where the Marquis would visit the chief of the Senoussites. De Morès apparently had in the back of his mind the idea of using El Oued as the starting point for his expedition later in the year.

The Marquis pushed farther south, calling on military and tribal leaders in the area, and then struck back to the north and Constantine. One of his first stops there was to see General de La Roque, who had received him warmly before he set out. A chill was on this time. De La Roque tried assiduously to discourage de Morès from going on with his expedition, telling him that a year's study would be indispensable before setting out.

De Morès bluntly asked the general if he could count on the cooperation of the French army officers to the south. De La Roque said no and added that he could do nothing for the Marquis' expedition unless it were permitted by an order from the French government in Algeria. This convinced the Marquis that he would have to go through Tunisia in order to penetrate the Sahara.

He returned to France, meeting the Marquise in Cannes on the Riviera to celebrate their seventeenth wedding anniversary—they had been married there. The visit lasted less than a month, but it was a delightful interlude. Then the de Morèses went to

Paris, he for the last time. A friend took him to see Mme de Thèbes, a well-known palmist. She studied the lines in his hand with rapt attention, turned her eyes away, and said nothing. De Morès waited a few minutes, then asked her to tell him what she had seen.

"What I see," she said, "will not be agreeable for you to hear."

"No matter, speak!" de Morès commanded.

"You are going on a long voyage. You will not return from it."

This sinister prophecy didn't discourage de Morès, but it did bother him. He said nothing about it to the Marquise; indeed, he put up a gay front, emphasizing the favorable aspects of the journey and his high hopes for its success. One of the last things he said while in France was that "for me, danger is everywhere, and much more in France than elsewhere, with the powerful and obstinate enemies I have made. I shall feel safe only in the desert." He apparently believed it.

In early 1896, when de Morès left for Algeria, Africa was in a turmoil. English and French conquest had been arrested for a number of reasons, some of them domestic. The British held a tenuous grip on Egypt; the Mahdi, leader of a well-trained army of Muslims, controlled most of the Sudan after defeating (and killing) General Charles G. Gordon at Khartoum. De Morès planned to join the Mahdi at Omdurman, near Khartoum, and offer his services. The Marquis probably thought the Mahdi harbored ambitions toward taking Egypt, which may have been the case, but at the same time there was plenty of other territory to which aspiring conquerors could address themselves and much of it was occupied by Arabs.

The voyage from Marseilles was pleasant. The Marquise went with de Morès as far as Tunis. En route, the Marquis pointed out the mountains of Sardinia, where his ancestors fought for Spain and where the village bearing his name lived on. Tunis was jammed with visitors attending a convention, and de Morès quickly took advantage of this audience by renting a hall and delivering an anti-Semitic speech. He was well received, for the people there had been subjected to extortion by the Jews, or so they said. But de Morès did more than excoriate the Jews. He pleaded for the continuation of the provisions of the Treaty of Ghadames between France and the Touaregs, which was ironic —the Touaregs eventually killed him. He also recommended an alliance uniting the French, the Muslims, and other Mediterranean peoples to drive the British out of Africa. In effect, de Morès was declaring war on Britain; his speech was so interpreted by an American newspaper identified only as the *Providence Telegram.*

It was time for the Marquise to depart, for de Morès was soon to leave on his fatal journey. At the dock, the Marquis' last words to his wife were: *"Travaillez et priez!"* Neither work nor prayer would help him.

But that was not de Morès' fault, any more than his defeat in Dakota could be laid entirely at his door. He made some bad judgments about people, which was perhaps his greatest weakness, but he was one of the most thoroughgoing organizers one can imagine. When he said good-bye to the Marquise, he had spent nearly four years studying and traveling in anticipation of the journey he was to undertake. An authoritative Frenchman, wrote that both Napoleon and de Morès matched audacious thinking in the conception of a plan of action with infinite prudence in the execution of it. That was true in the Marquis' African venture; had it not been for the complicity of the French government, the odds are that he would have succeeded.

De Morès' first step was to hire a crew. In Tunis on April 29, 1896, the Marquis signed an agreement with El Hadj Ali to guide him and his caravan from Gabes, Tunisia, to Ghāt, some one thousand miles over the desert as the crow flies. The fee: the equivalent of two thousand dollars in gold francs. The Arab had been highly recommended by people de Morès thought he could trust. As things turned out, El Hadj Ali's honesty ranked with that of Jake Maunders, whose position as "adviser" caused the Marquis so much grief in Dakota.

In addition to the guide, de Morès hired Abdel Hack, an Arab interpreter who was formerly an employee of the Algerian Department of Agriculture. Several Arab and Negro servants were engaged, two of whom spoke dialects of the areas through which the caravan would pass. Significantly, no professional soldier, no Frenchman or other European (other than de Morès) was in the party.

As usual, de Morès was well equipped. All of his gear, including tents, gimcracks, merchandise of real value, and presents, cost the equivalent of three thousand dollars. Arms consisted of eight repeating carbines, but considering the hardware de Morès habitually carried in Dakota, he was somewhat lightly armed with just one pistol in addition to his carbine.

A caravan such as de Morès' offered a tempting prize to bandits, and even though it was privately sponsored and outwardly commercial, the fact that it was led by a Frenchman put the prestige of France on the line. De Morès had been entertained at the home of the resident-general of Algeria, where he met Commandant Rebillet, military attaché and chief of information. He now turned to Rebillet for information and maps and at first seemed to be getting what he wanted—he was also eager to obtain the blessing of the resident-general's government for his mission. But aside from his official duties, Rebillet had been doing some commercial trading with merchants at Ghadames and other oases south of Algiers, and on the surface, de Morès seemed a competitor. Relations with the Residence cooled. The Marquis' guide was summoned and informed that the expedition would have no sanction or protection from the French government, and functionaries were told that they could do nothing to facilitate it.

On May 4, 1896, de Morès wrote the Marquise:

I write to you with your portrait, made in America, before me, and the most tender feelings for you. I have just passed a hard and difficult week. I believe I got the run-around at the port. When the occasions presented themselves, the means were lacking. At last everything is signed, and I am ready to leave, but this shows me how closely I have been watched.

The next day, de Morès called to pay his respects to Rebillet. The conversation quickly became pointed, with Rebillet waxing eloquent. He dragged out all of the objections to de Morès' plans that had been made before. De Morès didn't budge, nor did he lose his poise. On leaving Rebillet, he said to a companion: "I have everything to fear from that man." He was right.

(The mystery is why he didn't see through the machinations of the Third Republic's African officials who were plotting to lure him into a trap at Beresof, south of Algiers, where Touaregs were to have killed him. The Marquis apparently did suspect that particular gambit, but he did not perceive the final and fatal move against him.)

Rebillet was not finished. The day after de Morès' farewell visit, the day set for sailing—he was going to Gabes—two of his men were arrested on the charge that their papers were out of order. De Morès exploded. Bursting into Rebillet's office, he said: "If my men are not released in two hours, I am going to give you two of the most beautiful pokes in the face you have ever received." (Clearly, either Rebillet or the French government or both was trying to abort de Morès' venture and discredit him before the French and Arab public, to say nothing of the crowds that had gathered at dockside to see him off.) Rebillet gave in, and with much cheering, waving of hats, and shaking of hands, de Morès and the members of his caravan embarked on the first leg of the journey.

After a port call at Sousse, Tunisia, de Morès and his party landed at Gabes, where he was cordially received by the French governor of the area, General Allegro. He and two other senior officials had orders from headquarters in Tunis, apparently signed by the resident-general. The orders specified that no obstacles should be put in the way of de Morès' expedition, but at the same time, no responsibilities should be accepted for it;

French and indigenous authorities were to be instructed to do the same. Attached to the official document, however, was a personal note to General Allegro (the writer undisclosed) saying: "M. de Morès proposes to ask you for information on the Sudan and trans-Saharan commerce. I do not see any inconvenience if you were to put this at his disposition because he will ask for nothing but information. According to his own declaration, he does not want to cross the Tunisian-Tripolitanian frontier, nor ask our authorities to assure guides or transport."

Charles Droulers asks if there were not secret orders in addition to the official ones and the informal note. He thought the purpose of the resident-general was twofold: either to obstruct the departure of the caravan or, if de Morès left anyway, to put the expedition in front of a checkmate. "Double play, play *terrible*," Droulers wrote, "because a checkmate is slow death or assassination in the sands of the desert."

General Allegro did everything he could to facilitate de Morès' final fitting out in Gabes, the terminus for desert caravans. He arranged to get horses and forty camels with drivers, and other preparations went so well that de Morès wrote the Marquise he was departing under the best conditions. His letter of May 12, 1896, continued:

> The best that I am able to do now is to succeed. I see more and more the importance of my reaching my objective, and I sense that I am being watched everywhere by people ready to profit from my errors or weakness. I am not able, under the pressure of circumstances, to describe a panorama that changes continually. My enemies are around me, behind me, here and in Paris, but not in front. . . . My expedition has taken on an importance which I did not expect. It has become a national affair. It must succeed. . . . I believe in the protection of God and hope for the future.

The Marquis was devoted not only to his wife, but to his children. He wrote his older son:

> *Mon chèr Louis,*
> A last word before leaving. For me it is a great regret not to be

near you for your first communion. I wished I could have been by your side to attend the most important act of your life, and to pray with you. I could only do it at a distance and give you this counsel.

LIFE IS A VOYAGE AND A FIGHT. Eternal life is the end, the human life is a proof and a means. There are weapons to cross it: work and prayer. Never get tired of it.

In the moments of difficulties, you must never give up—remember that. Remember in seeking, toward and against everything, justice and truth, you bring yourself nearer to God. Remember, that in *NOTRE PÈRE* is the essence of a response to everything. As for life, seek to have a productive one. Guard, if you can, everything you have. It is much more difficult to produce than to destroy. Be good: THE FEELING OF ATTACHMENT [for one's fellow man] IS THE STRONGEST ARM. Be a devoted son to your mother, and be united with your brother and sister.

I hope to open for you a way here in Africa, and prepare for you both interests and friends.

Au revoir, mon chèr Louis, que Dieu te protège!

Ton père affectionée,
Morès

Across a map of the area the Marquis was to traverse, written in a strong hand, were these words: *"Toujours en avant avec l'aide de Dieu."* The note was signed "Morès." He did always go forward, and with divine aid, but that was not enough.

De Morès left Gabes on the morning of May 14 and headed his caravan west toward El Hamma, his first stop. While his travel plan in general is known, one can only surmise that he intended to cross the Algerian-Tunisian border at Beresof, probably to visit the Touareg tribes in that area. Before leaving Gabes, however, the Marquis received a telegram from the son of General de La Roque saying that an officer had been dispatched to Beresof to arrest him if he crossed the frontier there. De Morès avoided that by heading south, still in Tunisia.

At Kebilli, some seventy-five miles from Gabes, the Marquis called on the French army post commander, Lieutenant Leboeuf. The lieutenant had received a wire from the resident-general saying that de Morès' expedition was private and to give him no help, *but to keep him under surveillance to ensure that he kept his word and came across the frontier at Beresof, and to report back.*

Leboeuf had also received a personal letter from Colonel Cauchemetz (de Morès had met him in Gabes) asking Leboeuf to help the Marquis as best he could. The lieutenant followed Cauchemetz's wishes. Then de Morès received a wire signed by La Roque saying that Touareg guides awaited him at Beresof, ready to escort him. How did this mesh with the warning message from La Roque's son? It didn't. Droulers believes young La Roque was attracted by de Morès' philosophy and chivalry, as were others of his age, and wanted to save him.

De Morès told Leboeuf before leaving Kebilli that his promise to go through Beresof had been extorted from him and that not only did he fear arrest there, but "perhaps brigands would kill me." He was right, but even though de Morès didn't fall into the trap at Beresof, it made no difference. The Touaregs were not to be put off from taking their victim by some desert travel. Why General de La Roque should have been so open in his move against de Morès remains a mystery.

The next lap of the journey was quite pleasant. Even the weather favored de Morès. He wrote to his wife that he had suffered from the wind en route from Gabes to Kebilli—imagine his admitting that—but since leaving Kebilli the breeze during the day was most agreeable and the nights cool. He even picked some flowers, and while Droulers says he sent them to the Marquise, it is somewhat difficult to see how that was done. The caravan was now skirting the Tunisian-Tripolitanian border and making good progress; the Marquis, after circumventing the obstacle the government had put in his way, was happy and in good spirits. Had he been lulled into a sense of well-being? Maybe.

On May 30, de Morès reached Djenaien, where he wrote to the Marquise:

My dearest Medora,
Twenty-seven days since the caravan left Gabes. . . . The day after tomorrow I hope to exchange my camels from the coast for

those of the Touaregs and to be in Ghāt in 20 days. [De Morès had been cheated on the camels he got in Gabes; they were soft and undisciplined.]

We have made friends all along the route, and if you pass this way, you will find them. It is a second Far-West, full of wonders if ever so little you enter into the spirit of the country and in harmony with the native people.

We have had many incidents. Rebillet set a trap for us on one route [the ambush planned at Beresof.] We took another, and the officers [his guides, apparently] agreed with me.

We are positively in the process of opening a route, and, if I am able to say, creating great excitement in the desert.

Near Djenaien, de Morès encountered a band of Chambaas and hired one of them, Ali ben Bessis, as a guide, since he knew all of the trails de Morès wanted to use. The new man quickly discovered he was in a den of thieves and told the Marquis so, but at this point de Morès could do nothing more than sharpen his vigilance.

June 1, 1896. De Morès had eight days to live. The caravan was crossing a large pasture when suddenly seven Touaregs, mounted on fast dromedaries, rode up. They said they were to head up and guide the Marquis' caravan, but they were actually the henchmen of the Touareg Bechaoui, who was waiting to kill de Morès at a place called Mechiguig.

Should not de Morès have become alarmed at this point and distrustful of the Touaregs, especially in view of the double talk he had received by telegram from French government authorities? Droulers remarks that the only course de Morès could have taken would have been to surround himself with four hundred rifles, and he asks how de Morès was to cross the desert without guides. Then he adds that a man named Duveyrier (apparently an explorer or merchant) had succeeded in doing what de Morès was attempting.

June 2. Seven days on earth left for the Marquis. He put the guidance of the caravan in the hands of Ali Sinaouni, who was in league with the assassins. The next destination was Mechiguig, where de Morès was to have met more Touaregs who were to guide and protect him and furnish him with additional mounts. But Sinaouni led the caravan in a wide circle. After a halt and rest at a well with undrinkable water, de Morès tried to push on. The camel drivers refused. The Marquis then sent all the guides except one to look for water. They found it, and en route ran into a Touareg named Bechaoui and Sinaouni, who was supposed to be leading the caravan. That night, de Morès posted guards all around his camp and stayed up himself, watching.

June 3. Only six days remaining. Standing on some high ground near the camp that morning, de Morès looked down on a plain enclosed by cliffs. This desolate spot, speckled with a few tamarisk trees and bushes, was El Ouatia.

The Marquis' guides had left the caravan. He sent a man to find Abdel Hack, his interpreter. Hack was located and returned with Bechaoui. The latter was enormous, well built and dressed, and imposing in his martial bearing. He commanded a tribe of Touareg Ifgohas, desert pirates. The desert was dotted with thirty tents of them encamped near El Ouatia. Bechaoui recognized El Hadj Ali, the Marquis' chief guide, who had been engaged in Tunis and who was to have been paid two thousand dollars for de Morès' safe passage. The two quickly fell into conversation in the Touareg dialect. Bechaoui said the assembly of the Touareg Ifgohas at Mechiguig had sent him "to cut the route of the Frenchman." El Hadj Ali responded by saying that he had been ordered by *"les gouvernants* [he must have meant French governors] to conduct the Marquis to his doom."

Ali wanted to kill de Morès immediately. Bechaoui hesitated, saying he wanted to be covered by two leaders of the Touareg Ifgohas named Djabour and Okka, who, Droulers said, *"were allied with the French government"* [italics supplied]. He therefore sent them this message: "A Christian has come who intends to go as far as Ghāt. Is it necessary or not to guide him?"

Meanwhile, Bechaoui's Touaregs, armed to the teeth, infiltrated de Morès' camp in small groups. Even at this late date, de Morès was seemingly unsuspicious of the Touaregs. On the contrary, he shared Polignac's admiration for their courage, chivalry, and appearance, reminiscent of Gallic warriors. The Frenchman invited them to a dinner of *couscous*, rice, and canned fish, which they reveled in.

The time for prayer arrived. The Muslims gathered to recite the first chapter of the Koran and to prostrate themselves on the ground in supplication. De Morès, near by with arms crossed, said his *Notre Père*, ending with the plea *"et déliverez-nous du mal."* The Marquis was deeply moved by the scene, for he described it in his last letter to the Marquise: "The camp was magnificent. . . . It was a reunion of two worlds."

When asked about guards for the night, he replied to his trusted man through an interpreter: "Tell him that we are with the Touaregs and that we have nothing more to fear." (The Touaregs had stretched out to sleep all over the camp.) About 9 P.M., de Morès asked to have sentries posted around the camp and near his tent. "It has already been done," he was told.

Bechaoui and El Hadj Ali talked until 2 A.M.

June 4. Five days left. De Morès wrote to Lieutenant Leboeuf, still content with the Touaregs—*"de véritables hommes,"* he said. Since they were to furnish camels, he sent those he obtained at Gabes back with the guides he had engaged there. "He's a dead man," the guides said among themselves. De Morès was now alone except for servants, guide Ali ben Bessis, and his interpreter.

June 5. Four days to go. De Morès still awaited the Touareg camels. He distributed small presents to visiting bands of chieftains and their people.

June 6. Three fateful days remaining. In the afternoon, five Chambaas, led by El Kheir, appeared on camels, which they offered to the Marquis. He refused, saying he had made a deal for camels with the Touaregs.

Despite traditional animosity between the Chambaa and Touareg tribes, they fraternized, and that night they counseled—the Touaregs were those who had waited at Beresof to kill de

Morès. El Kheir wanted to murder the Marquis immediately. Bechaoui argued that they could rob him without killing, that he was a friend of Islam, and further, he was waiting word from his chieftain. Finally, however, the decision was death.

June 7. Two days. In a letter to Leboeuf, de Morès revealed for the first time that he was uneasy, but it was laid to the Chambaas. He again wrote admiringly of the Touaregs.

June 8. Next-to-the-last day. Up early, de Morès discovered that his prize white dromedary had disappeared—it had been stolen by the Chambaas. Toward nightfall, several Negroes arrived with some puny camels. De Morès took them and said the caravan would depart the following day. That night, two Negroes crept into his tent and stole a trunk containing maps and papers. Why didn't they, or others, kill the Frenchman while he slept? Could it have been his strong features, his nobility in repose, that discouraged them?

June 9. The end. De Morès now realized he had been betrayed and couldn't possibly go on. He ordered the caravan to the north, hoping he might find a tribal chieftain to whom he had given presents and who would perhaps offer protection. Soon he discovered the caravan was traveling south. He rode to the head of the column, reversed it, then continued, surrounded by his executioners. Droulers wrote: "Indifferent to danger, he left his coat of mail in his baggage. He abandoned himself to his destiny."

The attack was to have been made upon departure, but no one dared to strike the first blow. Then, about 8 A.M., as the column passed through some tamarisks, Bechaoui grabbed de Morès' carbine while several others pulled so hard at the thong holding his revolver holster that the Marquis was thrown to the ground. There he was hit in the forehead with a saber blow. The thick felt of his hat broke some of the force, and although he received a light wound, it bled freely. De Morès killed his attacker with one shot, duplicated his marksmanship on another Chambaa, and wounded still others. The attackers retreated, their mission a failure. De Morès backed up against a tree and reloaded. The enemy then encircled the Marquis at 150 yards, out of his revolver's range, firing their rifles ineffectively.

At 10 A.M., the murderers lifted their fire and sent El Hadj Ali to de Morès in an effort to make him surrender. He and his former guide and supposed confidant talked for fifteen minutes. No deal. The brigands obviously didn't know de Morès: for him to surrender under any circumstance was completely out of character. But then why should he give up when it was clear that he would be killed anyway? Better to take a few more of the enemy with him in death. De Morès held Ali as a hostage, and when he tried to escape, while the Marquis was momentarily diverted, the Frenchman dropped him with a single shot.

Now some forty killers surrounded the Marquis. The fusillade intensified, with de Morès taking a toll with his revolver. He gave his life dearly. Two shots felled him, one in his side, the other in his neck. De Morès was still on his knees, in firing position, when the leader of the Chambaas charged up and plunged a knife between his shoulders. He fell dead. His money belt was ripped off. Now the tribesmen set upon his body, stripped it, mutilated it in a grisly fashion, and, tying a rope to one ankle, dragged it to some bushes. De Morès' servants, loyal and brave, stayed with him to the end; they, too, were slaughtered.

The murderers thought they had left no one on the Marquis' side alive. They were wrong. Several days later, a native survivor arrived at a French army outpost and told of the massacre. The news was telegraphed to Gabes and Tunis and from there to France, England, and the United States.

A week passed. The French authorities did nothing. Lieutenant Leboeuf received a wire ordering him not to go personally to find de Morès' body. However, he sent two natives to search for it, and on June 27, they found the corpse and brought it back. Van Driesche and a doctor made positive identification.

XXIII

THE ASSASSINS TRIED—
FRENCH GOVERNMENT COMPLICITY

France was plunged into shock by news accounts of the Marquis' death. The story of his expedition had appeared only a few days earlier.

In New York, the *Herald* ran a story on June 10, 1896 (the day after the assassination), quoting the French journal *Gaulois* as saying that de Morès' foray into the desert had begun. Eight days later, the *Herald* stated that his death had been rumored. This was followed by a long account the next day, played prominently under these headlines:

SLAIN BY HIS
NATIVE ESCORT

————

CONFIRMATION RECEIVED OF THE MASSACRE OF
THE MARQUIS DE MORÈS AND HIS COMPANIONS

————

FIVE CRUELLY MURDERED
SET UPON BY ATTENDANT TOUAREGS
KILLED AND STRIPPED OF ALL
THEIR CLOTHING

————

MADE A VIGOROUS DEFENSE
NEWS OF CRIME BROUGHT BY TUNISIAN WHO
WAS CAPTURED BUT ESCAPED

The lengthy dispatch was datelined Tunis, June 18, and it checks closely with other accounts of the assassination, notably Charles Droulers' which must be considered the most authoritative in the light of subsequent investigation and checking on behalf of the Marquise.

The *Herald* dug into its files for information on the Marquis' life in America, including, of course, the fact that "no less than 18 attempts were made on his life in Dakota." The paper also used a rather lurid account of two cowboys' shooting a cigarette out of de Morès' mouth and the Marquis, in turn, besting the two with his deadly pistol fire. Quite accurately, the *Herald* observed that the many friends de Morès had made in the United States would mourn his death.

So did those in France and her possessions. In Tunis, the primate of the Catholic church delivered this eulogy in the cathedral: "In his Saharan expedition, the Marquis de Morès was not pursuing the seductive shadow of glory for himself. He wanted, in the highest sense, to devote his efforts to his country, to win over a people [Africans] through good works, and he had undertaken this rash but sublime enterprise in a Christian manner."

When the Marquis' coffin, draped with the French Tricolor, was drawn through the streets of Marseilles on July 14, the day of French independence, an emotional crowd with bowed heads threw flowers in the path of the cortege. It was the same in Paris. At the Cathedral of Notre Dame, the most imposing church in the city, distinguished Parisians pressed into the edifice for the services. As an indication of the esteem in which de Morès had been held by the common people, the butchers and others from La Villette, the city's wholesale meat center, joined those who mourned when the Marquis' casket was lowered into the grave at the cemetery in Montmartre.

Across the English Channel, Edward VII recognized the stature of the Marquis. Even though the Frenchman had been working vigorously against British interests in Africa, the sovereign said: "If he had been English, I would have made him a viceroy."

The French government evinced none of this feeling. Quite the opposite. Worse still, the government did nothing about the assassins, who went scot-free; they circulated at will in territories which, on paper at least, were French protectorates. A year passed, with the Marquise trying everywhere in Paris to get someone to act. Although the doors to every important ministry and legal authority were politely opened to her, nothing ensued. It was clear that she would have to initiate action herself. She did.

At the end of 1897, a year and a half after the assassination, the Marquise wrote an open letter to the people of Algeria and Tunisia in which she pleaded for their help in bringing her husband's murderers to French authorities for trial. She offered the equivalent of one thousand dollars as a reward for each of the assassins and two thousand dollars each for Bechaoui and El Kheir, the two ringleaders, who had been identified through the Marquise's efforts but about whom the French government had done nothing.

Early in 1898, Naib Mohabed Taieb, an influential native chief, brought the murderers, El Kheir, Hamma ben Cheik, and Hamma ben Youssef, to the French authorities in Tunis. Under most circumstances, the feat would have to be rated as a daring and commendable piece of work. But how did the French authorities reward Taieb? They threw him in jail for nineteen days on a flimsy pretext. During that time, some friends of the assassins pillaged and ransacked his house and devastated his fields. His family had to flee to avoid being killed. When Taieb got out of jail, he was forced to return the reward money he had collected from the Marquise. Some time later, he was involved in a military action under the French. He fell in battle. The bullet came from behind.

Scandalous as the treatment of Taieb may have been, the French were greatly embarrassed about the prisoners and felt they had to do something with them, so they jailed the culprits in Sousse to await trial. Meanwhile, the Marquise had engaged Jules Delahaye, a newspaper editor and former deputy, to investigate the events that led to the assassination and to be sure that evidence was ready for presentation at the trial.

On April 5, 1899, the *New York Tribune* ran a Paris-datelined story under these headlines:

"THE AFFAIR MORÈS"
A PROSECUTION WHICH INVOLVED HIGH FRENCH OFFICIALS IN TUNIS

THE WIDOW OF THE MURDERED MARQUIS DE MORÈS IS DETERMINED TO BRING TO JUSTICE THE ASSASSINS OF HER HUSBAND

The account said M. Delahaye had spent six months in Africa probing for facts, and as a result, he "brings grave charges of complicity in the assassination of the late Marquis against the Resident General of Tunis [M. Millet] and especially against the officer who was his military attaché at the time" [Colonel Rebillet]. Delahaye was quoted as saying:

With her [the Marquise] I said that those who executed the crime were a number of native agents of the French authorities [in Africa] and that these agents acted by order. . . . We by no means accuse M. Millet of active complicity. He is incriminated only for having allowed the trap to be prepared and the ambush to be carried out by agents who are under his direct orders.

The *Tribune* story related that Delahaye's accusations were focused on Colonel Rebillet, "under whose personal command were the native agents who, he alleges, executed the assassination." Delahaye pointed out that "no officer in Tunis, from the generals down to the sub-lieutenants, will vouch for him" [Rebillet]. He also noted that after the crime had been committed, "M. Millet himself demanded Rebillet's resignation, and no one in Tunis doubts that the chief reason was the compromising part which Rebillet seemed to him to have played in the expedition of the Marquis de Morès."

When the *Tribune* correspondent asked Delahaye to substantiate his grave charge, he answered: "I have the best of proofs—the confession of the assassins themselves, made in the desert, under their tent, at a time when they had neither hopes nor fears, and spoke only through need of telling the truth. Their confession is confirmed by all the circumstances of the expedition, ambuscade and murder from Tunis to El Ouatia." Delahaye boldly continued by presenting information which he believed proved the involvement of French authorities in de Morès' death:

Strictly speaking, we can understand that, for reasons of government, M. Millet should seek to save the French officials who are compromised in the matter. But why should he protect the natives? God knows how easily they put their hands on any Arab accused of no matter what misdemeanor! Well, in this affair . . . notorious brigands are protected by the Resident General, and even by the courts. Our struggle at present is precisely with the officers of justice, not to destroy hostile witnesses, but to get our witnesses heard. The Court of Indictments, in spite of the insistence of the public prosecutor, has put aside our evidence, to limit its own work to the place where the crime was actually committed, El Ouatia.

It will take no cognizance of all that passed before or elsewhere, supposing that in such a corner of the desert it will never find any trace of the order to assassinate. It is impossible for us even to throw suspicion on notorious wretches. For example, Ibrahim-el-Acheya was the guide furnished to Morès by the Cadi of Nafzoua. Now at the time of the expedition he was known to have had a hand in 59 murders. Why are such bandits spared, unless they are afraid that if they touch one they shall hit others with them?

This was a strong indictment of the government and the courts, but Delahaye said the Marquise "will yield to no one and before nothing. If need be she will give her life to the struggle [to avenge her husband's death]. She will prove, if not with the help of the impartiality of the judges, at least by the publication of the proofs in her possession, that Morès was indeed a victim or a martyr. She knows that she will have to encounter indifference and skepticism, but the truth will end by triumphing, for moral strength in the long run always triumphs over material force. This was the faith of de Morès, and it is the faith of his widow." Delahaye was overoptimistic.

The account of his action in the case continued to attract widespread attention. The *New York World* ran a long story on October 28, 1900, reviewing the facts and noting that the Marquis' "widow has been collecting evidence for a year that his death was instigated by the French government." What was the motive? the paper asked, answering that those who would avenge de Morès' death charge that *"the Marquis possessed personal knowledge of many of the undisclosed secrets of the Dreyfus case—knowledge menacing the peace of men high in the army and the government. In order that those secrets might be buried forever, the Marquise and her friends say, he was first packed off to Africa and there assassinated"* [italics supplied].

Delahaye is quoted prominently in the *World* story, which appeared about a year and a half after the *Tribune* piece. During the interim, Delahaye had hardened his accusation of the French government and its officers. He was now saying that

... all stories hitherto given to the world about the murder are lies invented by French officials.

It has been stated that the caravan was composed of brave men devoted to their master. We can prove, on the contrary, that the caravan was organized expressly to lead de Morès to his death. It has been the boast of the chief assassin that he was entrusted with the work of conducting the unlucky Marquis to the place where he was to meet his fate. *We accuse Colonel Rebillet of directly causing the death of the Marquis* [italics supplied]. This officer, notwithstanding his rank, carries on trade in Southern Tunisia, which he seems to consider almost a private possession. We also accuse of complicity the Resident General, M. Millet, who knew what was going to happen, but took not a single step to prevent a foul crime. The manner of the assassination shows how determinedly it was plotted. For three hours the Marquis withstood a desperate siege with gallantry which those who knew him can well picture. When his body was found, some 20 bullet wounds were counted in it. Another discovery of importance that we have made is that the Marabout of Guemar, of the tribe of the Tidjanies, promised the murderers full pardon and all the loot they could get if they killed the Marquis de Morès. [This is the only indication that anyone other than the Touaregs and the Chambaas, at the instigation of the French, had any designs on de Morès.]

Much legal skirmishing preceded the trial of the three assassins. It was clear to the Marquise that Judge Poisson, the jurist at Sousse before whom the case was to be heard, looked upon it with somnolent casualness. She asked for a replacement and got M. Geoffray. He was little better. Indeed, he was preoccupied with drawing a protective screen between the Marquise and the government functionaries who had been incriminated. The jurists in charge of arraignments refused to go after the identified assassins who were still at large: Ali Sinaouni, Brahmin, and Bechaoui. The Marquise, of course, deplored this abdication of judicial responsibility and asked that the case be tried before the highest court of appeals. Her motion was denied, and the trial was set for July, 1902, before the criminal court at Sousse.

By that time, Hamma ben Youssef, one of the accused, had died in jail. El Kheir was sentenced to death, Hamma ben Cheik got life. The Marquise asked that the death sentence be commuted. It was—to life at hard labor. But no French government official was touched at the trial. The ineffable Ali Sinaouni, Brahmin, and Bechaoui went free because, as Droulers put it, they were "under the protection of the government."

The Marquise passed on to her children a firm conviction of French complicity in the murder of the Marquis. This opinion is shared by his grandson, Antoine Manca de Vallombrosa de Morès, who told me: *"My grandfather was killed in the Libyan Desert by Touaregs paid by some of his political enemies"* [italics supplied].

The Marquise had avenged, but only in part, the heroic death of her husband. She returned to France.

In 1911, French officers put up a small obelisk at Mechiguig, overlooking the plain of El Ouatia. And at El Ouatia itself in 1928, the Duchesse d'Aosta, Hélène, Princess of Orléans, erected a large granite cross in de Morès' memory. Among the Touaregs, de Morès remained a legend, and only a few decades ago, this expression was still heard among them: "Brave as Morès."

XXIV

RETURN TO THE BAD LANDS

Back in France, the Marquise decided she had done all she could to avenge her husband's death. To attempt to prosecute his political enemies would be useless. She let the record of the trial stand as her witness, and the prestigious house of Plon-Nourit et Cie. published a 252-page transcript of the proceedings under the title *Le Crime d'El Ouatia, Assassinat du Marquis de Morès*.

Madame de Morès had the Marquis' remains removed from the cemetery in Montmartre and buried near Cannes on the Mediterranean. She, too, was eventually interred there.

By the early 1900's, the de Morès children were in their teens. They had been toddlers when they left the United States for the last time, but the influence of Dakota on their parents, especially their father, had rubbed off on them. Long before most French youngsters knew anything about *Le Far Ouest*, the young de Morèses had considerable knowledge of their parents' exploits in that part of the world. The result: in the meticulously groomed and espaliered garden of the de Morès home in the Boulevard Suchet, one of the most recherché addresses in Paris, the de Morès *fille* and *fils* played cowboy. They had a pony and enacted scenes from the Old West with all the verve and delight of American youngsters—and to the envy of their young friends.

It is easy to understand that the de Morès children should have urged their mother to take them to Dakota and that she, too, should have wanted to make a pilgrimage to the land in which she and her husband had spent such happy (albeit also trying)

257

days. So, in 1903, the Marquise, her daughter Athenaïs, and her son Louis made a trip to Medora. Paul, the younger boy, did not go.

Once again the *Pacific Express* rumbled out of Chicago, this time with the Marquise and her children, rather than the Marquis and van Driesche, riding the varnish. Two decades had passed since the Marquis and his man made their presence known in Dakota and the Marquise came out from New York for the first time. The scenery was much the same, and her feeling for it had changed little. As the *Express* knifed across the prairies, Dakota spread out before the Marquise and her children. It fascinated her once again and brought back a myriad of memories, most of them happy. For the de Morès children, it was an unfolding panorama in which they saw their father as the central figure. In a way, the three de Morèses were seeing the Marquis' vision of the empire he had hoped to build and almost did.

In its way, the de Morès episode in Dakota was a dream, the kind of American reverie of business empire; but for de Morès it embraced something noble: not just money grabbing (he had enough cash of his own), but the kind of enterprise that would have helped the common man. He had a vision that was attained several decades after his time in Dakota, for the antitrust laws and other factors operated in favor of the kind of enterprises de Morès mounted. He was, indeed, a man far ahead of his time.

The news coverage of the Marquise's return was sketchy, but she was quoted as saying that nothing could have been more delightful for her than to return to Medora. "I loved Medora. I love it still," she said, "and it will always be very dear to my memory. I will not let Medora die until after I do. . . . I must see the old ranch."

The Marquise and her two children spent six weeks in the château, high on the bluff overlooking the Little Missouri. The place had been maintained by caretakers, so the three moved in just as if they had been gone for a week or two. In many ways, they relived the days of the 1880's when life in that part of

Dakota was centered there. As late as 1967, Athenaïs, then in her eighties, wrote me from France that she still remembered the wonderful rides on horseback through the Bad Lands with her mother, brother, and Dakotans. The cowboys, she wrote, were *très aimable*. She recounted that her parents had fond memories of the Old West and that the homecoming was touching for her mother. Both of the children took to the country, just as their parents had.

Only goodwill prevailed when the Marquise came back to Medora. She gave a party in the Medora town hall for just about the entire population of Billings County, the area that surrounds Medora. It was apparently great fun for everyone, especially the de Morès children—Athenaïs danced tirelessly with the cowboys and others while the Marquise greeted everyone who came and chatted throughout the evening.

In the fall of 1903, the three left Medora, Louis for Yale, the Marquise and her daughter for France. The Marquise lived in Paris and Cannes until she died in 1921, but before her death she deeded the property in what had become North Dakota to her two sons.

Not long after the de Morèses' visit to Medora, the packing plant burned to the ground. The origin of the fire has never been established. Some speculated that a spark from a passing locomotive may have started the conflagration or that hoboes holing up there had been careless while preparing food. Others guessed that it was a case of arson, perpetrated by someone who harbored a grudge against the Marquis. Whatever the cause, nothing remains of the packing plant except the yellow brick chimney, standing gaunt against the sky (conductors on the railroad point it out to passengers as they pass through Medora).

The de Morès children, deeply touched by the history their father had helped to write, were determined that a memorial to him should stand in the town he built. They commissioned a life-size statue of him. It was executed in Paris and shipped to Medora in June, 1926. The piece was wrapped carefully to pro-

259

tect it from the elements, both en route and while awaiting its dedication, which was to be led by Louis Vallombrosa, the Marquis' elder son. Not long after it arrived, vandals set fire to the covering—apparently burlap—which defaced the statue badly. Why this fire and the burning of the packing plant? It is pure speculation, but both could have been the smoldering residue of twisted thinking that resulted in the animosity toward the Marquis during his stay in the Bad Lands. The statue was cleaned and the ceremony held, with Louis Vallombrosa delivering the dedicatory address.

By the mid-1930's, the Marquis' sons had disposed of most of the ranch properties, but they guarded the château religiously, keeping caretakers on duty there constantly. The church their mother had built for the Catholics of Medora was given to the parish, and the tract on which their father's statue stood was their own gift to Medora.

In 1936, Louis Vallombrosa presented the château and the surrounding grounds, along with the packing-plant site, to the state of North Dakota, with the state historical society as trustee.

There was a proviso in the deed stipulating that the château be considered as a museum, to be open to the public. It is there today, complete with furnishings and personal effects of the de Morès family, a memorial for everyone to see as evidence of the reign of the Marquis de Morès as Emperor of the Bad Lands.

NOTES ON CHAPTER SOURCES

THE EMPEROR OF THE BAD LANDS
The Pacific Express

Letters to the author from the Northern Pacific Railway Company, dated Nov. 13 and 23, 1959, and enclosing: a description of the *Pacific Express*, especially the 4-4-0 locomotive; a memorandum by Howard Eaton about the Marquis de Morès and Medora; a letter from the company's general freight agent, dated Apr. 13, 1920; and the terms of an agreement between the Northern Pacific and de Morès, dated June 8, 1883, concerning freight rates. Lucius M. Beebe and Charles M. Clegg, Jr., *The Age of Steam*, 125.

De Morès the Man

La Grande Encyclopedie, XXIV, 336. Pierre Frondaie, *Deux Possédés de l'Heroïsme*, 113. Usher L. Burdick, *The Marquis de Morès at War in the Bad Lands*, 5. *Bismarck Tribune*, Aug. 15, 1939. *Sioux Falls* (South Dakota) *Press*, undated. Photographs and a sketch of de Morès from the Duchesse de Sabran. *Dakota Territory in the 1880's*.

Patrick Donan, *North Dakota, The Land of the Golden Grain, The Lake-Gemmed, Breeze-Swept Empire of the New Northwest*, 5. Lincoln Lang, *Ranching with Roosevelt*, 26–31. *Bismarck Tribune*, June, 1883; July 4, 1883. Dzena Trinka, *Medora, passim*. Wayne Gard, *The Great Buffalo Hunt*, 5–6, 27–28, 206–207. John A. Hawgood, *America's Western Fron-*

tiers, 314. Arnold Goplen, *The Career of the Marquis de Morès in the Bad Lands of North Dakota*, 4–5. Lewis F. Crawford, *Ranching Days in Dakota*, 75.

CHAPTER II

DE MORÈS' BACKGROUND

De Morès' Ancestry, Upbringing, and Early Career
Goplen. *North Dakota Historical Quarterly*, VIII, 1 (October, 1940), 4, 7. Charles Droulers, *Le Marquis de Morès 1858–1896*, 1–18.
Living in New York and Preparing To Go West
Personal account books of the Marquise de Morès. Droulers, 19–21. Letter from General William Tecumseh Sherman to army officers on behalf of de Morès. Letter from H. Price, Commissioner of Indian Affairs, to Indian agents, dated Feb. 21, 1883.
Gorringe Option
New York Evening Post, Jan. 3, 1903. *North Dakota* (American Guide Series), 283.

CHAPTER III

THE TOWN OF LITTLE MISSOURI—THE BAD LANDS

Goplen, 9. A. T. Andreas, *Atlas of Dakota*, 194. Report of the Secretary of War, *House Executive Document*, 46th Congress, 3rd Session, Vol. V, Part 2, 59–61. Charles L. Brooks and Ray H. Mattison, *Theodore Roosevelt and the Dakota Badlands*, 2–13. A. C. Huidekoper, "My Experiences and Investments in the Bad Lands of North Dakota and Some of the Men I Met There," 4. Lewis F. Crawford, "Interview with Charles O. Armstrong, Grassy Butte, North Dakota, August, 1929," 4–6. Pamphlet of the Northern Pacific Refrigerator Car Company, 3–4. *New York Times*, Sept. 21, 1884. Herman Hagedorn, *Roosevelt in the Bad Lands*, 58–59. *North Dakota* (AGS) 8–11. Droulers, 22–23. Trinka, *Medora, passim. New York Evening Post*, Jan. 3, 1903.

CHAPTER IV

THE BUILDING OF MEDORA

Building Medora—Competition With Little Missouri
Huidekoper, 6. Goplen, 9–11. *Bad Lands Cow Boy*, May 15,
June 19, Feb. 15, Oct. 1, 1885. *North Dakota Historical Quar-
terly*, VIII, 4 (July, 1941), 273. Lang, 71.
The Northern Pacific Refrigerator Car Company—Cattle Deals
Goplen, 13. Hagedorn, 60–61. *Bismarck Tribune*, July 10,
1883.
Land Purchases
Goplen, 14. U.S. Department of the Interior, Bureau of
Land Management, memorandum, "Script Information," dated
March, 1957. Lang, 71.
Personnel
Hagedorn, 62–63. Droulers, 39.

CHAPTER V

DE MORÈS FENCES HIS LAND

Lang, 71–73. *New York Evening Post*, Jan. 5, 1883. Goplen,
57. Huidekoper, 25–26. *Bad Lands Cow Boy*, Aug. 27, 1885.
Attitude Toward de Morès
Tabor, Iowa, *American Nonconformist*, July 5, 1883. Burdick, 8–9. *North Dakota* (AGS), 284.

CHAPTER VI

OPEN WAR ON DE MORÈS

Burdick, 9–13. Hagedorn, 37–64. Lang, 75. Droulers, 25–30,
59–73. *New York Times*, June 28, 1883. *New York Sun*, June
28, 29, 1883. *New York Evening Post*, Jan. 3, 1903. *Bismarck
Tribune*, June 27, 1883. *American Nonconformist*, July 5, 1883.
Bad Lands Cow Boy, Aug. 27, 1885.

CHAPTER VII

JUSTICE-OF-THE-PEACE JUSTICE

Bismarck Tribune, July 2, 4, 13, 18, 28, 1883. *Mandan Pio-*

neer, July 1, 3, 4, 13, 1883. *New York Evening Post*, Jan. 3, 1903. Rayford W. Logan, *The Negro in American Life and Thought*, 76.

CHAPTER VIII
MEDORA IN 1883 AFTER THE FIRST TRIAL

Pamphlet of the Northern Pacific Refrigerator Car Company, 6. Goplen, 15. Hagedorn, 69. Brooks and Mattison, 13–14. *Bismarck Tribune*, July 28, 1883. *New York World*, Feb. 16, 1884. *Dickinson Press*, Sept., 1883. Letter from Antoine de Vallombrosa to the author, dated New York, N.Y., Feb. 5, 1960.

CHAPTER IX
MEDORA IN 1884 AND 1885

Helena (Montana) *Herald*, about April 24, 1884. *Bad Lands Cow Boy*, Feb. 21, Aug. 7, Oct. 30, Nov. 7, Dec. 11, 18, 1884; Jan. 15, Jan. 22, Jan. 29, Apr. 16, May 1, June 18, 1885. *New York Times*, Sept. 21, 1884. *Detroit Free Press*, Aug. 18, 1883. Hagedorn, 48. Lang, 78.

CHAPTER X
THE *Bad Lands Cow Boy*

Bad Lands Cow Boy, Feb. 7, 1884, through Nov. 25, 1886. Hagedorn, 73–77.

CHAPTER XI
DE MORÈS AND THEODORE ROOSEVELT

Brooks and Mattison, 17–23, 34–35. Hagedorn, 331–50. *North Dakota Historical Quarterly*, VIII, 1 (October, 1940), 19–20.

CHAPTER XII
LIFE IN THE BAD LANDS FOR THE DE MORÈSES

North Dakota Historical Quarterly, VIII, 4 (July, 1941), 271–83. Household accounts of the Marquise. *St. Louis Globe*

Democrat, June 29, 1885. *Bismarck Tribune,* Dec. 8, 1884; Sept. 5, 1885. Huidekoper, 25–26. Richard O'Connor, *Wild Bill Hickok,* 17. *Bad Lands Cow Boy,* July 16, 1885. Granville Stuart, *Forty Years on the Frontier,* II, 229.

CHAPTER XIII
DE MORÈS' BUSINESS AND THE BEEF TRUST

Bad Lands Cow Boy, Feb. 14, 21, June 27, 1884; Jan. 8, 1885. *Montana Stock and Mining Journal,* Nov., 1884. Duluth, Minnesota, newspaper clipping, not otherwise identified. *Weekly Yellowstone Journal and Live Stock Reporter,* Oct. 24, 1885. *Bismarck Tribune,* July 10, 1883; Feb. 24, Mar. 28, Apr. 2, 1886. *New York World,* Apr. 20, 1902. *New York Times,* July 1, 1883. *New York Tribune,* Aug. 27, 1886. *Mandan Pioneer,* July 10, 1883. *Fargo Argus,* undated. 22–24. Hagedorn, 339–40, 448–50. Huidekoper, 24. Louis Pelzer, *The Cattlemen's Frontier,* 207.

CHAPTER XIV
DE MORÈS' OTHER BUSINESS ENTERPRISES

Household accounts of the Marquise. Goplen, 30, 41–43. Hagedorn, 79–80. *Bad Lands Cow Boy,* May 7, 15, June 5, July 10, 1885. *New York Times,* Sept. 21, 1884. *Bismarck Tribune,* Oct. 4, 1887. Unidentified clipping from the North Dakota Historical Society files, probably from the *New York Times,* on the salmon-shipping operation. Pelzer, 208.

CHAPTER XV
THE MEDORA-DEADWOOD STAGE LINE

Crawford, Lewis F., *The Medora–Black Hills Stage Line. South Dakota,* (AGS), 36–37. *North Dakota Historical Quarterly,* VIII, 4 (July, 1941), 27. *Bad Lands Cow Boy,* Feb. 14, Sept. 25, Nov. 27, 1884. *Black Hills Daily Pioneer,* Apr. 19, 20, 1884. Goplen, 31–41. Hagedorn, 119–24, 209–14. *Dickinson Press,* Mar. 22, 1884. *Chicago Daily Inter-Ocean,* Feb., 1884.

CHAPTER XVI

THE THIRD TRIAL

New York Herald, Aug. 22, Dec. 8, 1885. *New York Times*, Aug. 22, 1884. *New York Evening Post*, Jan. 3, 1903. *Mandan Daily Pioneer*, Aug. 31, 1884. Indictment for murder, *Territory of Dakota* v. *Antoine de Vallombrosa, Marquis de Morès*, County of Morton, District Court, Sixth Judicial District, dated Aug. 19, 1885. *Bad Lands Cow Boy*, Aug. 27, Sept. 19, 1885. *Bismarck Tribune*, Aug. 22, 27, Sept. 3, 5, 6, 25, 1885. Petition of the Marquis de Morès to Judge William H. Francis of the Sixth Judicial District for a change of venue, subscribed and sworn to Aug. 27, 1885. Huidekoper, 26. *Jamestown Alert*, Sept. 12, 1885. *Weekly Yellowstone Journal and Live Stock Reporter*, Sept. 26, 1886. *North Dakota Historical Quarterly*, VIII, 1 (October, 1940), 11–12. Goplen, 60–61. Hagedorn, 342–47.

CHAPTER XVII

RUSTLING AND "THE STRANGLERS"

North Dakota Historical Quarterly, VIII, 1 (October, 1940), 16. Hagedorn, 139–47. Brooks and Mattison, 14–17. Pinkerton Detective Agency reports and letters, Aug. 30, 31, Sept. 2, 4, 7, Oct. 8, 1884. *Glendive* (Montana) *Times*, Jan., 1884. *New York Sun*, undated story but obviously early 1884. Stuart, II, 195–225.

CHAPTER XVIII

THE COLLAPSE

Bismarck Tribune, Dec. 4, 8, 1884; Oct. 4, 8, 11, 1887. *New York Tribune*, Oct. 11, 1886. *New York World*, Oct., 1900. Lewis F. Crawford, *History of North Dakota*, I, 105. Lang, 69, 263. *North Dakota Historical Quarterly*, VIII, 1 (October, 1940), 17–18, 22.

CHAPTER XIX

PARIS AND THE ORIENT

Droulers, 53–70.

CHAPTER XX

RECONNAISSANCE AND INTRIGUE IN FRENCH INDOCHINA

Droulers, 71–81.

CHAPTER XXI

FRANCE—POLITICS—DUELS

Droulers, 83–160. *New York World*, Jan. 31, 1890. *New York Herald*, Feb. 2, 3, 1890; Mar., 1892; June 24, 25, 1892.

CHAPTER XXII

AFRICA—THE ASSASSINATION

Droulers, 161–241, frontispiece map. *New York Herald*, June 19, 1896.

CHAPTER XXIII

THE ASSASSINS TRIED—FRENCH GOVERNMENT COMPLICITY

New York Herald, June 10, 18, 1896. *New York Tribune*, Apr. 5, 1898. *New York World*, Oct. 28, 1900. Letter to the author from Antoine Manca de Vallombrosa, dated Feb. 5, 1960. Droulers, 243–52. Las Cases et Broussais, *Le Crime d'El Ouatia, Assassinat du Marquis de Morès, Chambre Criminelle de Sousse, Juillet 1902, Plaidoiries pour Madame la Marquise de Morès, passim.*

CHAPTER XXIV

RETURN TO THE BAD LANDS

Goplen, 66–69. *North Dakota Historical Quarterly*, VIII, 4 (July, 1941), 272–84. Zdena Trinka, *Out Where the West Begins*, 235–36. *Dickinson Press*, Mar. 23, 1907. *Billings County Republican*, Mar. 27, 1907. *Golden Valley Chronicle*, Mar. 21, 1907.

BIBLIOGRAPHY

I have limited this bibliography to works that bear rather directly on the Marquis de Morès, the area in which he lived, and the tenor of the times during his stays in Dakota Territory, France, the Orient, and Africa. I do not try to account for every source of information about him.

MANUSCRIPTS AND OTHER PRIMARY SOURCES

The North Dakota Historical Society provided me with its complete file on the Marquis de Morès, including household accounts, scrapbooks, bills, reports, letters, etc., totaling 461 pieces, and also including notes made by Arnold Goplen for his study *The Career of the Marquis de Morès in the Bad Lands of North Dakota*. The items from the Society that bear directly on *Emperor of the Bad Lands*, and some from other sources, are listed below.

Burdick, Usher L. "Life and Exploits of John Goodall."
Crawford, Lewis F. Interviews with Charles O. Armstrong, Erasmus Deffenbach, A. C. Huidekoper, and Orgain.
Gorringe, Henry. Letter to the Marquis de Morès, dated January 11, 1884.
Huidekoper, A. C. "My Experiences and Investments in the Bad Lands of North Dakota and Some of the Men I Met There." Manuscript.
Indictment for Murder, *Territory of Dakota* v. *Antoine de Vallombrosa, Marquis de Morès*, County of Morton, District Court, Sixth Judicial District, dated August 19, 1885.

Pamphlet of the Northern Pacific Refrigerator Car Company.

Petition of the Marquis de Morès to Judge William H. Francis of the Sixth Judicial District for a change of venue, subscribed and sworn to August 27, 1885.

Pinkerton, William, superintendent of the Western Division, Pinkerton Detective Agency. Letters and reports of September and October, 1884.

Price, H., Commissioner of Indian Affairs. Letter to Indian agents, dated February 21, 1883.

Report of the Secretary of War, *House Executive Document*, 46th Congress, 3rd Session, Vol. V, Part 2.

Sherman, General William Tecumseh. Letter to army officers on behalf of the Marquis de Morès.

U.S. Department of the Interior, Bureau of Land Management. Memorandum, "Script Information," dated March, 1957.

Wishnek. "The Marquis de Morès and the North Dakota Bad Lands."

PERSONAL INTERVIEWS AND CORRESPONDENCE

Correspondence with Antoine de Vallombrosa, grandson of the Marquis.

Correspondence with Athenaïs de Vallombrosa de Graffenried, daughter of the Marquis.

Northern Pacific Railway Company. Letters to the author about the Marquis de Morès and his business arrangements with the company and especially about the *Pacific Express*.

Notes of conversations between the author and Antoine de Vallombrosa.

NEWSPAPERS AND MAGAZINES

Bad Lands Cow Boy, all microfilm issues from late 1884 to 1886, Medora, Dakota Territory.

Bismarck Tribune, 1883 through 1903, Bismarck, Dakota Territory and North Dakota.

Tabor, Iowa, *American Nonconformist*; *Billings County Re-*

publican; Black Hills Daily Pioneer; Boston Leader-Herald; Chicago Daily Inter-Ocean; Dickinson Press; Detroit Free Press; Fargo Argus, Glendive (Montana) *Times; Golden Valley Chronicle; Helena* (Montana) *Herald; Jamestown Alert; Mandan Pioneer; Montana Stock and Mining Journal; New York Evening Post; New York Herald; New York Times; New York Tribune; New York World; St. Louis Globe-Democrat; Sioux Falls* (South Dakota) *Press;* and *Weekly Yellowstone Journal and Live Stock Reporter*—all from the years 1883 through 1886 but extending in some instances to 1907.

Miscellaneous newspaper clippings, sources unidentified, in an album of the Marquise de Morès.

Point de Vue, a Paris magazine, undated but surely 1967.

BOOKS, MONOGRAPHS, AND PERIODICALS

Andreas, A. T. *Atlas of Dakota.* Chicago, 1884.

Beebe, Lucius M., and Charles M. Clegg, Jr. *The Age of Steam.* New York, Rinehart & Co., 1957.

Brooks, Charles L., and Ray H. Mattison. *Theodore Roosevelt and the Dakota Badlands.* Washington, National Park Service, 1958.

Burdick, Usher L. *The Marquis de Morès at War in the Bad Lands.* Fargo, N.D., 1929.

Crawford, Lewis F. *The Medora–Black Hills Stage Line.* Grand Forks, N.D., Normanden Publishing Co., 1925.

———. *History of North Dakota.* Chicago, American Historical Society, 1931. 2 vols.

———. *Ranching Days in Dakota.* Baltimore, Wirth Brothers, 1950.

De Morès, Antoine, and Ses Amis. *Rothschild, Ravanchol & Cie.* Paris, 20 Avril, 1892.

Donan, Patrick. *North Dakota, The Land of the Golden Grain, The Lake-Gemmed, Breeze-Swept Empire of the New Northwest.* Chicago, Chas. R. Brosic, 1883.

ican; *Black Hills Daily Pioneer*; *Boston Leader-Herald*;
·ago *Daily Inter-Ocean*; *Dickinson Press*; *Detroit Free Press*;
·o *Argus*, Glendive (Montana) *Times*; *Golden Valley
·nicle*; Helena (Montana) *Herald*; *Jamestown Alert*; Man-
·Pioneer*; *Montana Stock and Mining Journal*; *New York
·ning Post*; *New York Herald*; *New York Times*; *New York
·une*; *New York World*; *St. Louis Globe-Democrat*; *Sioux
· (South Dakota) Press*; and *Weekly Yellowstone Journal
Live Stock Reporter*—all from the years 1883 through 1886
·xtending in some instances to 1907.

·iscellaneous newspaper clippings, sources unidentified, in an
·m of the Marquise de Morès.

·int de Vue*, a Paris magazine, undated but surely 1967.

BOOKS, MONOGRAPHS, AND PERIODICALS

·reas, A. T. *Atlas of Dakota*. Chicago, 1884.

·e, Lucius M., and Charles M. Clegg, Jr. *The Age of Steam*.
·ew York, Rinehart & Co., 1957.

·ks, Charles L., and Ray H. Mattison. *Theodore Roosevelt
·d the Dakota Badlands*. Washington, National Park Service,
·58.

·lick, Usher L. *The Marquis de Morès at War in the Bad
·nds*. Fargo, N.D., 1929.

·vford, Lewis F. *The Medora–Black Hills Stage Line*. Grand
·rks, N.D., Normanden Publishing Co., 1925.

·—. *History of North Dakota*. Chicago, American Historical
·ciety, 1931. 2 vols.

·—. *Ranching Days in Dakota*. Baltimore, Wirth Brothers,
·50.

·lorès, Antoine, and Ses Amis. *Rothschild, Ravanchol & Cie*.
·ris, 20 Avril, 1892.

·an, Patrick. *North Dakota, The Land of the Golden Grain,
·he Lake-Gemmed, Breeze-Swept Empire of the New
·orthwest*. Chicago, Chas. R. Brosic, 1883.

CHAPTER XX
RECONNAISSANCE AND INTRIGUE IN FRENCH INDOCHINA
Droulers, 71–81.

CHAPTER XXI
FRANCE—POLITICS—DUELS
Droulers, 83–160. *New York World*, Jan. 31, 1890. *New York Herald*, Feb. 2, 3, 1890; Mar., 1892; June 24, 25, 1892.

CHAPTER XXII
AFRICA—THE ASSASSINATION
Droulers, 161–241, frontispiece map. *New York Herald*, June 19, 1896.

CHAPTER XXIII
THE ASSASSINS TRIED—FRENCH GOVERNMENT COMPLICITY
New York Herald, June 10, 18, 1896. *New York Tribune*, Apr. 5, 1898. *New York World*, Oct. 28, 1900. Letter to the author from Antoine Manca de Vallombrosa, dated Feb. 5, 1960. Droulers, 243–52. Las Cases et Broussais, *Le Crime d'El Ouatia, Assassinat du Marquis de Morès, Chambre Criminelle de Sousse, Juillet 1902, Plaidoiries pour Madame la Marquise de Morès, passim*.

CHAPTER XXIV
RETURN TO THE BAD LANDS
Goplen, 66–69. *North Dakota Historical Quarterly*, VIII, 4 (July, 1941), 272–84. Zdena Trinka, *Out Where the West Begins*, 235–36. *Dickinson Press*, Mar. 23, 1907. *Billings County Republican*, Mar. 27, 1907. *Golden Valley Chronicle*, Mar. 21, 1907.

BIBLIOGRAPHY

I have limited this bibliography to works that bear rather directly on the Marquis de Morès, the area in which he lived, and the tenor of the times during his stays in Dakota Territory, France, the Orient, and Africa. I do not try to account for every source of information about him.

MANUSCRIPTS AND OTHER PRIMARY SOURCES

The North Dakota Historical Society provided me with its complete file on the Marquis de Morès, including household accounts, scrapbooks, bills, reports, letters, etc., totaling 461 pieces, and also including notes made by Arnold Goplen for his study *The Career of the Marquis de Morès in the Bad Lands of North Dakota*. The items from the Society that bear directly on *Emperor of the Bad Lands*, and some from other sources, are listed below.

Burdick, Usher L. "Life and Exploits of John Goodall."

Crawford, Lewis F. Interviews with Charles O. Armstrong, Erasmus Deffenbach, A. C. Huidekoper, and Orgain.

Gorringe, Henry. Letter to the Marquis de Morès, dated January 11, 1884.

Huidekoper, A. C. "My Experiences and Investments in the Bad Lands of North Dakota and Some of the Men I Met There." Manuscript.

Indictment for Murder, *Territory of Dakota* v. *Antoine de Vallombrosa, Marquis de Morès*, County of Morton, District Court, Sixth Judicial District, dated August 19, 1885.

Pamphlet of the Northern Pacific Refri[...]

Petition of the Marquis de Morès to Jud[...] of the Sixth Judicial District for a chan[...] and sworn to August 27, 1885.

Pinkerton, William, superintendent of [...] Pinkerton Detective Agency. Letters [...] ber and October, 1884.

Price, H., Commissioner of Indian A[...] agents, dated February 21, 1883.

Report of the Secretary of War, *Hous[...]* 46th Congress, 3rd Session, Vol. V, [...]

Sherman, General William Tecumseh. L[...] behalf of the Marquis de Morès.

U.S. Department of the Interior, Bureau [...] Memorandum, "Script Information," [...]

Wishnek. "The Marquis de Morès and [...] Lands."

PERSONAL INTERVIEWS AND C[...]

Correspondence with Antoine de V[...] the Marquis.

Correspondence with Athenaïs de V[...] ried, daughter of the Marquis.

Northern Pacific Railway Company [...] about the Marquis de Morès and his bus[...] the company and especially about the *P*[...]

Notes of conversations between the [...] Vallombrosa.

NEWSPAPERS AND MA[...]

Bad Lands Cow Boy, all microfilm [...] 1886, Medora, Dakota Territory.

Bismarck Tribune, 1883 through 1[...] Territory and North Dakota.

Tabor, Iowa, *American Nonconforn*[...]

Droulers, Charles. *Le Marquis de Morès 1858–1896*. Paris, Librairie Plon, 1932.

Frondaie, Pierre. *Deux Possédés de l'Heroïsme*. Paris, Librairie Plon, 1939.

Gard, Wayne. *The Great Buffalo Hunt*. New York, Knopf, 1959.

Goetzman, William H. *Exploration and Empire*. New York, Knopf, 1967.

Goplen, Arnold. *The Career of the Marquis de Morès in the Bad Lands of North Dakota*. Bismarck, North Dakota Historical Society. Reprinted from *North Dakota History*, Vol. XIII, Nos. 1 and 3 (January and April, 1946).

Hagedorn, Herman. *Roosevelt in the Bad Lands*. Boston, Houghton Mifflin, 1921.

Hawgood, John A. *America's Western Frontiers*. New York, Knopf, 1967.

Howard, Joseph Kinsey. *Montana: High, Wide, and Handsome*. New Haven, Yale University Press, 1943.

Lang, Lincoln. *Ranching with Roosevelt*. Philadelphia, Lippincott, 1926.

La Grande Encyclopedie. Paris, Librarie Larouse.

Las Cases et Broussais. *Le Crime d'El Ouatia, Assassinat du Marquis de Morès, Chambre Criminelle de Sousse, Juillet 1902, Plaidoires pour Madame la Marquise de Morès*. Paris, Plon-Nourit et Cie., 1904.

Lewis, Meriwether. *Lewis and Clark in North Dakota*. Bismarck, North Dakota Historical Society, 1947–48. Reprinted from *North Dakota History*, Vols. XIV and XV, 1947, 1948.

Logan, Rayford W. *The Negro in American Life and Thought*. New York, Dial Press, 1954.

Lounsberry, C. A. *Early History of North Dakota*. Washington, Liberty Press, 1919.

Moody, Ralph. *Stagecoach West*. New York, Crowell, 1967.

North Dakota. New York, Oxford University Press, 1950. American Guide Series.

North Dakota Historical Quarterly, Vol. VIII, Nos. 1 (October, 1940) and 4 (July, 1941).

O'Connor, Richard. *Wild Bill Hickok*. New York, Doubleday, 1959.

Palmer, Bertha Rachael. *Beauty Spots in North Dakota*. Boston, Richard G. Badger, 1928.

Pelzer, Louis. *The Cattlemen's Frontier*. Glendale, Calif., Arthur H. Clark Co., 1936.

Sandoz, Mari. *The Buffalo Hunters*. New York, Hastings House, 1954.

South Dakota. New York, Oxford University Press, 1938. American Guide Series.

Stuart, Granville. *Forty Years on the Frontier*. Cleveland, Arthur H. Clark Co., 1925. 2 vols.

Trinka, Zdena. *Out Where the West Begins*. St. Paul, The Pioneer Co., 1920.

——. *Medora*. New York, First Award Books, 1940.

Waldo, Edna La Moure. *Dakota*. Bismarck, Capital Publishing Co., 1932.

Webb, Walter Prescott. *The Great Plains*. Boston, Ginn & Co., 1931.

INDEX